ST MARTIN'S
TRUE CRIME
CLASSICS

Jill had the rare ability to spot vulnerabilities in a man, and she focused in on their weaknesses like a hungry cheetah surveying a herd of wildebeest to pick out a prey animal that was too young or too old, lame or sick. Men were her prey, and when she was on a blood scent she didn't deviate from her target. She was a sultry temptress who could addle male minds with her sexual charisma, serve as a charming dinner companion, or chat knowledgeably about sports cars, guns or business.

ST. MARTIN'S PAPERBACKS TITLES BY CLIFFORD L. LINEDECKER

THE MAN WHO KILLED BOYS
NIGHT STALKER
KILLER KIDS
MASSACRE AT WACO, TEXAS
DEADLY WHITE FEMALE
POISONED VOWS
DEATH OF A MODEL
SMOOTH OPERATOR
THE VAMPIRE KILLERS
BABYFACE KILLERS
BLOOD IN THE SAND

Poisoned Vows

Clifford L. Linedecker

St. Martin's Paperbacks

Acknowledgments

Books dealing with true events do not come into being solely through the efforts of the authors, but are the result of the active assistance and cooperation of many people. This is especially true when the primary subject of the book was so peripatetic, who crisscrossed the country and repeatedly settled in one state and then another.

Some of the individuals and organizations the author wishes to thank for assistance in tracking Jill Billiot-Coit around the country and unraveling her story include:

In New Orleans: Jeannine Macaluso and Irvin L. Magri, Jr.

In Houston: Ed Wendt of Texas Media Services; and B. B. McCurdy.

In Indiana: Carl V. Steely; Worth Weller of *The News-Journal* in North Manchester; and a number of friendly folks in North Manchester, Plymouth, and Culver who shared personal recollections with me and helped dig through dozens of documents and files.

In Steamboat Springs: The helpful staff at the *Steamboat Pilot* and *Steamboat Today,* especially reporter Joanna Dodder; staff at the Routt County Courthouse; and the waitresses, clerks, shoppers, and others who willingly shared experiences and stories with me.

My special thanks to the Reverend and Mrs. Charles Coit of Orange Park, Florida, who were so helpful in passing on recollections of their brother and brother-in-law, William Clark Coit, Jr.

Finally, thanks go to my editor at St. Martin's Press, Charles Spicer, and to my agent, Tony Seidl of T. D. Media, for their encouragement and support.

Author's Note

This book is totally nonfiction. Nothing has been made up. The events happened, and they are recounted here as accurately and faithfully as it is within the ability of the author to do so. No names have been changed. Conversations and quotes are taken from the recollections of law-enforcement officers; other participants who were interviewed by the author; journalists and other news sources; statements in legal files; or testimony from court proceedings. In cases where accounts or recollections conflict with each other, I have used the story that is most plausible or presented both, while pointing out the sources so the reader can decide for him- or herself. In a few instances, accounts are given slightly out of chronological order for the purposes of smoothing out the narrative and making the story more readable.

October 1994

Contents

Introduction

It's not news that society in the United States is violent. At this writing, according to the latest statistics available, the FBI's annual Uniform Crime Reports show that approximately 24,500 people were murdered in this country during 1993.

And through the early months of 1994 there was no indication of any significant let-up in the rate that Americans and occasional visitors to this country, shoot, stab, strangle, poison, and beat each other to death. Violent crime in the United States has shot up a mind-boggling 560 percent during the past thirty years, according to US Justice Department figures.

The unwary, unlucky, and sometimes grossly foolish, can become murder victims in myriad ways.

Drug deals go bad and turn into violent shootouts; women and children of both sexes are murdered by rapists; serial killers troll for male and female prostitutes, barroom pickups, or hitchhikers; longtime drinking buddies kill each other in drunken brawls; men and women are shot down for a few dollars after making withdrawals at ATM machines; other die in coldly-calculated, carefully-planned executions; and family members are turning on each other with increasing frequency.

It is a continual struggle between good and evil that provides plotlines for countless movies, television series, newspapers, and books. There is a fascination with murder that is unequalled by any other crime. And the obsession with homicide is especially keen when the accused killer is a woman.

Women aren't supposed to do such things. They create and nurture life. It is the testosterone-driven male with his naturally-aggressive, competitive, and territorial instincts who most often kills on the battlefields during wars between nations or during the ongoing war that rages on America's streets and in its homes.

When a woman abandons her more traditional function in the deadly game of homicide as victim, survivor, or observer and assumes the role of killer, it's especially disturbing—and sensational. Even then, her behavior is often linked to ties with a homicidal male companion that gives their crimes a Bonnie-and-Clyde patina.

They are women like Judith Ann Neely, who was barely fifteen when she ran off to marry husband, Alvin, and began to make babies and murder anyone unlucky enough to stray into their path during a rape, robbery, and murder spree in Alabama, Georgia, and Tennessee; of Debra Brown, who joined boyfriend Alton Coleman in a savage orgy of sex and murder that linked them to the slayings of more than a half-dozen men, women, and children in the Midwest. Both murder teams went about their bloody work in the early 1980s.

Women with homicide on their mind also tend to look for a man to do the dirty work for them. Or they use poison to do the job themselves. Any crime historian worth his or her salt can compile a long list of "Arsenic Annies," who have inflicted agonizing deaths on unsuspecting victims with poisons. Cyanide and strychnine are other lethal compounds that are sometimes used by both female and male poisoners.

Occasionally, homicidal females freelance on their own, but with rare exceptions such as serial killer Aileen Wuornos, a hitchhiking prostitute now on Florida's death row, their victims are people who have been dependent on their care in hospitals and nursing homes—or family members. When women kill, the victim is likely to be someone who knows and trusts them, or did trust them at one time. It's a tragic fact that a disproportionate number of women who kill tend to murder boyfriends, husbands, and former mates.

The woman who is the subject of this book fits neatly into that mold. Jill Coit has been described by a private investigator as a "black widow," a lethal creature who murders her mate then feeds off his corpse.

That term, when applied to humans, is usually reserved for women who have killed a series of husbands. At this writing, Jill was charged with a single murder of an ex-husband who was shot to death with a .22 caliber pistol in Steamboat Springs, Colorado. But an earlier husband she was feuding with in Houston died in disturbingly similar circumstances.

Jill has had a lot of husbands. And the fact she was married multiple times, to nine different men, was a big factor in my decision to examine her life and try to figure out what makes this particular woman tick.

It was a bit of serendipity when I began checking into her tumbleweed travels around the country and learned that three of her husbands live within a forty-mile radius of my small hometown in Indiana. In fact her most bitter divorce was fought out in the Marshall County Courthouse in Plymouth, the bucolic farming community where I grew up.

But it became quickly obvious to me that regardless of whether or not she was living in a small town like Culver, Indiana, or Steamboat Springs, or in a big city like Houston or New Orleans, Jill was one of those women who had the ability to attract boyfriends and husbands almost at will. And she held on to them until she was ready to cut them loose and move on.

Jill wasn't a woman with a reputation for stealing other women's men. She didn't prowl back alleys looking for husbands locked into boring or unhappy marriages who were ripe and ready for plucking. With one exception, none of her men were married to other women when she became involved with them. Her husbands were men who were lifelong bachelors or were already divorced when she met them. She was too intelligent to get herself into situations where she had to waste valuable time and energy fighting another woman over a man.

She was a charming woman, an engaging Lorelei who wore her many marriages like trophies, continuing to hold on to the loyalty of some of her husbands and enlist their help in her various personal and business ventures long after they were divorced. Her husbands represent a richly diverse range of professions and activities that include a bricklayer, student, lawyer, auctioneer, engineer, educator, merchant, Marine officer, and retired Navy chief petty officer. At one time or another, they all fell under her spell.

Some were luckier than others.

Clifford L. Linedecker
October 1994

"But before this, you could ask any of my husbands and they would tell you I was an excellent wife."

Jill Coit
Interview with
Rocky Mountain News

Prologue

Debbie Fedewa didn't like the looks of the two heav-ily-bundled-up strangers loitering in the neighbor-hood. It was about nine o'clock Thursday morning on October 21, 1993, and she was leaving her house with her son to go to a health club when she first noticed them wandering along West Hillside Court with their hands stuffed in their pockets.

There were no strange vans or trucks parked nearby, and they weren't wearing uniforms to indicate they were there to deliver or repair appliances or fur-niture. Considering their weird get-ups, it was also ob-vious that they weren't door-to-door salesmen. They didn't look like the type of characters anyone would willingly open their door for.

That was one of the bothersome aspects of their dis-turbing appearance in the quiet, small-town neighbor-hood. They weren't recognizable as people who lived in any of the nearby homes, and they didn't appear to have any special business in the area.

They looked so menacing and alarming, in fact, that Debbie turned her car around, returned to the house, and locked the doors. It was something she didn't usu-ally do, even when she was home alone. But one of the characters had turned and glanced at her as she drove

past them. There was something about the furtive look
that was intensely disturbing.

So it was a relief when they drove away down the
street after a few minutes. But by about two o'clock in
the afternoon they were back again wearing the same
ludicrous outfits and once more cruising slowly and
aimlessly through the neighborhood. Their outlandish
getups were downright weird, almost like something
for a Halloween party.

But Halloween was still more than a week away. It
was a typical early Autumn day in the Rockies, and
temperatures were pleasantly invigorating. It was still
far too warm during the daylight hours to be as heavily
dressed as the strangers were, and people were still
wearing T-shirts outside. Winter wouldn't officially
settle in with its bone-chilling winds and heavy snows
for a couple of months.

From the top of the ragged ridge the neighborhood
was built along, the scarred face of Mount Werner
could be clearly seen looming with its dull-green crisscross of ski trails extending from Storm, Sunshine,
Thunderhead, and Christie Peaks, as well as lower
levels cut out through the stands of fir and pine. In
late October the trails were still empty, and it would
be several weeks yet before they filled with hardy locals and vacationers plummeting down the steep
slopes and slogging along cross-country trails. For
now, the pace of life in Steamboat Springs, Colorado,
was comfortably slow and relaxed. The vans, pickup
trucks, passenger cars, and rugged utility vehicles that
navigated the roughly seven-block-long downtown
area on Lincoln Avenue were mostly filled with locals.

The drivers and passengers lived in the ski town, or
in the growing clutter of suburbs, trailer parks, and
one-horse Routt County hamlets with names like
Hahn's Peak, Milner, Oak Creek, and Hayden. Most
of them had come to work, shop, or relax in the retail

outlets with names like Go-Fer Foods, the Steamboat Smokehouse, F. M. Light & Sons, Boggs Hardware, and other businesses and restaurants that lined the main drag.

All that would change during the season, when the tourists showed up in full force to ski, snowboard, snowmobile, and take advantage of other winter sports. Steamboat's resort hotels, motels, bed and breakfasts, and condominiums would fill up with visitors. The winter resort would then come into its own as "Ski Town USA," and Lincoln Avenue (US Route 40) would be snow-lined and clogged with vehicles.

But for now, Steamboat's roughly 5,000 year-round residents were taking a breather and enjoying the brief respite and relative privacy that settles over the community between the winter and summer sports and tourist seasons. Strangers were a rarity.

That was one of the reasons the curiously-dressed couple was so disturbing.

Ms. Fedewa lived in a quiet, private, upper-middle-class neighborhood of two- and three-story terraced homes built into the rugged hillsides. For the most part, the people who lived on Hillside Court were members of families headed by merchants and professional men who knew each other. During the summer the streets were spotted with adults and children on bicycles, and during the winter months the bike racks atop Jeeps and Broncos were replaced with skis and other cold-weather toys suitable for the snow country.

It was a neighborhood where strangers, even well-dressed strangers, were immediately noticed. And this couple wasn't well dressed. They stuck out like a sore thumb.

It was fairly obvious that the shorter of the two strangers was a woman dressed like a man. Her bulky jacket couldn't completely hide the generous breasts, and the hips were definitely feminine. Her rear-end

was palpably flat. When she walked it wasn't with the
confident stride or easy lope of a male, but with the
more fluid, graceful movements and the feminine rolling of the hips of a woman.

The conspicuously odd cross-dresser was about five-
foot, five-inches tall. An absurd and obviously false
mustache was plastered over her upper lip. It was
much darker than the hair on her head. The mustache
and the ponytail dangling from the cap were so ridiculous it was frightening.

Her companion was bigger: an athletically-slim man
who appeared to be at least six feet tall, perhaps more.
He was wearing a brightly-colored cap over a thicket
of light-colored hair, a tan canvas-like rancher's jacket,
and blue jeans. Both he and his companion were white
and appeared to be between thirty-five and forty-five-
years old.

The strangers didn't look like the kind of people
anyone would want lurking around the neighborhood
when local kids returned home from school. By the
time children began bursting noisily through front
doors and heading for kitchen refrigerators or bath-
rooms after school, however, the disturbing mystery
couple was gone.

Gerald William Boggs didn't show up for work on Friday and he hadn't been in touch with any of his family
or friends since he left the Boggs Hardware Store at
about one PM, the previous day. That wasn't at all like
the tall, fifty-two-year-old merchant and lifetime resi-
dent of Steamboat Springs.

"Gerry" to his friends and family, he was athletic
and adventurous and traveled frequently to indulge his
passions of scuba diving and undersea and outdoor
photography. Photography was only a hobby, but
Gerry was good at it, and he set up a darkroom in his
house where he developed his own film and made

prints after trips into the mountains or forays farther afield to islands or offshore Pacific reefs.

He and his brother, Douglas, had grown up with the Boggs Hardware Store, and they took their responsibilities seriously at the business their father, William Harold Boggs, founded more than a half-century earlier. Gerry wouldn't let down his brother and their partner, Bob McCullough, by cavalierly skipping out on the job without at least telephoning to say he wouldn't be in to work that day. But he didn't call, and he didn't answer when other people tried to telephone him to ask about his bewildering and troubling out-of-character absence and see if he was okay.

Doug was worried about his brother. Gerry was healthy as a horse, and he took good care of himself. He wasn't a problem boozer, and he ate right and got plenty of exercise. Summer and winter, he was either working or outdoors enjoying the clear mountain air and taking advantage of the recreational opportunities.

But he had been living alone since he and his wife had had their marriage annulled a couple of years earlier, after barely nine months as man and wife. Gerry agreed to an annulment after he learned his wife hadn't bothered to divorce her previous husband. Their split followed an ugly confrontation over their personal lives and business matters.

Failing to get a divorce before remarrying was an inexcusable oversight, because if anyone should have known better, Jill Lonita Steely should have. She already had more experience with marriages and divorce than almost anyone, except Hollywood queen Elizabeth Taylor and longtime USO entertainer Martha Raye. When Jill and Gerry linked up she had been married to seven different husbands.

When word got out around Steamboat about Jill and Gerry's marital shoot-out, some of the local comedians, titillated by the development affecting one of the community's oldest and most prominent families, joked that the former Mrs. Boggs changed husbands almost as often as she changed her panty hose.

But the star-crossed union was no joke to Gerry or other members of his family. In recent months the dispute between Jill and him had turned especially nasty and was becoming embarrassingly public, while they clawed at each other in Routt County Court with a rush of motions, depositions and writs. The smalltown merchant was visibly wilting under the pressure. Douglas Boggs climbed into his car and steered toward his brother's house at 870 West Hillside Court.

After parking in the drive and approaching the house, Doug found his brother curled up dead on the floor of a utility room just off the kitchen. His high forehead was a smear of scarlet. Blood was everywhere, splattered on the floor and smeared on the white wall and the kitchen door a few inches behind Gerry's head. The kitchen door was unlocked, as it usually was, but it was blocked by Gerry's body.

Lying on his left side, he was dressed warmly in a flannel shirt, blue jacket, pants, and heavy shoes, as if he had either just come into the house from outside or was about to leave. Curiously, the handle of a dust mop was balanced at a forty-five-degree angle on his right hip, with the business end resting on the floor. There wasn't the slightest sign of life.

ONE

Jill and Larry

Jill Lonita Billiot and her only sibling, Marc, weren't exactly the Smothers Brothers, but at least as far as she was concerned they shared a common experience with television's famous singing comedy team: sibling rivalry. She was jealous of her baby brother and convinced that her parents loved him more than their only daughter.

Eventually, as an adult with children of her own, she would confide to a reporter for Denver's *Rocky Mountain News:* "I was raised that women were to entertain, to get married, and have babies."

Jill's father, Henry Albert Billiot, was a New Orleans-area towboat captain who worked the waterways of the world's largest and busiest port city. He was owner and operator of his own business, Billiot Tug Boat. Her father traces his ancestry to the Houma Indians. Billiot is an especially common name around New Orleans and Houma (population 30,000), seat of local government in Terrebonne Parish, fifty miles southwest of New Orleans in the middle of the Louisiana Bayou country. In fact, seven bayous converge in the town, and there are so many canals and bridges that tourism promoters and many locals call it the "Venice of America."

Established in 1834, only nineteen years after the Battle of New Orleans, the bustling seafood-packing and shipping center's name is taken from the Houma tribe, which is now settled in Terrebonne and La-Fourche parishes in southeast Louisiana. The name of the small tribe and the closely-related Chakchiuma homma can be translated as the "Red Crawfish (People)."

Although Jill's father's family roots are sunk deeply into Louisiana's crawfish and alligator country, her mother is a native Midwesterner from a state that proudly touts itself on license plates and tourism brochures as the "Crossroads of America."

She grew up as Juanita Engelman, and traced her ancestry to hardy Germans who settled in the rich, fertile farm country of northern Indiana. Some family members and other acquaintances who were on a friendly basis with her shortened her first name when addressing her and called her "Nita." When her children were born Nita Billiot was a full-time New Orleans housewife.

By her own admission, after Jill matured and began her marrying ways, she altered her birth-date, gradually advancing it a year or two at a time into the early 1950s. But she was probably born during one of the most momentous periods of America's history, while World War II was raging, either on June 11, 1943, or on the same day and month a year later in 1944.

The little dark-haired, dark-eyed girl was as brown and feisty as one of the crawfish that prowled the Louisiana bayous and canals, but she arrived too late to remember the war years and homefront hardships like ration books and shortages of gasoline, tires, and silk stockings. By the time she was old enough to begin elementary school, the American economy was experiencing the immediate post-war boom years and the country was already confronting the Soviet Union in the Cold War.

Jill was far too young to worry about such convoluted problems as the economy and the Cold War, however. Her world was smaller, more warm and secure. And until the arrival of her brother, Marc, it appeared she was at the center of her parents' world as well.

Before and after the squalling interloper made his appearance however, Jill's world was filled with the odor of spicy Cajun cooking, as well as with fried chicken and dumplings prepared Indiana-style. She learned early how to crack the shell of a blue crab or snap open a crawfish steamed bright red before sucking out the sweet pale meat and juices. As she grew up she was also taught in Sunday school about Jesus and the Ten Commandments; she grappled with the three R's; played with dolls; and competed for attention with a younger brother she may not have liked at all.

Her home was in one of the most colorfully exotic locations in the country. Despite its catchy nicknames such as the "Queen City of the South" and the "Crescent City," (because of the way it's snuggled between the scythe-shaped shoreline of Lake Pontchartrain and lazy loops of the Mississippi River) New Orleans has a bawdy history that few cities can match. Since the 1987 release of Hollywood's sexy crime thriller, *The Big Easy,* which was set there, New Orleans has become more firmly attached to its most popular modern nickname. Somehow, in many ways, the "Big Easy" seems more appropriate today than its longtime predecessors.

The city of a half-million people sprawls between the huge lake and the serpentine meanderings of the country's grandest river as it nears the end of its journey in the Gulf of Mexico. Tourism authorities would prefer that potential visitors associate their community with positive images like the fine seafood and other savory cuisine epitomized by the famous chef, Paul Prudhomme and his colleagues, along with standard local favorites like black iron skillet corn bread, blackened redfish, Cajun seafood jambalaya, turtle soup, and Louisiana pecan pie.

The history of jazz in New Orleans is another source of civic pride and the city sponsors an annual Jazz Fest that attracts enthusiasts from all over the world. One of America's most captivating and enduring music forms, jazz was born on Basin Street and adjoining arteries in what is now the French Quarter. The Queen City has produced or nurtured the careers of a long line of musical geniuses ranging from pianist Jelly Roll Morton (Ferdinand LeMenthe) to Joseph "King" Oliver with his hot cornet; from the famous trumpeter and scratch-voiced vocalist Louis "Satchmo" Armstrong to fellow trumpet player Al Hirt.

The unique colonial and antebellum architecture, which includes some of the most elegant examples of wrought-iron courtyard gates and iron-lace balconies and balustrades in the world, is yet another aspect of the city that local movers and shakers are especially proud of. Even the otherworldly shadowland of the above-ground cemeteries, with their historical tombs laid out in blunt, flat, simple slabs and their showpiece elaborate sculptured monuments draw tourists with curiosities whetted by the unique blend of the artistic and the macabre.

New Orleans earned a reputation for wet graves centuries ago because of its high water table. Many early settlers buried their dead only after boring holes in the coffin then lowering it into the moist ground where a couple of slaves stood on it until it filled with water and settled into its final resting place.

Wealthier residents of the old city, repulsed at the idea of after-death immersion, began burying their loved ones in wall vaults and stone sepulchres anchored only a few inches into the ground. Sealed in stone, the corpses didn't share the wet graves of their predecessors. Under the hot southern sun, they baked inside their stone ovens instead.

For decades, the unique burial vaults in century-old graveyards like the Garden District's Lafayette Cemetery Number One were a huge tourist attraction. Spontaneous tours of some of the more notable graveyards have been stifled in recent years, however, by hoodlums from nearby public housing projects who have taken to mugging and raping unwary tourists wandering around the ancient burial grounds.

The Mardi Gras in New Orleans, of course, is famous throughout the world. The annual celebration attracts thousands of tourists to the city and surrounding communities before its raucous windup on Shrove Tuesday, or Fat Tuesday, the final day before the beginning of Lent.

But mention New Orleans and serious historians as well as many other people are likely to think of Storyville, which was the Queen City's notorious official red-light district for roughly twenty years before it was closed by the US Department of the Navy in 1917 and absorbed by the rough-and-tumble *Vieux Carré*, the French Quarter. The exotic old neighborhood is synonymous with New Orleans as the slightly sinister playground of generations of flatboatmen, sailors, and tourists.

Voodoo was a part of the New Orleans mystique even before Storyville. The mysterious and menacing blend of West African animism and shamanism with Roman Catholicism is the stuff of legend as well as religion in New Orleans. And no historical character has been so closely related with the mystical rites, magic, and lore of voodoo than a series of menacing priestesses collectively known as Marie LaVeau.

The original Marie, a beautiful free mulatto who worked as a hairdresser for elegant white ladies and arranged sex orgies for rich white men when she wasn't concocting magical spells, is believed to be buried at the foot of Basin Street in Cemetery Number One. A few years after she passed the mantle of voodoo queen on to a successor, the occupants of the city's ubiquitous brothels and crib houses were still doing such big business with the spell peddlers that members of a so-called benevolent association of madams got together and officially agreed not to use the voodoo women against each other.

The Crescent City's dark side has been well chronicled in literature, film, and song, much more so than its record of positive accomplishments. Director Louis Malle's blockbuster movie, *Pretty Baby*, starred young Brooke Shields as a child prostitute in a Storyville brothel and the movie launched her career. A few years earlier, country music crooner Bobby Bare scored big with a hit single that was a comic version of a Marie LaVeau story penned by former *Playboy* cartoonist, author, and composer Shel Silverstein.

The New Orleans that Jill grew up in had undergone massive changes since the days of Storyville and the birth of jazz, but they weren't all necessarily improvements. New Orleans was still a rough-and-tumble rivertown populated by people whose appetites were often too big and their tempers too short for their own good. Although the brothels and crib houses of Storyville closed long ago, prostitutes of both sexes were still more easily available than parking spaces on many of the streets. The opium that Storyville whores and their clients smoked in private had been replaced by heroin—later cocaine—that was openly available from street peddlers in the same neighborhoods.

As late as 1993, when Jill was having serious trouble of her own with the law, her hometown was tagged with the unofficial title, "Murder Capital USA." New Orleans took the title from Washington, DC, which had held the dubious distinction as the nation's most violent city for four years in a row.

New Orleans eased the nation's capital out of the top spot for cities of 250,000 population or more by recording 389 homicides. According to the FBI statistics and the most recent census figures, that worked out to 78.2 murders per 100,000 people. Most of the slayings occurred in and around public housing projects, and a large number involved narcotics.

Washington, DC, which is a larger city and actually had more slayings, 467, came in a close second, with 76.6 homicides per 100,000 of population. Detroit ran a distant third. By mid-1994, a concerned bar owner in the French Quarter was keeping a public tally sheet comparing homicides in New Orleans with those in Boston, a city with approximately the same population. The kill rate in New Orleans was running more than five to one ahead of homicides in Boston.

But when Jill was a girl growing up in the New Orleans area, it was not nearly as violent. When she was fifteen years old and her family was living on Yetta Avenue in Metairie, a bedroom community of 172,000 snuggled between the New Orleans International Airport and the western edge of the Crescent City between Lake Pontchartrain and the river, she moved out of her family home. The teenager traveled north to live with her maternal grandparents in northwest Indiana's tranquil farm country.

The Englemans lived just outside Servia, an unincorporated village at the intersection of Nehr and Klutz roads about a ten-minute drive southeast of North Manchester. Servia is a smattering of a half-dozen or so houses surrounded by farm fields and cow pastures that makes the bucolic North Manchester look like a metropolis by comparison.

North Manchester, which became the new center of Jill's school and social life, is a quiet little farming community and college town that is about as different from New Orleans as it can be. Once the site of a village of Potawatomi Indians, and roamed even earlier by Miami tribesmen, the area welcomed its first white settlers in 1834. That was barely eighteen years after the state, which English settlers named for the "Land of the Indians," was admitted to the union.

Many of the families living in North Manchester when Jill arrived still traced their ethnic roots to Great Britain and Germany. The ancestors of most were hardy farmers who made their living by tilling the soil. Dairy cattle, hogs, and poultry are important elements of the local agricultural industry.

During the growing season Wabash County fields are filled with wheat, hay, oats, corn, sorghum, soybeans, and a variety of other crops. Many farmers double-crop, planting and harvesting wheat and other grains early in the season, then sneaking in fast-growing yields of sunflowers that successfully resist early frosts for late-season harvests.

The town of roughly 5,000 people is also a center for the Church of the Brethren and its immediate offshoots, including the United Brethren Church. The United Brethren founded a seminary in 1816, which eventually became Manchester College, and was operated by the Church of the Brethren. Today it hosts about 1,400 students and is one of six Brethren-related co-educational colleges of liberal arts and sciences. The Brethren also sponsor a graduate school, Bethany Theological Seminary, in Illinois.

The Brethren organized in 1708 in Schwarzenau, Germany, after breaking away from the Lutheran Church. Within roughly twenty years almost all of them had emigrated to the United States. Also referred to in their early days as "Dunkers" or

"Dunkards," because of their practice of baptizing members by threefold immersion, they are one of the historic peace churches along with the Quakers and the Mennonites. Even during World War II, many young Brethren men refused military service as conscientious objectors. Some of the more pious still refuse to press lawsuits.

The quiet and unadorned lifestyle followed by some of the more conservative members of the Brethren and German Baptist neighbors is still obvious in North Manchester. German Baptist women lend an Old World charm to the community as they attend church services, do their shopping, and tend to other activities and chores dressed in simple blue or white ankle-length dresses set off with delicate plain white bonnets.

North Manchester's most famous citizen was Thomas R. Marshall, governor of Indiana from 1909 to 1913, and vice-president of the United States from 1913 to 1921. Marshall served with Woodrow Wilson during the first World War.

Many of Jill's new schoolmates in the junior class at North Manchester High School were farm kids who did the chores in the mornings before boarding buses and heading for school. In the afternoon and evening after returning home they did more chores. They fed, watered, milked, and cleaned up after cows; slopped hogs; gathered eggs; pitched hay; and helped out with the cooking and cleaning. On weekends and during spring and summer breaks, children drove tractors, hauled combines, or maneuvered shovels and hoes in the fields alongside brothers and sisters and parents.

For fun, they paired off and dated at nearby drive-in theaters, went on hayrides, and skated at area rinks. But the most popular recreation for North Manchester teenagers was provided by the high-school basketball and football teams. There was little that could compare with packing the stands around the football field on a crisp late September or October night to cheer on the Squires while chewing on popcorn or hot dogs and sipping fresh, sweet apple cider.

During the fierce northern Indiana winters the Squires moved indoors and exchanged their bulky football gear for T-shirts and shorts to test their prowess on the basketball court against prep squads from Cherubusco, Columbia City, Rochester, Tippecanoe Valley, Wabash, and other nearby communities. Once or twice a year the Squires squared off against one of the big-town high schools in Fort Wayne. The schoolmates of the players, along with many of the town's adults, filled the gymnasium with their cheers.

On winter weekends, if Manchester College was playing home games, they could also assemble to watch the Spartans match their football and basketball skills against teams from other small Midwest schools such as the Rose Hulman Institute in Terre Haute, Ball State in Muncie, and Rockford College in Illinois.

North Manchester High was a small school in a small town, and Jill didn't slip in unnoticed by the other teenagers. She exploded on the high-school dating scene like a rocket. Although she was not necessarily prettier, or more attractive than most of the other girls, there was something about the combination of teenage charm, vivaciousness, her Southern accent, and the exotic locale of her former home that made the local teenage males sit up and pay attention. "All the boys were attracted to her like a magnet, and of course most of the girls hated her for that reason," Nancy Reed, her best friend from those high-school days, recalled years later.

When Jill posed for her junior picture in the 1961 edition of the school yearbook, *The Crest,* her dark curly hair was swept back from her forehead and was well above her shoulders. The features in her oval face were even, and her high, full cheekbones gave her a slightly plump appearance that was misleading.

Her photo was the last picture in the second row of the first page showing the junior class. The photos were arranged alphabetically, and her picture and name appeared between those of classmates Nancy Bickel and Allen Bitzell. Judging by the pictures of the neatly-dressed, well-groomed boys and girls, they represented a good cross section of wholesome Midwest American teenagers. There was nothing about any of the photos to indicate any of the juniors were destined to become especially famous—or notorious.

Jill's photo didn't appear with her classmates at North Manchester High School during their senior year. By the time the 1962 edition of *The Crest* was distributed and the graduating class began passing personal copies around to friends for autographs, Jill had interrupted her formal education to get married.

She eloped with Larry Eugene Ihnen, a rural North Manchester boy with a freshly-scrubbed handsomeness who graduated a year ahead of her with the class of '61. Larry's last name was pronounced "Ee-nan." His senior appearance in the 1961 edition of *The Crest* was unique. Other graduating seniors had lists of extracurricular activities with everything from football, basketball, and track, to the student council, class play, dance band, speech, Spanish and science clubs, or the National Honor Society. After four years of high school, Larry didn't have a single entry. Jill, apparently, was his primary extracurricular activity, at least during much of his senior year.

Judging solely by the photographs, he might easily have passed for the youngest of all the students in the graduating class. Wearing a light-colored sports jacket with a dark bow tie for his senior photo, the baby-faced schoolboy with the neatly trimmed dark hair could have been mistaken for a fourteen- or fifteen-year-old.

The young couple were joined in holy matrimony by the Reverend William A. Nangle, pastor of the United Methodist Church in the county seat town of Wabash about fifteen miles almost due south of North Manchester. It was July 24, a couple of months after the groom's high-school graduation.

Jill wore street clothes for the ceremony. She explained to a Denver newspaper reporter years later that she didn't have a big wedding and wear a white gown because white was for virgins. And she didn't qualify.

On the couple's application for a marriage license, Jill listed "student" as her occupation. Larry indicated he was an apprentice bricklayer. The eighteen-year-old groom's parents were divorced, and his mother, Donas L. Armey, signed her consent for the marriage. In the space on the application for consent of parents or guardian, Jill indicated that her father and mother were also divorced. There was no consent signature for the seventeen-year-old bride.

Like Jill, Larry was born under the sign of the twins, Gemini. His birthday was May 28, 1943, just less than one year and two weeks before hers. According to people who put store in such things, the birthdays of the bride and the groom indicated that they would be ambitious, alert, intelligent—and temperamental.

The teenage wedding may or may not have been fated by the stars to occur, but it was virtually unnoticed back in North Manchester. Page-one stories in the town's local newspaper, *The News-Journal* were devoted to a tornado that ripped through the nearby communities of Tippecanoe Lake and Goshen; high-school journalism students attending a workshop at Indiana University; a new budget adopted by the North Manchester Church of the Brethren; and a national story about President John F. Kennedy threatening Russia over the Cuban missile crisis.

There wasn't a word about the wedding that day in that issue of the paper, or in any subsequent editions.

The teenagers quietly moved into a mobile home at Cleveland's Trailer Court on the outskirts of Manchester. Larry went to work laying bricks. Jill found herself a job at the Heckman Bindery, one of North Manchester's most dependable and largest employers.

Whether or not it was moodiness or crabbiness on the part of the young bride, the groom, or both, the ill-fated marriage quickly shattered. The teenagers lived together less than a year before breaking up in March 1962. Larry moved in with his mother on Packerton Road in an area a mile or so out of town known as Damrod Heights. Jill continued to live in the trailer. Represented by a local law firm, Plummer & Plummer, she obtained a restraining order on March 7, preventing her husband from bothering her at her home or elsewhere. Wabash Circuit Court Judge John W. Beauchamp signed the order.

In her petition for divorce filed in the circuit court in Wabash, Jill also asked that her husband be directed to pay her attorney fees and half of the approximately $280 the couple had in a joint savings account with the Indiana Lawrence Bank & Trust company in North Manchester. She noted that she was a housewife and factory worker and said she had no funds to pay for the cost of the divorce.

Jill accused her husband of the catch-all offense of cruel and inhuman treatment and said it was no longer possible for them to live together as husband and wife. She also asked for restoration of her maiden name, Billiot.

Larry filed a cross-complaint claiming it was he who was the victim of cruel and inhuman treatment. He was represented by attorney Sarah Kelton Browne of

North Manchester, and he agreed that he and his wife could no longer live together.

On June 12, a couple of weeks after the graduation of Jill's former classmates at North Manchester High School, her marriage was formally dissolved. Jill dropped her complaint and the divorce was granted to her husband. Her maiden name was restored. The young couple had been married a few weeks short of a year.

Like the hurried wedding, the divorce of the former high-school sweethearts attracted little more than a whisper of attention from their neighbors and acquaintances. For awhile, Jill hung onto her job at the bindery while she put her disappointing marriage behind her. But she wasn't going to settle for very long for the life-numbing existence of a high-school dropout who lived in a trailer and worked at a dead-end job in a factory.

She was barely eighteen, single again, and just beginning to burst into the full bloom of her beauty and power as a mature woman. She was ready for challenge, romance, and adventure.

TWO

Steven and Clark

For your hands are defiled with blood, and your fingers with iniquity; your lips have spoken lies, your tongue hath muttered perverseness.

Isaiah 59:3

It was a typical Saturday night in the French Quarter: the tiny nightclubs, bars, and eateries were moist, sultry, and overcrowded with neighborhood regulars moving or seated elbow-to-elbow in the twilight darkness with a smattering of adventure-seeking tourists. They listened to the vagabond jazz riffs of a mellow sax, or a modern-day descendant of Storyville's old whorehouse professors tickling the ivories, enjoying the atmosphere while sipping idly at drinks and sharing the conviviality and sticky gloom. Ceiling fans droned overhead, slapping listlessly at the tobacco smoke and stale air.

William Clark Coit, Jr., was relaxing with a martini after another long day in the marshes when he got his first look at Jill.

She was a stunningly beautiful woman with long legs, exquisitely-swelling breasts that were shown off with a provocatively low-cut blouse, and a tiny waist that complimented the smooth feminine flare of her hips. Her long, dark hair was pulled back to accentuate the dramatic planes of her oval face.

Jill knew how to use clothes and cosmetics to en-

hance her natural loveliness and make the most of her
sensuous shape, smoldering brown eyes, and fine, high
cheekbones. Her makeup was perfectly applied, with
just enough accent to complement her dusky complexion, the inquisitive brightness of her big eyes, and the
stark sensuality of her full lips. Clark was enchanted
by the alluring temptress.

A lanky thirty-five-year-old bachelor, who had spent
the past decade working his way up through the ranks
with the Tennessee Gas Transmission Company and
Tennessee Gas Pipeline Company, he was a rolling
stone. By the time he began loping through French
Quarter jazz joints and watering holes, he was already
on the fast track at Tennessee Gas and was in charge
of all the company's construction in southern Louisiana. It was such a massive responsibility that he had
his own company-assigned float plane and pilot so he
could inspect and examine potential pipeline sites in
the bountiful marshes and gummy shallows of the tide-
water.

The job he was working would eventually involve
the laying of an intricate network of more than 300
miles of pipe through the swamps and across the Mississippi River. Company bigwigs as well as the men in
the field referred to the job as the Muskrat Line because of the proliferation of the fecund little rodents
in the marshes. They may have as easily and appropri-
ately named it the Nutria, Blue Heron, or the Alligator Line.

After the pipelines were connected, natural gas was
pumped through them and across the country to cus-
tomers as far away as the Midwest, New England, and
New York.

Clark wasn't a ladies man, and it was especially difficult for him to develop a serious relationship with a
woman. After fifteen years of moving around the
country from job to job and living in temporary apart-

ments, he was more experienced at casual short-term, hit-and-run romance. In large part, it was the nature of the job. There wasn't much of an opportunity to lay down solid roots.

But in other ways, it was exactly what he wanted. He didn't busy himself pursuing waitresses, barmaids, and other women he met on his travels like many of his colleagues did. He was quiet and professional on the job, and those characteristics marked his personal life as well.

He was midway into his thirties, however, and it was a time when even longtime holdouts like Clark were beginning to consider finding a girl and settling down. Jill was young, dark, beautiful, charming, intelligent, and had a tiny waist that would fit perfectly between his big, rough engineer's hands. She was everything that a man like Clark could wish for, or so it seemed.

The attraction appeared to be mutual. Clark was tall and as rawboned as a cowboy. He was also blond, lonely, and had an excellent job with a high income and even greater future earning potential. He was just what Jill wanted in a man.

The morning after meeting Jill, Clark telephoned his pilot and asked if he minded taking him on a rare Sunday flight over the marshes. The pilot said it wouldn't be a problem. Clark was a popular man among his fellow employees, and people did things for him because they liked him. All he had to do was ask.

When he showed up for the flight, his sexy companion from the previous evening was with him. She looked as sensuous and enticing in the bright light of the late Sunday morning as she had looked the evening before when she was shielded by the protective blue gray haze of the French Quarter. At twenty-one, there were no bothersome wrinkles to cover up. Her face and body were flawless, and when the pontoon plane took off for the rare Sunday morning inspection tour she was seated snugly inside with Clark and the pilot.

Clark was already falling under the spell of the enchanting woman beside him. But despite her youth she was a ruthlessly ambitious and complex individual with a life that was already rapidly filling with awkward secrets.

She was still married to her second husband, and was the mother of an infant son. And she was already, or would soon become, a woman who was reputed to be capable of monstrously greedy acts.

Jill was never cut out for production-line work or life in a trailer home. She had left the flat Indiana corn and soybean country with its barnyard odors to return to New Orleans a few months after her divorce from the teenage swain she left school to marry. She came alive as she drove along the canals and levees, dined on delectable seafood, and strolled past the walled gardens and terraces that sheltered brilliant splashes of blooms and smells from jasmine, camellias, magnolias, and sweet olives.

She returned to her interrupted studies and quickly completed work for her high-school diploma. In 1963 she signed up for a single course, British literature, during the fall term at Tulane University. Tulane is the fulcrum of a trio of colleges whose campuses are lined with magnolia trees and flower beds stretched along the eastern shore of the Mississippi. Newcomb College and Loyola University of New Orleans are the neighboring schools.

Early in the new year, Jill traveled north to enroll at Northwestern State University of Louisiana in Natchitoches, one of the oldest schools of higher learning in Louisiana. The university was established in 1884. This time she committed herself to a more ambitious class load.

The oldest settlement in the Louisiana Purchase, Natchitoches is solidly anchored in an area known as the "crossroads country," where the rich French and Spanish traditions of the southern part of the state meet with the stolid values of the old cotton plantations and modern-day sugarcane fields and dirt farmers. Natchitoches is four years older than New Orleans. The popular comedy, *Steel Magnolias*, was written in Natchitoches by local playwright, Robert Harling, and the 1989 movie starring Dolly Parton, Sally Field, and Herbert Ross was filmed there.

Back on her home ground in the Pelican State, Jill was confident, ambitious, and full of energy. She was a gifted student with a talent for entrepreneurism. Her mind soaked up information, then sifted through it, analyzed it, and figured out how her newfound knowledge could be put to the best use to further her dreams of luxury and wealth.

Among the business and other down-to-earth classes designed to prepare students for their pragmatic workaday future, Jill managed to jam in an acting course. She was a natural actress, who had always shown a gift for drama and comedy. She could turn on and turn off emotions as quickly as flicking her long eyelashes.

Any baby fat she may have retained or expanded on while she was living in Indiana dining on a traditional Midwestern diet of mashed potatoes, dumplings, gravies, and pork roasts was quickly trimmed off her lithesome five-foot, six-inch frame after she returned to Louisiana.

The confidently-poised and charming beauty didn't go unnoticed by the male students when she strolled with other coeds among the magnolia trees, lofty spires, and gothic arches on the Northwestern State campus. She was always pert, bright, and impeccably dressed. She was already perfecting her skills at dealing with men in business and on a more personal level. She didn't denigrate or overlook her own attributes and accomplishments, but she knew how to make a man feel like he was the most important person in the world.

Jill had an innate sense of the delicate art of seduction, a natural understanding of how and when to send out sexual signals. She knew how to fix a man with a long, smoldering glance that attracted his attention and signaled that she might be interested. She knew the dynamics of silent communication between the sexes.

Steven Moore, a handsome student from downstate was one of the most impressed and persistent of her suitors. Casual campus dates soon developed into intimate *tête-à-têtes*, then mushroomed into a full-blown love affair. On May 5, 1964 when the gardenias were in full bloom, Jill took her second plunge into matrimony. The couple first married in a civil ceremony in Mississippi, and the following October, they had a religious ceremony in Abbeville, Louisiana, in marshy Vermilion Parish, midway between New Orleans and the Texas state line.

Jill's demanding schedule and busy life became even more complicated a few weeks after the marriage, when she realized she was pregnant. On March 28, 1965, she gave birth to her first child, Steven Seth Moore.

By that time her new marriage had already broken down, and she had been separated from her husband for several months. She was too much of a party girl and had too many independent interests for the union to have much of a chance of surviving.

Steven Seth was still in diapers when she met Clark. The rugged construction engineer was an easy conquest. He was bowled over by the dark-eyed temptress who was so well-versed in the delicate art of seduction.

Jill didn't waste much time attempting to maintain a balancing act between the husband she was still tied to, the new man in her life, and her infant son. She was a formidable woman who had a robust lust for living and charged head-on at life. Along with her beauty and sexual charisma, she was smart, focused, and tireless. To many of her acquaintances, and to others who knew her more intimately, it appeared that she never ran out of energy and enthusiasm.

On August 27, 1965, she filed a petition for divorce in the Jefferson Parish Courthouse in Gretna, across the river from New Orleans. It is an odd fact about the southern Louisiana parishes in and around New Orleans that although the lion's share of the population has settled north of the Mississippi, the courthouses and seats of local parish government are all located on the more marshy and isolated south side of the river. Moore was served with the divorce papers at his Fig Street home in Harvey. He filed his own cross-action divorce suit a hundred miles or so west of New Orleans in Vermilion Parish.

Jill moved into Clark's apartment in the French Quarter. The lonely engineer thought he was the luckiest man in the world, and as he enmeshed himself further into the relationship, he plunged deeply and irretrievably in love. Jill also enrolled once more at Tulane, taking classes during the fall term of 1965 in US history, the history of public address, and in astronomy. And she kept in touch with Nancy, her close friend from high school in North Manchester.

In November, 1965, eight months after the birth of her son, Jill and her boyfriend flew from New Orleans to Cleveland where he showed her off to his family during the Thanksgiving holiday. Jill was her usual charming self when the family gathered around the dinner table at the house in the comfortable upscale bedroom community of Gates Mills just outside the east edge of the city. Neither Clark nor his girlfriend mentioned that she was the mother of an infant son, left behind in New Orleans.

Jill was attractive and pleasant, and Clark was as proud as a peacock. She seemed to settle into the warm, friendly rhythm of the close family group with a minimum of awkwardness. She had a delightful sense of humor, and her table manners were refined. If there were any warnings in her behavior that she might not be exactly the genuinely sincere young woman she appeared to be, the signals were either too subtle to be picked up by anyone or they were simply overlooked because of the happiness of the occasion.

Clark was too stunned by her tantalizing sexiness to notice or care about the possibility of any defects of character or moral blemishes. His pride in his companion was obvious. He was attentive and courteous, pulling out her chair to help her seat herself and taking special pains to include her in the conversation.

Because William C. Coit Sr., had already laid claim to the names William and Bill, family members and many of his friends and acquaintances called Jill's boyfriend by his middle name, Clark. It avoided mix-ups. Clark was one of two children, and his brother, Charles H., was three years older. The small family was close. William C. Coit Sr., made a good living, and his wife, Anna Dix-Coit, made a good home for her little brood. During most of his working career William Sr. was a salesman, peddling everything from real estate to cars, although he worked in an aircraft plant in Cleveland during WWII helping to build bombers.

Despite the gap in ages, his sons were close while they were growing up in suburban Cleveland. They played and roughhoused and tangled with each other in occasional spats as most siblings do. Years later, Charles recalled that he quit fighting with his brother when Clark got too big to handle. It was also about that time when the family stopped calling the younger son "Clarkie" and settled into use of the more grown-up "Clark."

As the boys grew up and approached full manhood, Charles went off to theological school. A few years later, Clark traveled catty-corner across the state to the college town of Athens where he enrolled in classes at Ohio University.

Clark continued dating in college as he had in high school, but unlike his older brother, who married and fathered three children, he never took the plunge. Even after graduating and going to work for a friend of his father's who was a land buyer for Tennessee Gas, he tenaciously hung onto his bachelorhood. He was enthusiastic about his job and quickly began working himself up in the giant multi-national business that today has interests in everything from natural gas and chemicals to packing and farm products.

He traveled from state to state working in the field on major construction sites and was project manager on various operations in the Midwest and elsewhere before he moved up to his job in oil-rich southern Louisiana and a position as head of construction on field projects. One of the earliest and most challenging jobs he oversaw was the Ohio River Crossing Project, laying pipes during the winter of 1963. Despite his traveling and constantly-shifting location, he maintained his close emotional ties to his family.

The brothers kept in touch by telephone and by mail while Clark worked his way up the company ladder, and Charles ministered to the congregations of Episcopal churches closer to home in Ohio. A few years after the Thanksgiving gathering, when both his parents, William Sr. and Anna Dix-Coit were seriously ill, even though he was in Houston some 3,000 miles away from Gates Mills at the time, he shouldered his share of responsibility along with his older brother for their care. He had a strong sense of family.

Clark was also a loving and attentive uncle to his brother's two boys and one girl. He loved children, and during family get-togethers he showered them with toys and with exciting yarns about his travels around the country. He was a good storyteller, and if he embellished a few details now and then to make the tales more exciting for his nephews and niece it merely added to their enjoyment and affection for their uncle.

As Clark moved up to increasing levels of responsibility he was in and out of the company headquarters in Houston. He loved the east Texas metropolis. Once nicknamed the "Bayou City" before most of the bayous were covered in a blanket of skyscrapers, cement parking lots, streets, and highways, Houston was a vibrant, exciting place to live.

Houston is as well known as a hub for national and multi-national businesses as for any of its other accomplishments.

With its deep-water Houston Ship Channel giving it easy access to Galveston Bay and the Gulf of Mexico, Houston is one of America's busiest centers of commerce. Billion dollar businesses like Tenneco, with its various subsidiaries, are headquartered and thrive in Houston. Tenneco is only one of a glittering number of major multi-national corporations with headquarters there.

Clark quickly adopted many of the characteristics and much of the lifestyle of longtime residents of Texas and other states in the far South and Southwest. He was outdoors much of the time when he was on the job and when he was relaxing. He bought hmself a pair of pointy-toe cowboy boots and began collecting a little Western art. But he never took to ten-gallon hats, and he usually made his pipeline rounds wearing the same beat-up, faded old beige porkpie hat to shield his head and face from the blistering sun.

He made friends easily and was a good party guest or host. He had a good ear for music and taught himself to play the piano without ever taking a lesson. But once he met Jill, Clark's bachelor days, if not all his carefree playboy ways, were numbered.

A couple of months after the Thanksgiving dinner, he telephoned his brother to make a surprise announcement.

"We're married," he said.

The development was about as unexpected as it could be. There had been no forewarning to the family and no invitations to the wedding. The longtime bachelor had simply driven west across the Louisiana border to Orange County, Texas, with his girlfriend, and on January 29, 1966, they were united in a simple ceremony. Clark was thirty-six years old, and Jill was twenty-two.

His older brother reflected years later, "He was no spring chicken. I mean he was beyond the age of the first juices running."

Clark's behavior in shutting his family out of one of the most important events in his life was out of character for William and Anna Coit's youngest son. His brother was an Episcopal priest, and it wouldn't have been either surprising or inappropriate for him to have been asked to officiate at the ceremony. But he wasn't. In fact, the family couldn't even figure out exactly where the marriage took place. Clark and his new bride never told them. Nevertheless the news was more pleasing than distressing. It was about time Clark settled down and began raising a family of his own.

The Coits didn't know that cutting families out of her marriages was Jill's style. It was a pattern she would follow for three decades, slipping off to marry men in quiet little ceremonies performed in court-houses, wedding chapels, or churches without bother-ing to invite members of her family or those of her grooms.

Clark and his puzzled family were unaware that the bride hadn't yet bothered to legally divorce her former husband. Jill's divorce from Moore didn't become final until March 23, 1967. By that time she had already been married bigamously to the laid-back, fun-loving engineer for more than fourteen months.

For awhile after their marriage, the couple rented an apartment in the town of Harvey, on the south bank of the Mississippi River just across from New Orleans. Clark's company was occupied in a big off-shore drilling project there. The first summer the cou-ple were together in Harvey, Clark's brother and sister-in-law visited them. Charles tagged the little town with the personal nickname, the "Big Pookah," for the Pulitzer prize-winning Broadway play and blockbuster 1950 movie *Harvey*, starring Jimmy Stew-art. Stewart was cast as a likeable tippler with a six-foot rabbit sidekick named Harvey, only he could see. The rabbit was a "pookah," a friendly otherworldly entity who came and went with the ease of a Cheshire cat's smile.

Clark brought his family to Ohio once to visit Gates Mills and the Findlay area where Charles was pastor of a church. Jill also took her husband back to North Manchester one Christmas to show him off to relatives and to Nancy and her other friends.

While Clark was roaming the marshlands of Jeffer-son, Plaquemines, and LaFourche parishes exploring, taking soil samples and running lines to the offshore drilling rigs, he learned how insular and protective of their territory some of the Cajuns and other locals could be. They were suspicious of outsiders and let him know they didn't like him poking around in their swamps and wetlands. He stuck around anyway and completed his job, but he was careful.

After nearly two years in the New Orleans area, Clark moved to the company's home offices in Houston, where Tenneco occupied an imposing structure that covered an entire city block in the downtown area. The building loomed more than thirty stories high and in those years before construction of the Houston National Bank building and other skyscrapers, it was the third tallest structure in the city. Although the Bayou City became his home base, he continued to take assignments to jobs throughout the South and the Midwest that lasted months at a time.

A friend, B. B. McCurdy, was already working at the home office. Like Clark, McCurdy was an engineer and the two men had become friends when their paths crossed at various times while they were pipelining during their early years with the company. But they didn't work together until they both wound up in Houston, and that was when their friendship began to bloom in earnest. McCurdy was a native of the little oil-rig town of Ranger, near Abilene in west Texas.

McCurdy and his wife, Virginia, "Ginny" to her family and friends, were about the first people from the Tenneco "family," whom Clark introduced to Jill. Ginny McCurdy, a former Georgia peach who met her husband while he was pipelining in Monroe, Louisiana, liked Clark as much as her husband did. It was difficult for anyone who worked with him or spent any time around him not to be captivated by his boyish enthusiasm and charm.

Men enjoyed him for his rowdiness and camaraderie; and many women thought he was adorable. He had a high, prominent forehead with blue eyes that had a hint of leprechaun orneriness about them and diverted attention from the slightly-noticeable cleft lip that was the only flaw in his leathery-faced handsomeness.

The McCurdys were happy for their friend when he introduced Jill. "We just felt good for him when we first saw her and he married her, because she was so beautiful," McCurdy later recalled. "He had waited this long in his life, then he married this beauty." Clark was proud as he could be, and he could hardly stop grinning.

For awhile the couple rented an apartment in the Sharpstown area of southwest Houston, four or five blocks from the McCurdy home. It was large enough to provide a separate bedroom for young Steven Seth. Then they put a down payment on a single-story, four-bedroom, white-brick home at 8923 Sharpcrest about two-and-a-half miles away in the same development and moved in. The house had a two-car garage but no basement. Basements are rare in Houston residences because of the moist gumbo-like earth, and most builders simply pour huge slabs of concrete on a housing site and build the structure on top.

During the late 1960s and early 1970s when Clark settled his family into the spacious house, a bride could hardly have asked her husband for a nicer home in a more attractive neighborhood. Several Tenneco families bought homes there, and at that time, Sharpstown was one of the most prosperous and affluent neighborhoods in the city. The comfortably attractive subdivision even had its own country club, and along with communities with names like Tanglewood and River Oaks it was part of the Silk Stocking congressional district where George Bush got his start in politics. Houston, like many southern cities, was a longtime Democratic stronghold, and Bush breathed life into the local Republican party. From 1966 to 1968, when Clark and Jill were setting up housekeeping together, the World War II hero Navy pilot and future president was their congressman.

Clark and his pal, whom he called "Mac," about as often as he called him "B. B.," worked hard, and when it was time for recreation, they played hard. The two couples visited back and forth, and they were such close friends they didn't need invitations to show up at one another's house.

McCurdy loved Thunderbirds, and he had two 1957 models that he kept in perfect running condition and glossed to such glistening high sheen that they would have satisfied a Marine Corps drill sergeant. Clark fell in love with his buddy's Thunderbirds and decided he had to have one of the high-performance machines for his own to tool around in.

Eventually McCurdy heard about someone who had a 1957 T-Bird to sell, and the two pals drove over to the owner's house for a look. It was a beauty. Clark and the owner dickered for awhile, made a deal, and the engineer drove the sleek, black sportscar home. It ran perfectly, but one of the first things he did was take it in for a new paint job. He had it painted bright red.

With the exception of Jill, the Thunderbird was the love of his life. He kept the car washed and polished until it glittered so brightly he could have used the reflection to shave in. The elegantly designed and engineered little T-bird was his passion, and he enjoyed wheeling around Houston. It wasn't at all unusual on a Saturday or Sunday afternoon to hear the roar of the engine as the T-Bird whipped down the street and screeched to a stop in front of the house. When they went to the door, Clark and Jill would be outside in the car with the fiberglass top removed and a martini precariously balanced on the dashboard.

"Hi, B. B. Hi, you guys," Clark would call out. "Just thought I'd come over and pay you a little visit." Clark had been in the Lone Star State long enough and enjoyed it enough to pick up the raw east Texas nasal twang and rhythm.

During one of the more memorable visits, Clark brought another of his toys with him: a miniature steel cannon about eight or ten inches long that could fire. It worked like a muzzle loader. The men trooped out to McCurdy's big backyard, and Clark poured a load of powder in the cannon, stuffed in some wadding, and fired it. After a couple of dish-rattling explosions, McCurdy suggested to his pal that maybe they should quit. Neighborhood kids were already hanging over the fences, and he was worried one of the neighbors was going to call the police.

"Well, then, I guess we better stop," Clark agreed. He called off the noisy demonstration, packed up the cannon, and went inside the house to mix a fresh martini. He was easy to get along with.

Clark and McCurdy were members of a local Thunderbird club, and their wives shared in the activities. One year, Jill served as the club secretary and recorded minutes of meetings and took care of the paperwork. She also loved the T-Bird, but it was her husband's toy. The club, which was nameless at first but eventually evolved into the Classic Thunderbirds of Houston, sponsored rallies and joined with other groups for shows, picnics, and parades. There was a very active club in San Antonio, and every year several members from the Houston group drove there to appear in the St. Patrick's Day Parade. Other car owners drove in from Dallas and Fort Worth for the event. Yet another group of T-Bird owners from Arkansas and Louisiana met in Shreveport and invited the Houston club to many of their events.

An annual picnic is held in the little town of Katy—about ten miles west of Houston—for owners of sports cars, Model-T's, and just about any vintage Ford vehicle that catches the eye of a driver or collector.

Every September, Clark, McCurdy, and colleagues from Tenneco went off for a rowdy boys-only jaunt to south Texas and Mexico for a weekend of bird-hunting or golfing and all-around carousing. Contractors who dealt with the company had developed the custom of treating some of Tenneco's top talent to the trips. One of the contractors established a golf tournament at a course near Brownsville and named it the Martini Open. It was rumored that to compete, the golfers had to drink a martini at every hole.

Clark played a little golf, but he liked the annual September whitewing parties the best. Sponsors of the hell-raising forays paid for almost everything, including the leasing of ten or twenty acres of the orange groves where the doves congregated.

One of the contractors provided a bus outfitted with a big stock of beer and liquor and gobs of man-sized sandwiches and other food for the trips to the border. The old bus was painted bright orange and white, the colors of the University of Texas. During those years, McCurdy assumed an important role as one of the designated drivers. He and the other driver stayed sober and made sure that the party animals got safely to and from the marathon frolics along the Rio Grande. They usually followed US Route 59 to Victoria, where they dropped down to the city of Alice about fifty miles inland from the curving Gulf Coast, then cut a straight line south to the orange, lemon, and grapefruit groves in Hidalgo and Cameron counties near McAllen and Brownsville.

"Wasted Days and Wasted Nights," "Raindrops Keep Fallin On My Head," and a variety of other Tex-Mex, hard country, and Texas Outlaw tunes blasted non-stop from the stereo, while the rowdy passengers partied, drank, and played gin rummy all the way downstate. Native Texas crooners Freddy Fender and B. J. Thomas were riding high on the country and pop charts in those days.

There wasn't much that was exciting to see during the last hundred miles or so of the trip, except dry, desolate scrub land and mesquite trees, until they reached the Lower Rio Grande Valley. Irrigation brought the previously sun-parched valley to life with graceful palm trees, fields of lettuce, tomatoes, and cucumbers, and huge orchards filled with row after row of orange, lemon, grapefruit, and lime trees. South Texans and visitors today sometimes refer to the area as the "Magic Valley" because of its fertility and the abundant crops produced there.

McCurdy knew the area well. One year he and a crew just completed a surveying job around Edinburg a few days before Christmas. Their boss told them to take a few days off, then get up to Zanesville, Ohio to begin a new project. After working in the balmy weather of the Valley, they spent the worst months of the winter in the ice and snow of east central Ohio. That was standard operational procedure for the men like McCurdy, Clark, and their colleagues when they were working the pipelines. It was a gypsy life.

The citrus groves near McAllen and Edinburg were teeming with a flutter of whitewing doves. The tiny game birds didn't make easy targets, especially for a hunter with a few drinks under his belt. When whitewings were flushed from the groves, they took off fast, skimming low over the tops of the trees with the swiftness of a World War II Japanese kamikaze. At the first flustered rustle of wings, the Texans started blazing away.

Sparrows, crows, starlings, and an occasional wild parakeet were sometimes blasted into oblivion or dispatched in a scatter of feathers and pinwheeling death dives along with the real targets of the hunt. When the birds were flushed, it was shoot first and ask questions later. McCurdy had developed a hobby as an amateur photographer into a professional skill and he took pictures of the hunters with their trophies. One year Clark mailed one of the photos to his brother in Ohio, showing him standing outside an orange grove with a drink in one hand and a tiny feathered trophy in the other. It looked about the size of a hummingbird, but Clark was proud of it.

The hunters stayed in local motels, and men were hired there to pick and clean the birds.

After a day of hunting, McCurdy loaded his rowdy charges into the bus and drove them across the border to Matamoros for some serious carousing. Just about any male who has grown up or spent much of his youth and young manhood in or near south Texas, has at one time or another checked out Boys' Town—the utilitarian name for the red-light districts—in Matamoros, Reynosa, Nuevo Laredo, Juarez, and other cities or villages that hug the Texas border. As politically incorrect as it may be today, for generations of south Texans the practice has been followed as a virtual rite of manhood.

Not everyone headed straight for Boys' Town; some of the restless men settled for the noisy cantinas where they tipped one icy longneck bottle of Corona and Dos Equis after another or squared off in friendly contests to see who could drink the most tequila, lick the most salt, and crunch and swallow the largest number of the fat little cactus worms embalmed in alcohol and curled up inside the bottles.

The girls and the madams at the cathouses in Boys' Town knew McCurdy by his first name. He usually made his appearance, still stone sober, at two or three o'clock in the morning, solely to round up his hell-raising sidekicks for the trip back across the border. One night he drove through three or four miles of narrow streets and alleys before he was satisfied with his final head count. Some of his charges were very important people with the company, and McCurdy was determined to get them safely back.

Despite his enjoyment of the whitewing parties, Clark wasn't a big gun collector. He knew how to use and care for a gun, but he never developed the same obsession with them as he did for his T-Bird. Shotguns were provided by the sponsors or loaned by friends for the hunts. At the end of the hunt a company aircraft flew down to pick up most of the weary revelers and save them the long trip back to Houston by bus.

Wives went along on other outings that were more subdued, and Clark and Jill once posed for a photo with another engineer and his wife while they were dining on a trip to Mexico. Jill was pregnant.

While she was tending to her duties as a new housewife, belatedly divesting herself of her marital ties to Moore in Louisiana, and building on her relationship with her new husband, she was also marking up other important milestones in her life.

On Veterans Day, November 11, 1966, she gave birth to another boy. He was named William Andrew. The tiny newcomer had Clark's blond hair, and as he grew up friends described him as looking like a carbon copy of his father with the same distinctive features. On March 1, 1968, a third son was born. The baby of the family was named William Clark Coit III, after his father and paternal grandfather. With two boys in the family sharing the same name, the middle son was called Andrew or Andy. Like his grandfather, the youngest Coit was called William, Billy, or Bill. Jill's dark-haired oldest son used his middle name, Seth. It would be the only portion of the name given to him at birth that survived.

The birth of William Clark Coit III also reportedly marked the end of his mother's childbearing years.

Doctors are said to have performed a partial hysterectomy on her at the time of his birth. Jill claimed years later however she did not have a hysterectomy, although she conceded some cancerous cells were removed from her cervix during the operation. At any rate, she was no longer capable of giving birth.

During the first few years of the marriage, the couple got along well together. Clark was a man with a ready sense of humor, and he enjoyed his bride's quick wit and zest for life. She was not only the kind of beauty who stopped men in their tracks, she was fun. He was proud of the boys and was generous with toys and presents. During good weather he hauled out the barbecue grill, and cooked hot dogs, hamburgers, chicken, or steak.

Gradually, however, their relationship began to change, and admiration turned to suspicion and doubts. Jill was a shameless narcissist who was hung up on her good looks, and she tended to be overly dramatic. She was also an outrageous flirt, and men who didn't know Clark well and weren't his close friends usually responded to her come-ons. Her behavior was embarrassing to Clark and to the couple's friends. It was creating serious strains on the marriage.

As the 1960s drew to a close and the messages of love from flower children were giving way to the violence and easy slogans of Vietnam War protests, the Coits' marriage was in serious trouble, despite the birth of two sons.

Disturbing stories about Jill were circulating among Tenneco couples at the home office, linking her to a series of tawdry affairs with other men.

One summer when she and Clark temporarily settled in Lexington, Kentucky, in the center of the bluegrass and thoroughbred country while he was working on a job there, Jill took riding lessons. She was a natural equestrienne, and she easily learned to ride and jump her mounts. Within weeks however, the story was being whispered around that she was having a romance with her riding instructor.

Shortly after Clark was sent to Syracuse on another job, the rumor mill began buzzing again about a torrid liaison she was reputedly having with a doctor who had treated one of the boys.

Jill and Clark were back in Houston when she began taking scuba-diving lessons, and a new round of stories started circulating. This time she was said to be having an affair with her diving teacher. She was flaunting her infidelities and almost deliberately inviting attention, as if she enjoyed being at the center of the feast of spicy gossip.

B. B. McCurdy didn't like what he was hearing. None of the company gossips seemed to have any real evidence to back up the stories, but they were troubling, nevertheless. There were so many of them, and how, he wondered, did they start? Furthermore, if the nasty tales were untrue they were grossly unfair and damaging to his friends. And if they were true, Jill's behavior was a tragedy of major proportions for Clark, who was as deeply in love with his wife as he was when they married.

It was Jill herself who crushed any doubts McCurdy may have had about the stories that she was cuckolding her husband.

Clark and Jill were hosting a Christmas party for some of their friends from Tenneco, and McCurdy was in the kitchen by himself mixing a drink when she opened the back door and slipped inside, according to his recollections. A bitter wind, which locals call a "Canadian Norther" was sweeping across the prairie.

Despite the frigid weather outside, Jill didn't have a coat on. She had a reputation for wearing flashy, revealing outfits that showed a lot of skin, especially her long legs and breasts. The cold clung to her body like an envelope as she moved up close to McCurdy.

"Has anybody missed me?," she asked in her velvet voice.

McCurdy hadn't expected the question, but he wasn't really surprised. Nothing about Jill Coit was surprising anymore.

"Well, I don't know. Where the hell have you been?" He couldn't have asked a question she was more anxious to answer. She was steaming mad, and she spit out more information than McCurdy really wanted to hear.

"That sonofabitch I'm taking scuba lessons from. He knew I had to run this party tonight," she snarled. She had called him a bit earlier from the telephone in a back bedroom and suspected from the way he talked to her that he wasn't alone. So she drove over to his home to take a look for herself.

"I just went over there and caught him shacking up with somebody," she said. "That sorry sonofabitch."

Any image of a sweet Southern belle Jill may have planned to maintain for her friend that night, had exploded into a nasty torrent of jealousy and vitriol. It seemed nobody hates a cheater as much as another cheater.

Jill spent a lot of time away from home on her own. A fledgling modeling career and public relations work she was doing were taking up big chunks of her time. Her boys were being looked after by professional baby-sitters or accommodating friends. After awhile she began taking overnights, weekends, and then breaks of a week or two at a time to deal with her busy business affairs. Sometimes she headed back to New Orleans.

Another Tenneco couple were close friends with Clark and kept the boys a few times while Jill was on one of her trips. They later told McCurdy that one day they found ugly bruises on one of the boys where Jill had whipped him with a belt buckle.

When the boys were picked up, the woman who had been taking care of them had a little talk with Jill. She made it plain that if she ever saw evidence again on one of the boys that they had been beaten, Jill was going to be in big trouble. She was a woman who wouldn't stand for permitting children to be abused.

She and Clark began an on-again, off-again series of separations and reconciliations. Clark was embarrassed by his wife as she played out her bold ritual of betrayal. The relationship quickly turned from warm and exciting to cool and bleakly ominous.

She openly boasted about her lovemaking skills. Stunningly lovely, Jill had a keen sense of the power of her beauty and femininity to go along with a convenient set of elastic morals. She was a sassy, sexy temptress, and she had no difficulty—or compunctions about—attracting admirers and lovers.

She knew how close McCurdy was to her husband, and perhaps that's why she tried to tease him with boasts of her erotic skills and accomplishments. One time she confided to him that it was too bad he wasn't a blond or she would already have had him in bed, he recalled. He joshed back that he guessed he would have to dye his hair. But Jill responded that wouldn't help anyway. The blond hair had to be natural.

She loved to boast, and he figured she thought it was safe to use him as her sounding board because he was too loyal to break Clark's heart by saying anything to him. But B. B. didn't want to hear that kind of talk from his friend's wife, and he told her so.

"Jill, don't tell me any more about your exploits," he finally told her. "Honey, I just don't want to know it."

That was too bad, Jill reputedly said, because she gave the best blow job on earth.

By now Clark was humiliated and his self-confidence and sense of manhood were being hopelessly smothered. The effect of Jill's reputation for runaway infidelity in the marriage was devastating. He stepped up his boozing. His tippling grated on his wife's nerves and made things worse. She was basically a teetotaler and preferred going out for a nice meal in a fancy restaurant to spending an evening draining a bottle of fine wine or stronger spirits.

The couple broke up the first time on October 10, 1969. Jill filed in the Court of Domestic Relations in Harris County for divorce. She accused her husband of almost non-stop boozing during his time off from work.

According to her complaint, Clark would begin drinking "on many occasions" after returning home from work and continue boozing late into the night. There was more of the same on weekends, despite her abhorrence of his habit. He made matters worse by badgering her with "unpleasant invectives" that kept her "continuously upset and nervous," she added. Jill claimed his behavior was so troubling they could no longer live together.

"Plaintiff would show that while married to Defendant she conducted herself with propriety and attempted at all times to do everything possible to please Defendant," she declared. Clark filed a reply denying the accusations made against him.

Jill asked for custody of the boys, an unspecified amount for their temporary support, community property, and $1,500 in attorney fees. The requested lawyer fees had gone up considerably since her divorce from Ihnen, when the Indiana court ordered him to pay filing costs and $75 in preliminary attorney fees.

The second page of the petition contained a statement that, if true, would have made her ripe fodder for the supermarket tabloids. She noted that two children were born of the marriage, listing Andrew's birthdate as November 11, 1967 and Billy's as March 11, 1968. If the birthdays were correct and Jill was the mother of both boys, it would have meant that they were born four-months apart. If correct, it was a feat for the record books, but it was more likely a simple oversight or typographical error.

A few weeks after the divorce action was filed, the couple reconciled. In May, Jill dropped her petition for divorce and moved back into her Sharpstown home with her husband and boys. Clark earned a good salary, and he was a good provider who was generous with his money. And he loved the boys. Much of the time, Jill had a Mexican-American maid to help take care of them and the house while she and her husband were at work.

After four years of the still-shaky marriage, Clark formally adopted Seth. Jill also petitioned the District Court in Houston to have her oldest son's name changed. Steven Seth Moore became Jonathan Seth Coit. Seth's mother stated on the petition that her son had lived in the household of his stepfather for more than four years. He was expected to enter school within the next year and wished to begin classes with the new name, she said.

In accordance with Texas law, the adoption file was closed. No one bothered to inform the child's natural father in Louisiana of his boy's adoption or name change.

Seth was a bright, inquisitive, and energetic child. Nevertheless, he wasn't in school long before he became aware that he may have had a problem. He was eventually diagnosed with dyslexia, a condition usually reflected in reading difficulties. Dyslexia often reveals itself by causing victims to see mirror images of words or to mix up the letters.

For whatever reason, perhaps because he was her

first child, or because he was dyslexic, Seth grew up with an especially close and enduring attachment to his mother. Jill claimed she also suffered from a mild form of the disorder.

Even with Seth officially becoming a Coit, however, the household on Sharpcrest still wasn't one big happy family. Despite efforts to make the truce work and heal the corrosive wounds steadily eating away at the marriage, they weren't getting along well. It was difficult for the ambitious young woman, juggling tasks of public-relations executive, model, wife, and mother of three healthy little boys. She repeatedly complained that the kids were driving her up a wall, according to Clark.

The troubled couple temporarily joined forces in court however after Jill was involved in a rear-end collision while she was driving in the 4600 block of the Southwest Freeway. She was at the wheel of her new 1970 Mercury when she slowed for a line of cars ahead and a vehicle driven by an employee of the Floyd West & Co., hit the car immediately behind her, knocking it forward into her vehicle, according to her account.

Jill was treated at a nearby hospital and ultimately claimed in court that she suffered a whiplash that left her with frequent headaches, pain in the shoulders and upper back, dizziness, and nervous shock. In a lawsuit filed against the company and the driver by the same attorney who represented her in the divorce action, she was identified as a twenty-five-year-old woman who was employed as a model and in public-relations work, earning approximately $800 per month. She complained she had been unable to work since the accident and asserted that unless her condition improved, work in her profession and in her job as a housewife would be carried out under the handicap of pain and suffering.

Jill asked for $50,000 for pain, suffering, and cost of

medical care. As part of the same suit, Clark asked that the defendants be ordered to pay for the cost of repairing the car. The defendants claimed the mishap was an unavoidable accident and that Jill had neglected to exercise ordinary care.

The lawsuit was eventually settled in January 1972 without a trial when a compromise was worked out by the court. But the litigation helped set a precedent for a flurry of divorce actions, civil lawsuits, and criminal charges that Jill would be involved in for the next twenty-five years of her life.

By the time the damage suit was settled, Jill and Clark had been separated again for four months. On September 7, 1971, Clark returned from work to find the boys alone in the house with the maid. His wife had cleared out and left without a word about where she was going or when she would return. Jill was back in New Orleans again, where she was said to be taking flying lessons. New stories were already making the rounds at Tenneco that she was having a torrid affair with her flying instructor.

Clark did his best to meet the challenge of his sudden role as a single parent. He made arrangements with the maid to care for the boys while he was at work in the city and during periods when he was on business away from Houston. Once while he was playing bachelor father he took a couple of weeks off from work, loaded the boys into an old Greyhound bus that had been converted into a motor home and drove to Ohio. He and the boys visited with his parents in Gates Mills, then drove back south with Charles and his wife, Alma, to Fostoria to stay the rest of the weekend. Charles was pastor of the Trinity Episcopal Church there and he hooked up the bus's electrical system to the church so his brother and nephews would have power Saturday night. Clark talked about some of his domestic problems to his brother and sister-in-law, but didn't mention his wife's reputed infidelities.

His troubles were waiting for him back home. It was only 350 miles from the Big Easy through Baton Rouge, past the sugar cane fields, bald cypress, and Cajun country bayous of southern Louisiana, across the Texas line at Beaumont, all the way to Houston.

Jill was a long way from being permanently out of her husband's hair. In those days the drive could be made along Interstate 10 in about seven hours. And a flight from the New Orleans International Airport to one of the Bayou City's two major airports, Houston Intercontinental on the far northside or William P. Hobby at the southern edge of town could be made in little more than an hour.

Jill returned to Texas a few times to see the children, but continued for several months to leave them in the care of her husband and the maid. Then on February 22, 1972, she returned to the house again while he was at work. When Clark returned, he discovered that much of the furniture had been carried out of the house and the boys were nowhere to be seen.

He was still trying to figure out what to do when he heard a child crying. It was Billy, his youngest, who was three years old. Clark later said the three brothers were in a car with their mother when she told Billy to get out. He wasn't going along with his older brothers. Clark also claimed his mother-in-law had helped Jill while his furniture was loaded into a truck and hauled away.

Two days later, Jill returned to the house, removing almost all the rest of the furniture. This time she also took little Billy along with her. Jill was back in New Orleans with the furniture and the boys.

Clark confided in his older brother during their telephone calls, telling him about his troubles. Charles asked him if he had cancelled his credit cards, and

Clark said he planned to. But it was too late; his wife was continuing to rachet up the pressure. About the time he learned that his boys and furniture were gone, he was informed that Jill had run up a whopping $1,800 bill at Foley's Department Store, one of the classiest stores in Houston.

Clark's life was suddenly plunging out of control, and he was facing financial ruin and personal disaster. Alone, with Jill and his boys gone, the disconsolate husband continued drinking more than was good for him. He confided to a couple of friends from Tenneco at different times that he thought someone was planning to kill him, but he didn't name names.

On March 1, his youngest son's fourth birthday, Clark filed a petition for divorce in the Harris County domestic relations court, accusing his wife of abandoning her husband, home, and family. The subsequent raids on the house to take the boys and the furniture were carefully detailed in the complaint.

The complainant described himself as a man who was a good and dutiful husband, father and provider who conducted himself properly during the marriage. But his wife's personality had changed so radically and the marriage relationship was so badly damaged, the couple could no longer maintain any reasonable expectation of reconciliation, he claimed.

Clark asked for custody of the three children, and a fair division of the community property. Curiously, the petition cited a different set of birthdays for the two younger boys from the dates provided with the divorce action previously filed by their mother. The date of Andrew's birth was listed as November 11, 1966, and Billy's was given as March 1, 1968. None of the three divorce petitions filed over two-and-a-half years cited the same combination of birthdays for the younger boys.

Two weeks after Clark filed his divorce petition, Jill

cross-filed against him. It appeared that just about everything that could turn sour in Clark's personal life had, but he was still hopeful of salvaging enough of his property and savings to start over. He told his friends that his wife was doing her best to clean him out of everything he owned.

McCurdy was concerned about his friend. Clark was going through a rough time, and with his brother three thousand miles away in Ohio, he was pretty much enduring it alone. When he wasn't working, he was in the quiet, spartanly-furnished house with just himself and the bottle. About the only furniture Clark had in the place was a narrow cot and a twelve-inch television set.

Despite all the ugliness and hurtful things that had happened, Clark bared his heart to his friend and talked about how much he still wanted his wife back. "Mac, it's very simple," he confessed one night. "I just love the woman." He was helpless when it came to Jill.

But Jill was keeping the pressure on, and Clark was beginning to wilt. The stress and heartbreak were wearing him down. After work Tuesday evening, March 28, Clark, McCurdy, and some of their colleagues from Tenneco trooped across the street to the Normandy, one of their favorite watering holes, to tip a few cool ones. It was Seth's seventh birthday, but he was in New Orleans with his mother and brothers and Clark wouldn't have an opportunity to share the occasion with him. The troubled engineer reluctantly conceded to his friends that it seemed to be inevitable that he and Jill would be divorced, and he had given up trying to salvage the marriage.

She was so determined to clean him out financially, that he withdrew $10,000 from the company credit union that day, he said. "At least she won't get this away from me," he glumly told his audience. Everyone

was doing their best to cheer him up, but after awhile
McCurdy decided it was time to head for home.

"Clark, I'm goin' on home now. Goddamnit, don't
stay out here too late," he told his friend.

There wasn't anything waiting for Clark at home except loneliness and an empty house, and he was in no
hurry to leave. But he assured his pal that he wouldn't
hang around the bar drinking all night.

"I'll be on home, don't worry," he said. "I'll call you
when I get there." One of the Tenneco secretaries
stuck around and had another drink or two with him,
and he showed her the wad of money he had withdrawn from the credit union a few hours earlier. She
stared in surprise at the stack of $100 bills for a mo-
ment, then with an intake of breath she cautioned:
"Clark you shouldn't be carrying that much money
around."

"Don't worry, I'm goin' on home," he assured his
friend. "But this is one bunch of money that she won't
get her hands on." A few minutes later he walked out
of the Normandy, climbed in his old station wagon,
and headed for Sharpstown.

About 10 o'clock that night, McCurdy telephoned
his friend at the house. "You okay?" he asked when
Clark picked up the telephone. "Yep, everything's
fine," Clark replied. "Gonna take a little nap, and I'll
see you in the morning."

According to McCurdy, another, more curious telephone call was accepted by the wife of one of Clark's
fellow engineers in Houston roughly a half-hour earlier that night. She was the same woman pictured with
her husband and the Coits in the photograph taken
during the trip to Mexico. Her husband was on business in St. Louis when she answered the phone and a
woman posing as a long-distance operator said she was
trying to reach him or a Mr. Coit. Her husband was
out of town, the Houston woman replied.

"Well, how about Mr. Coit then?" the caller asked.

"So far as I know, he's in town," the housewife replied.

The next time she talked with her husband she told him a funny thing had happened. Jill Coit called while he was gone, pretending to be a long distance operator and asking for him or Clark. The housewife wasn't fooled by the transparent ruse. She had been around Jill too many times not to recognize her on the telephone. Jill's soft, sexy voice, with its distinctive hint of a Louisiana accent was unmistakable.

The official workday for most of the employees in Tenneco's main office began at 8 AM, but many of the engineers and executives came in early, especially if they were involved in a construction project or dealing with people in the field. Clark was usually in his office by 7:15 or 7:30. At about eight that morning, McCurdy dialed his friend's extension for a quick checkup to make sure Clark was okay.

One of Clark's co-workers answered the call and said he hadn't showed up yet. That was out of character for him. Despite all his troubles he was too serious about his work to allow his personal difficulties to affect his performance at Tenneco. He already held down an important position with the company, and appeared to have a brilliant future. He never shirked his responsibilities.

He didn't have any business appointments elsewhere in Houston or out of town that colleagues at Tenneco knew about, and he hadn't telephoned to say he would be late or taking a day off. He wasn't a man who missed work without a good reason. But no one answered the telephone when co-workers tried to contact him at his house.

McCurdy was alarmed and sincerely concerned about his friend. Clark's drinking had become especially heavy since Jill left, and his chum was afraid he might have had a heart attack. The possibility of suicide even crossed McCurdy's mind. But he didn't really believe Clark would kill himself. He loved the three boys too much to run out on them that way.

McCurdy telephoned his wife and explained that their friend hadn't shown up for work and he was worried about him.

"Sweetheart, get in the car and go over to Clark's house and see if he's okay," he told her. "Now if his old station wagon's parked out there, don't go inside. You either go to a pay phone, or you go home and call me." Clark kept his prized Thunderbird in the garage.

Ginny was a gentle, steady woman who raised a fine family and made a good home for her little brood. She was devoted to her family and friends, and she was especially fond of Clark. Her husband didn't want her walking in on some grisly situation that would leave her with unpleasant memories.

In late March there was still an east Texas chill in the air, and she slipped on a light jacket before climbing into her car and beginning the twenty-minute drive to Sharpcrest. The big 1966 station wagon was standing in the driveway. Ginny parked her car and rang the bell at the front door. There was no answer, so she rapped on it a couple of times with her knuckles. The door didn't open, no one called out, and there were no sounds of activity inside, so she walked around to the back entrance.

She knocked at the back door, and when there was still no reply she tried the knob and realized it was unlocked. Cracking the door open a few inches, she called out Clark's name. The house was silent. Ginny appreciated her husband's concern for her and his caution not to enter the house, but she couldn't resist checking out the situation for herself. She was worried about their friend, and she eased inside. Entering a small alcove where the washer and dryer were kept, she walked through the kitchen into the den and peered into the hallway.

Clark was lying on the floor in his blue boxer shorts and a T-shirt. Blood was all over the place. His trunk and underclothes were soaked in it. Blood was gathered in pools under his head and upper body, and ugly smears stained the walls.

Ginny took one horrified look and retreated to the kitchen. She called her husband from the wall phone and told him something terrible had happened to their friend.

"I-I don't know if he's dead or not," the shaken woman stammered. "But there's blood all over, and he's laying in the hall."

McCurdy's first thought was getting help for his friend as quick as possible. He might still be alive.

"Honey, you call an ambulance. The first thing you call is an ambulance, and call the police, and get out of there," he instructed his wife. It was still a few years before the 911 system was initiated in most cities. In those days, he says, "You just dialed zero and begin to holler."

As soon as his wife hung up the phone, McCurdy dialed Clark's office and talked with Reavis L. Maggard, one of the men who worked with him.

"There's something wrong at Clark's house and I'm goin' down there," he said.

"I'm going with you," Maggard responded.

Minutes later the two men were in McCurdy's car, pulling out from the company-owned parking garage across the street from the Tenneco building. McCurdy's mind was racing, trying to figure out what had happened. He was scared to death that Clark had fallen in the shower, cut himself on broken glass and staggered into the hallway where he bled to death.

It took the men about twenty minutes to negotiate their way through the early morning traffic and reach

Sharpcrest. Clark's house was only two blocks from the corner, and his friends could see an ambulance and a couple of police cars clustered in and around the driveway.

McCurdy stopped behind a parked squad car, and he and his companion hurried along the driveway to the back door. He hardly noticed Clark's old Suburban station wagon sitting in the drive. A Houston Police Department uniform officer was standing just outside and asked them who they were and what they wanted.

"Well, I'm a real close friend of Mr. Coit's," McCurdy replied. "And my wife was the one that came over here and found him. She called me."

The cop motioned them inside. McCurdy and Maggard walked through the utility room and kitchen into the den and stopped about eight feet from the body of their friend. Clark was crumpled face-down in the hallway leading to the bedroom area, with his body turned at a slight angle against the wall. The head was toward the kitchen. He was still in the same position he had been lying in when McCurdy's wife found him there.

It didn't require the training of a homicide detective or a medical examiner to recognize the ugly gunshot wounds on the body. Clark had been shot from behind. McCurdy and Maggard didn't stick around and try to count the wounds. They took one quick, agonized look and retreated from the house as quickly as they could. Several homicide investigators and evidence technicians were busy at the scene, and they wouldn't have been permitted to stick around much longer anyway. It was no place for civilians—or for close friends of the victim.

Evidence technicians were inside and outside of the house dusting carefully-selected objects for possible latent fingerprints, shooting photographs from a variety of angles, taking measurements, studying the blood spatter-pattern, and scrutinizing the crime scene for trace evidence and potential clues. A detective interviewed Virginia McCurdy later at her home, and she described her discovery of the body.

There was no sign in the house of the $10,000 Clark had withdrawn from the credit union the previous day or of his billfold with the $500 to $600 pocket money he usually carried around with him. Two rings he wore were still on his fingers.

A prized .41 caliber Magnum, which he recently bought, was also missing from the little wooden case he kept it in. Models of the high-muzzle-velocity revolver had been on the market less than ten years and were used by several police departments around the country. Clark admired the sleek, powerful firearm for its stopping power and wouldn't have considered getting rid of it.

For awhile after police found some new wood and other signs of recent repair around the front door lock, they puzzled over the possibility of an earlier break-in. The door appeared to have been jimmied open and a new lock installed. The old lock, a hammer, and screwdriver were on a table in the front room. But McCurdy cleared the matter up and saved wasted time and effort for the investigators when he laid the blame for the damage on the home owner. Clark rambled home drunk one night and couldn't find his key, so he kicked the door in. Then he had to buy and install a new lock.

Several other suspicious holes were observed in the door, the door casing, and in the walls of the hallway that appeared to have been caused by bullets.

Early on the same afternoon, only three hours after Clark's body was found, the forty-two-year-old engineer was wheeled into the Harris County Morgue for an autopsy. There, among the cold, sterile surroundings of the morgue, Assistant Medical Examiner Ethel

E. Erickson performed a classic autopsy. Chief Medical Examiner Joseph A. Jachimczyk witnessed the procedure. The first step in the process was to make a close visual observation of the corpse to observe the condition of the body and record the presence of external injuries or other unusual marks. Then Clark was weighed and measured. He was seventy-inches long, just under six feet, and weighed 167 pounds. The body was stiffened with rigor mortis.

The pathologists observed lacerations of the upper right scalp, and a gunshot entrance-wound in his left temple. There were no powder burns or stipling to indicate the barrel of the gun may have been held within a few inches of his head when he was shot. A small inch-long abrasion also marked his right forehead.

Another bullet had grazed his jaw on the left side of his face. The path of the bullet was in line with three superficial grazing wounds extending from his left shoulder toward the left side of his neck. Two more entry wounds were found in Clark's back, one on the right side and one on the left.

The pathologist opened Clark's chest and abdomen by making a Y-shaped incision and peeling back the flesh. Small-caliber bullets like .22s can do more damage to someone's insides than slugs fired from more powerful weapons. A shot from a .45 can blast a hole straight through flesh and bone, but the smaller .22s may bounce around inside, richocheting off bones while zig-zagging through tissue and organs. Clark suffered dreadful internal damage. One of the bullets passed completely through the left ventricle of his heart; his liver was slashed in two places; his left lung was pierced in two places; and the second rib on the left side was fractured.

Dr. Erickson removed a small caliber, copper-jacketed slug from the left side of the victim's chest. It was the bullet fired into the left side of his back. The other bullet fired into his back was also recovered just under the tenth left rib. Like the first slug, it was marked and placed in a separate special evidence container. X-rays of his skull disclosed that the bullet shot into his forehead shattered into small bits. The fragments were recovered from Clark's brain and packaged as evidence.

Laboratory tests and other observations indicated Clark was a healthy, middle-aged man before the fatal assault. Blood tests for barbiturates and narcotics were negative. His blood-alcohol level was 0.164 percent. The formula for determining legal intoxication varies in different states at different times. But .08 or .10 are usually in the ballpark, and people have been arrested for alcohol levels as low as .05. Clark had tipped quite a few drinks before he was shot.

"It is our opinion that the decedent, William Clark Coit, Jr., came to his death as a result of gunshot wounds (1) of head and (2) of back—Homicide," the pathologists concluded in their autopsy report.

Clark wasn't shot with his .41 caliber pistol, or with a .38 caliber handgun that he also owned. The slugs recovered from his body and from the house were all fired from a .22. The murder weapon wasn't recovered.

One of the police detectives theorized Clark was lying in bed watching television Tuesday night or early Wednesday morning when he went to the back door to let someone inside and was attacked. The television was still turned on and playing in the master bedroom when police arrived. The sheets on the bed were rumpled.

McCurdy thought that was probably an accurate reconstruction of what happened. He figured Clark got out of bed to admit someone into the house, then was shot in the back after he turned around to lead them further inside or toward the front door. And he figured the bushwhacker had to be someone Clark trusted.

Clark's missing billfold was found several days after his murder, tossed into a ditch a few miles north of the city limits near the Intercontinental Airport. There wasn't so much as a single dollar bill inside, but the discovery sparked suspicions about why it was discarded at that particular location. Did Clark's killer leave town via the airport right after the murder?

A detective asked McCurdy if Clark would have agreed to let Jill come to the house or would have driven to the airport to pick her up if she had telephoned and said she was in town and wanted to see him.

"Yes, he would have done it," McCurdy replied. "He would have picked her up at the airport, or he would have said, 'Yeah, you can come inside.'"

The investigation began to bog down almost as soon as it began. In the early 1970s when the Tenneco engineer was murdered, the Houston Police Department was already developing a spotty reputation that would make it at least as well known for its failures as its triumphs.

When Clark Coit was shot to death in his house by a mystery killer, teenage boys from a shabbier neighborhood across town were being slaughtered by a vicious gang of sex-and-torture slayers. The murders of boys from the Heights had been going on since 1970. But worried parents couldn't work up much interest from the police in solving the mystery of their missing teenagers. The youngsters were disappearing one and two at a time, but when parents tried to enlist law enforcement officers to investigate the strange vanishings they were put off with suggestions the boys were probably runaways.

Houston police busied themselves with other matters while the killings continued. On August 8, 1973, the serial-murder case involving the missing boys finally resolved itself. Nineteen-year-old Elmer Wayne Henley telephoned police in suburban Pasadena and blurted out that he had just shot his friend to death.

The friend was Dean Corll, a thirty-three-year-old former candy-maker and mastermind of the murder ring. Henley had brought a thirteen-year-old neighborhood girl along with a teenage boy intended as a victim to Corll's house, setting off the fatal confrontation. Eventually the remains of twenty-seven victims were recovered from three burial sites, although one was later said to represent an unrelated homicide. Corll was a native Hoosier, who grew up just outside Fort Wayne, Indiana, about a half-hour drive from Wabash County where Jill married her first husband.

In the early 1970s, serial murder wasn't an everyday event in the United States, and the story flashed around the world, setting off a flurry of shock and outrage ranging from the Vatican to the Soviet government's official Communist press organ, *Izvestia*. Commentators for the party newspaper seized the opportunity to blast the Houston Police Department for cruel unconcern and crippling bureaucracy.

In Houston parents of the murdered boys were saying many of the same things. Some Houston police were defending themselves by blaming the boys, muttering that they were prostitutes who knew about the sex and paint-sniffing orgies at Corll's home and got into trouble because of their willingness to play for pay. The police department came in for additional criticism for reputedly cutting the search for bodies off short. The critics theorized that the search ended when it did because the people of the Heights were without significant political power, and the police weren't overly anxious for Houston to set a long-standing record for serial killing.

But Clark was murdered in a neighborhood where

the residents had plenty of political power and knew how to use it. The house on Sharpcrest was surrounded by comfortable up-scale homes of important people and respected well-to-do professionals like himself: teachers, lawyers, accountants, dentists, and engineers. On the rare occasions when a murder occurred in Sharpstown, concerned neighbors expected the police department to take a close look at the evidence and make a determined effort to bring the killer to justice. Sharpstown wasn't a neighborhood where there was a longstanding pattern of unsolved murders.

But for one reason or another the investigation of the engineer's slaying broke the pattern. Police couldn't find the murder weapon, they couldn't find a witness, and they never had a sit-down discussion with Jill about her stormy relationship with her late husband and his perplexing murder. The homicide probe quickly fizzled and lost steam.

About a week after the slaying, the *Houston Post*, one of the city's two major daily newspapers, offered a $4,000 reward as part of its "Public Protector" program for information leading to the arrest and conviction of the killer. Rewards in the same amount were posted in twelve other homicide cases and $2,000 was offered for help in the arrest and conviction of a stickup man, but the writer opened the major crime roundup with Clark's slaying. Along with everything else, Houston was also a violent city.

The anonymous author of the story observed that police believed robbery might be the motive for the slaying. The reward for help solving Clark's slaying was never claimed. And the paperwork compiled during investigation of his murder began gathering dust alongside others in the Houston Police Department's unsolved case files.

THREE

Major Brodie &
Daddy Johansen

Clark's violent death and the gruesome scene at the house were fiercely traumatic, and McCurdy was badly shaken when he returned to Tenneco and reported the tragedy to company administrators.

The somber group of executives agreed among themselves that someone had to notify Jill. Since McCurdy was one of Clark's closest friends and had a pretty good idea of where to find her in New Orleans, he drew the unenviable task of passing along the message about the shooting to the widow.

A year or two earlier when McCurdy flew into New Orleans International on business, he had driven the few miles from the airport to visit Jill's parents in Metairie, and he still had their address and telephone number.

He figured the home on Yetta Avenue was a good place to begin looking for her. When he dialed the number Jill was there.

She sounded a bit surprised, but was friendly and responded with a standard greeting:

"Hi, Mac. How are you?"

Speaking softly and struggling to suppress the lump in his throat, he replied he had bad news. "Clark has been killed."

"What? How?" Jill demanded.

"He was shot!"

Jill hesitated for a moment or so, before gasping, "Who would want to do that to Clark? Oh, Clark . . ."

It was a good question, one that would still be unanswered twenty years later, except for rumors and suspicions that somehow were never quite pinned down. But McCurdy wasn't an interrogator; he was a messenger with bad news, and he listened patiently and sympathetically while Jill apparently began to lose her composure.

She was reacting with the expressions of shock and agony that could be expected of any normal person in her position, considering the circumstances.

A couple of days later, McCurdy took a telephone call at his office from a man in New Orleans who identified himself as Louis A. DiRosa. He was Jill's lawyer, and he wanted to know about company death benefits and any other proceeds that might be coming to his client. McCurdy had not only been Clark's chum, but he was also Tenneco's manager of employee benefits for all the pipelines. He handled all the paperwork involved with the death or disabilities of pipeline employees and mailed out the checks to survivors. He was the right man to call.

Clark was killed twenty days after Jill cross-filed for divorce, and she was still his wife and next of kin. Tenneco had a generous package of death benefits and other extras for its employees. Clark had a hefty retirement policy and a company insurance policy with a double-indemnity clause for accidental death. Death by gunshot, if the victim wasn't shooting back at someone, was covered by the special provision.

Jill eventually wound up with roughly $156,369.41, solely from her husband's company benefits. The package included funds from a retirement plan, life insurance, and a company savings program in which he had 689 shares of Tenneco stock. At the time it was worth $24 per share, but the value doubled over the next decade. A portion of the estate of Clark's parents also eventually fell into her hands through $150,000 trust funds set up for each of the boys. The total estate was also shared with the other grandchildren.

The young widow collected a small fortune after everything was totalled. In 1972 when fast-track engineers like Clark were earning between $25,000 and $30,000 annually, she had come into a tremendous amount of money.

McCurdy wound up mailing most of the checks from the retirement policy to Jill at the Tower Advertising Company, which she had formed and operated in New Orleans. Jill's company offices were next door to those of her lawyer in the Pere Marquette Building. But Clark's old friend also turned over some checks and documentation directly to DiRosa in Houston. The high-powered New Orleans lawyer was in town within a couple of days or so of Clark's death, looking after his client's welfare and affairs.

DiRosa was an experienced attorney who was a member of a politically powerful New Orleans family. His older brother, Joseph V. DiRosa, was a longtime member of the seven-member city council, who held one of two at-large seats voted on in all precincts of the city. For awhile Joseph was council president and mayor pro tem.

The younger DiRosa was a shrewd and resourceful legal technician who understood politics and the subtle intricacies of the law. He was a skilled professional who knew how to get everything for his sexy client that was coming to her from her late husband's estate.

One of the first things DiRosa did when he got to the Bayou City, was sweep into the Houston Police Department homicide headquarters and begin going

over records of their investigation into the murder. He
also talked with B. B. about the company's survivor
benefits. One time DiRosa drove around the block until B. B. rode the elevator down from his office and
walked out to the curb to hand over benefits documents to the lawyer in his car.

DiRosa's client was safely back in New Orleans,
where she checked herself into a psychiatric hospital
for treatment of acute hysteria after slashing her
wrists. She was desperately worried about how she
would raise three little boys without her husband, she
claimed. But she was convinced at the hospital that
she had to put those feelings behind her and go on
with her life for the sake of the children.

While she was in the hospital, she was conveniently
removed from the direct attentions of homicide investigators in Houston. Under the circumstances, as a pa-
tient hospitalized for hysteria and emotional distress,
the fragile state of her mental health and her well-
being were too important to risk by submitting her to
questioning by inquisitive lawmen.

"We wanted to talk to her but she hid behind attorneys," Houston Detective Sgt. Jim Binford told the
National Enquirer twenty years later. Binford was also
quoted as saying Jill was the only suspect.

While DiRosa was collecting information and famil-
iarizing himself with his client's tangled affairs and Jill
was coping with her grief in the hospital, Charles Coit
was tending to funeral arrangements for his only
brother.

Charles had been home alone at five o'clock
Wednesday afternoon when he answered the telephone. A man on the other end of the line identified
himself as an officer with the Houston Police Department. The policeman asked if he was the brother of
William Clark Coit. A sick feeling of apprehension

was already sweeping over Charles when he replied affirmatively.

"Well, he's been shot," the officer said.

Charles dreaded the question he had to ask, but it couldn't be avoided.

"Is he dead?"

"Yes," the policeman confirmed.

Charles was standing up with the telephone in his hand, and his legs suddenly felt like strings of cooked spaghetti. He sat down on the floor. He asked the officer if his parents had been notified and was told they weren't.

"Well, don't tell them then," he said. "I will."

He was still sitting in a half-daze on the floor a minute or two later after hanging up the telephone, when his wife returned home from work. Alma Coit was filled in on the heartbreaking news. Then the couple began making arrangements to leave for Gates Mills to carry out one of the saddest tasks of their lives.

They had just broken the dreadful news to Charles's parents when the telephone rang and his father, William Coit, picked up the receiver. He was still shaken from the disclosure of Clark's violent death, and his face blanched. Charles asked who was on the line. It was Jill.

Charles picked up another phone and told his father to hang up, then took over the conversation. Jill said she just telephoned to tell them Clark was dead.

A few minutes later, the brief conversation ended. Then Charles and Alma began the long, mournful 150-mile drive back to their home in Findlay. Distraught and shaken, Charles notified his bishop at the diocese headquarters in Cleveland about Clark's murder. It was Holy Week, the most solemn and one of the busiest times of the year for the church, but Charles found it impossible to concentrate on his pastoral duties. He also had a funeral coming up for one of his parishioners, and the next day he telephoned his bishop again and said he needed help. He simply wasn't functioning as he should be.

A half-hour later a substitute pastor for the church was knocking at his door. The substitute handled the funeral. On Maundy Thursday, the two priests filed into Charles's church, Trinity Episcopal, in Fostoria, where he informed the congregation of his personal tragedy. Then his fellow priest conducted the services.

On Good Friday, Charles boarded an airliner and flew to Houston. His wife stayed in Findlay to care for their children. His parents also remained behind. The elder Coits simply weren't up to the trip. A Tenneco vice president arranged for Charles to be met at the airport and driven to a house where he spent the night. The next morning he talked with a company lawyer, who advised him that he was being made executor of his brother's estate.

No one had been able to find a will, and since Clark was estranged from his wife and she was in New Orleans, Charles was the obvious choice for the role. His brother's body had been transferred from the coroner's office to the George H. Lewis & Sons Funeral Home, and Charles arranged to have his brother cremated. He directed the morticians to ship the ashes back to Ohio.

The bishop in Cleveland had arranged through a counterpart in Texas to have an Episcopal priest from Houston conduct the funeral service. Charles sat in the front row at the church, flanked by close friends and colleagues of his brother during the somber ceremony. Jill didn't attend the funeral.

As they walked out of the church following the service, Charles told his companions that he needed a drink. But they had one more stop to make first. The company executive took Charles to the funeral home, where the mortician asked if he wanted to see his brother one last time.

"He's in the box isn't he?" Charles asked, nodding toward the closed coffin.

The mortician assured him that was the case. "Well, then I don't want to see the body," Charles responded. He preferred to remember his baby brother as he had been in life, and had no desire to inspect the results of the mortician's skilled efforts to smooth over the terrible damage to Clark's shattered face and ruined jaw.

Charles had his drink at the home of one of his brother's friends, where his friends and colleagues from the company gathered for an old-fashioned wake. They swapped stories about the easy-going, fun-loving engineer, and they mourned. The next day, Charles attended Easter services at a Presbyterian church with friends of his brother.

After returning to Ohio, he scattered Clark's ashes over the Chagrin River, a few miles from the home in Gates Mills where they spent their boyhood together. A few months later, in October, Anna Dix-Coit's ashes were sprinkled over the same river. About a year after that, the ashes of William Clark Coit Sr. were also consigned to the tranquil waters.

A few days after Charles left Houston, Clark's will was found in a safety-deposit box at a local bank. Clark had made out the will and signed it on March 14, 1967, when William Andrew was still an infant and about a year before the birth of his namesake, William Clark Coit III. He left everything to his wife. She was also named executrix in the document.

He stipulated that he was leaving nothing to either Seth, who was then twenty-three months old and hadn't yet been adopted, or to William Andrew, or to any future children of his. He did so because he was ". . . conscious of the fact that the well-being, upbringing, and the education of my said children is the primary concern of my beloved wife, Jill Lonita Coit, to whom I leave all of my estate as above stated."

In the event that he and Jill died together in an accident, or she failed to survive him by thirty days, his estate was to be used for the care and education of his children and the remainder should be equally divided among them at the time the youngest of them reached the age of thirty. Another Houston friend of Clark's was named to oversee the trust account that would be set up for them. Jill's mother, who at that time was living in Harvey, was named as the alternate trustee and as guardian for the children in the event his wife didn't survive him.

The will did not specifically mention Clark's considerable company-related benefits, except for $756.36 remaining in his Tenneco Credit Union account and $2,525 in wages and vacation pay due to him at the time of his death. But it included the house on Sharpcrest, which had a cancellation policy that paid off the mortgage in the event of the death of the primary wage earner. With his death, the house in the Sharpstown County Club Terrace became free and clear for the widow. It was worth roughly $30,000.

Also listed in the will were a $6,000 cashier check from the Houston National Bank payable to W. C. Coit Jr.; $1,081 in a checking account at the Houston National Bank; fifty shares of the Philadelphia Life Insurance Company worth a total of $928 at that time; and one share of Midwestern Gas Transmission Company stock worth $121.

Personal property included furniture and personal effects worth $1,260; escrow refunded on a repaid loan at the First Mortgage Company of Texas of $556; a federal income tax refund of $205; the 1966 Ford station wagon valued at $350; a 1967 Ford two-door valued at $200; a 1970 Mercury two-door valued at $2,250; and a 1967 Ford two-door valued at $200.

Clark did not have a 1967 Ford two-door, but he had the 1957 T-Bird which, considering the excellent condition it was in, would have been worth at that time about $8,000 to $10,000.

When a Houston lawyer had the will probated for the executrix on January 26, Jill's address was given as 9809 Joel Street in Harahan, Louisiana. DiRosa signed as notary public on a statement she signed in New Orleans appointing attorney William M. Schultz to represent her in the proceedings in Houston. It was also noted that all the debts against the estate had been paid, including several doctor bills, $1,250 to Foley's, and $1,632.79 to the mortuary for Clark's funeral. B. B. swore out a deposition in probate court confirming Clark's death, former residence in Harris county, and the fact that to his knowledge the will was never revoked.

With his role as executor cut short, Charles returned to Houston to sign more legal papers. He remained there long enough to be interviewed by homicide detectives, then returned again to Ohio. More than twenty years after he made the sad journey, the grieving brother still hadn't heard another word from the Houston Police Department about the investigation into his brother's murder. And he talked directly only once more with his brother's widow. Jill telephoned him in Fostoria and asked where he had interred the ashes.

Charles told her he scattered them over the river, where the brothers had played as boys.

"You mean there's no place where we can go and put a stone?" she asked.

"No," Charles replied. "Because this is what Clark wanted."

They didn't talk again. Jill eventually paid for Clark's name and the dates of his birth and death to be inscribed in a niche on a memorial at a cemetery in

New Orleans. A few years later one of Clark's friends visited the memorial, and was shocked at the dismal condition it was in. When a complaint was lodged with a cemetery employee the response was laconically blunt.

"Well, don't worry about it," the employee said. "There's nothing in there, anyway." Charles thought creation of the memorial was an odd thing to do. But people who knew Jill had learned to expect unorthodox behavior. It was in perfect character for her.

Houston police probably didn't contact Charles after their interview because they had nothing positive to report about the investigation. Efforts to solve the mystery began bogging down before the victim was even put to his final rest.

The *Post's* "Public Protector" program reward offer of $4,000 for information helping to solve the slaying was never claimed.

In the meantime, DiRosa obtained affidavits stipulating that Jill was attending a birthday party in New Orleans on the night her husband was murdered. Seth had just turned seven years old. One of the statements was from a guest at the party who claimed to have seen her at 7:30 PM. Another was from a guest who stated he saw her there around midnight.

The affidavits were impressive, but they still left a four-and-a-half-hour gap in her whereabouts that was unexplained. Homicide detectives checked out flights between Houston and New Orleans on the night of Clark's death, but if they learned anything suspicious they kept a tight lip about it with the public.

Jill made good use of the telephone while she was in the hospital, frequently talking with B. B. in Houston. She asked her old friend if he knew where Clark's T-Bird was. It was still in the garage at the house.

"Now, Mac, I want you to have that car," she said. B. B. conceded that he loved the car and would like to buy it because it had belonged to his friend. He insisted he wouldn't take it as a gift, and would only accept it if he could pay her the fair market price. Jill was equally insistent. She wanted to give it to him. The ultimate fate of the car remained a standoff, and neither of the two shifted their position when they discussed it during subsequent calls.

DiRosa also talked to McCurdy about his client's determination to sign over the title to the Thunderbird to him, according to the Texan. As soon as the estate was settled, the lawyer reportedly said, the Thunderbird would be signed over to him. Several times DiRosa telephoned him to discuss Jill's company benefits or other matters, and invited him to come by New Orleans for a visit. The lawyer said he would pick up some tickets for the Saints' games and McCurdy could watch some professional football as a guest of his and Jill's. The Tenneco executive was just as stubborn and determined as she was. There was no way he would accept the car as a gift. After one of his telephone talks with Jill at the hospital, he was more convinced than ever that he had made the right decision.

She might need a friend in Houston sometime who would be willing to talk about what a good person she was, he says she told him. But nobody was going to buy a glowing character reference from the engineer, by giving him Clark's Thunderbird—no matter how much he wanted it.

"Jill, I want the car and I'll buy it," he told her. "As far as anything I could tell about you, I don't know anything for a fact." He pointed out that although she had bragged to him a few times, he couldn't tell anyone he thought she was evil. The time would come however, when he would revise that opinion and became convinced she was about as bad as could be.

Three years after McCurdy started looking after the car, he finally had enough and dropped it off at a local auto storage which specialized in T-Birds. Then he wrote registered letters and mailed them to DiRosa at his office, to Jill at the Tower Advertising Agency, and a third copy to her at her parents' address in Metairie. He advised them where the car was and said he was washing his hands of the matter.

DiRosa telephoned him about two weeks later and asked what was going on. "Well, the letter explains it. You're a lawyer," McCurdy pointed out. He said he was sick and tired of the game-playing and the car was no longer his responsibility. DiRosa wanted to know what the storage fees were.

"I don't know, and I don't care," the crusty engineer replied. "I don't have to pay it."

DiRosa sent a young man to pick up the car from the garage and drive it back to New Orleans. Coincidentally, the driver's uncle was a vice president with Tenneco, and the youth mentioned meeting a beautiful woman in New Orleans whose late husband was with the company. He said her name was Jill Coit. The executive told his nephew to stay as far away from the woman as he could.

Soon after the Thunderbird was delivered to Jill in New Orleans, she obtained a personalized license plate for it with the slogan, "Q. T. BIRD."

Long before the matter of the Thunderbird was settled, it appears authorities in Houston never got anywhere in bringing the Tenneco engineer's killer or killers to justice, and the investigation died on the vine. The McCurdys still mourned their friend, but they had accepted his death and their loss. Ginny never failed to remember Clark on the anniversary of his death, however, and she always had a memory or observation to dredge up and share with her husband. Charles Coit also telephoned every year about that time to chat with the McCurdys and reminisce about his brother and their friend.

Jill finally walked out the doors of the hospital, presumably cured of her suicidal depression. She was refreshed and primed for new adventure. She had enough of New Orleans and Houston for awhile, so she collected her sons and headed west to seek her fortune in California.

The boys were told that their father had died of a heart attack. The thought of their father dying a quiet, natural death was less traumatic than forcing their young minds to cope with the idea of murder.

About the time Jill arrived on the West Coast and was settling down in the Los Angeles area, back in Houston the divorce suits she and her late husband had filed against each other were dismissed by the Harris County Court of Domestic Relations. With Clark's death, the matter of the divorce and the promise of bitter legal wrangling over the couple's property and the boys had become a moot point.

By that time two new men had emerged in Jill's life.

Edwin Bruce Johansen was a wealthy, older retired businessman who lived on Barrows Drive in Los Angeles. There are two versions of how the lives of this odd couple crossed. Jill claims they met when Johansen sold her a warehouse, that she was sorry for the old man and helped care for him for two or three years. Other sources indicate Johansen was a longtime acquaintance of her and her family when they crossed paths again in California.

Whatever may have sparked the relationship, Johansen was apparently as enchanted with Jill as so many younger men were. The frail eighty-nine-year-old man traveled to New Orleans, and on July 20, 1973, signed a document signifying his wish and intention to adopt Jill.

DiRosa handled the legal procedures and paperwork for the adoption. Jill loved to drive, and after moving to California she frequently made the trip by car back to New Orleans to visit with her family and follow up on her various interests there. She stayed in close touch with her lawyer there. He was the man she went to when she needed legal advice.

According to the act of adoption subsequently filed with the clerk of the court in Jefferson Parish, which lies due south of the western end of New Orleans, Johansen had not remarried after the death in 1969 of his wife, the former Mary Taney, and he had no surviving close relatives. The adoption was being carried out in Louisiana because Jill's residence at that time was in Jefferson Parish, according to the legal document.

The would-be adopted daughter added her consent to the procedure and both she and her prospective new parent declared that it was their wish that her name be legally changed at the same time from Jill Billiot-Coit to Jill Coit-Johansen. Jill, Johansen, and two witnesses signed the document. DiRosa added his signature and stamp as a notary public in the Parish of Orleans, state of Louisiana. Jill had observed her thirtieth birthday five weeks earlier.

But she wasn't the only woman who was showing intimate concern for the lonely, sometimes cantankerous old widower. Ann H. Schwartz, the wife of his longtime accountant, Morris Schwartz, was also demonstrating a strong personal interest in helping him wind up his financial affairs during his final days. On October 10, less than three months after he adopted Jill, Johansen made out a will leaving his total estate to his accountant's wife. She was also designated as the executrix.

Johansen was a devoted Mason, and he specified that in the event of Mrs. Schwartz's death, his entire estate would go to the Masonic Lodge #381 F&AM, in Oceanside, California.

His newly-adopted daughter wasn't even mentioned by name in the will, but it was carefully worded to specifically disinherit anyone claiming to be his "heir-at-law."

"If any person whether or not related to me in any way shall either directly or indirectly attempt to oppose or set aside the probate of this will or to impair or invalidate any of the provisions hereof and such person shall establish a right to any part of my estate, I give and bequeath to such person the sum of $1 only and no further interest whatsoever in my estate," the document stated. There seemed to be no question about it; Jill was cut out of any inheritance from her adoptive father. But the tug-of-war was just beginning.

On November 29, the old man again picked up a pen, and in his shaky handwriting, signed a new will leaving his entire estate after funeral and burial expenses to Jill. She was also named executrix. Similar to a stipulation in the earlier will, the new document carried a declaration that anyone challenging the provisions would be left with $1 and no further interest in the estate.

The will was witnessed by Louis A. DiRosa and an Oceanside, California, man, Noel L. Mares. In both wills, Johansen stipulated his wishes to be cremated and for his remains to be placed next to those of his wife in Santa Monica's Woodlawn Cemetery.

That was apparently the last of the wills, but the struggle over the disposition of his estate hadn't even gotten really started yet. Johansen died a peaceful, apparently-natural death on August 1, 1974, shortly after observing his ninetieth birthday. According to his wishes, he was given a Masonic funeral, cremated, and interred next to his wife. Then the fireworks began exploding in a three-way money squabble that would spark accusations that were incredibly bizarre even for California. Their echoes could still be heard around the court almost twenty years later.

Ann Schwartz filed for probate of the will naming

her as heir and executrix a month after Johansen's death. On November 25, Jill filed a petition in the Los Angeles County Superior Court seeking revocation of the action. Identifying herself as Johansen's adopted daughter, she said the document admitted to probate was not his final will. She produced a copy of the will naming her as heir and executrix. Although Jill was represented by a different attorney, she listed the Pere Marquette Building in New Orleans where DiRosa had his law offices, as her address.

By early the following year, relatives of the old couple had surfaced. Led by a niece of Mrs. Johansen, they were also becoming embroiled in the fray. In her own petition for revocation of the probated will, Frances Young Getze, of Newport Beach, accused the Schwartzs of taking grossly unfair advantage of a senile old man who was paranoid, belligerant, confused, and suffered from loss of memory. He was in such awful condition he didn't know what he was doing when he signed the purported will leaving his estate to Mrs. Schwartz, the niece contended.

The couple took advantage of Morris Schwartz's confidential relationship with Johansen and the old man's deteriorated mental health to ingratiate themselves with him and persuade him he was obligated to reward them, she said in the petition.

They allegedly convinced him he and Mrs. Schwartz were reincarnated souls who knew each other in a prior life. She was a queen and he was her slave, whom she had treated with kindness and consideration. Consequently, he owed her a debt for that kindness.

As 1975 neared its end, several additional distant relatives, including first and second cousins, had joined in the dispute to challenge both wills. Neither of them were valid because of Johansen's alleged senility and other mental problems at the time they were made out, they claimed. They also charged that Jill was not in fact his adopted daughter. And if he indeed made out a will naming her as his heir, he executed the document shortly before his death while he was "obviously sick in mind with a progressively deteriorating condition and . . . was easily influenced and controlled by anyone seeking to take advantage of him . . ."

When Jill filed her version of Johansen's will for probate in 1977, it was challenged by Mrs. Getze, just as the documents held by Mrs. Schwartz were.

The full story of the titanic struggle and its conclusion is still hidden in the awesome maze of the Los Angeles County Court system archives. But as recently as January 1990, a declaration for final discharge and order was filed releasing Ann Schwartz as executor of the estate. The document indicated she was the "sole distributee." Another document filed in superior court the previous year awarded a balance remaining in the estate of approximately $7,000 to Mrs. Schwartz after payment of a small amount of attorney and court fees.

So what happened to the rest of the estate? Despite later published denials by Jill that she didn't profit financially, according to her youngest son, she wound up with a considerable inheritance that included about $60,000 in cash, three or four houses, and some other property.

Jill didn't simply cool her heels while resolution of the dispute over Johansen's estate was being slowly played out in the courts. She had never been a woman known for letting grass grow under her feet, and she obviously would not be happy living the single life for long.

She had already changed her name again a few weeks before Johansen was bundled off to New Orleans to sign her adoption papers. On November 3,

1973, she tied the knot with a rugged thirty-three-year-old major in the US Marine Corps. Her married name wasn't really "Coit" when she was adopted. She was Mrs. Donald Charles Brodie.

The ceremony was conducted by a Lutheran clergyman, the Reverend Donald J. Fisher, in the city of Orange, a far suburb at the southwest edge of Los Angeles. Gerald and Mary Ellen Soma of Santa Ana stood up for the couple.

Jill indicated on her marriage license that she had been married only once before, and that her previous husband had died. She signed her name on the marriage certificate as Jill Lonita Coit and listed her date of birth as June 11, 1946, either two or three years after her true birth date. According to the information in the marriage certificate, she was twenty-seven years old, more than five years younger than the groom. Brodie had been married once previously, and was divorced in August 1969. He listed his occupation as the "USMC" and the kind of industry or business he was in as the "US Government." Jill gave her occupation as "model," and her industry or business as "advertising agency."

Both the bride and groom indicated they had sixteen years of formal education and listed the same address on South Ditmar Street in Oceanside, San Diego County. The picturesque coastal city of approximately 77,000 people is roughly midway between Los Angeles and San Diego at the southern edge of the sprawling Camp Pendleton US Marine Corps Base.

A native Hoosier and military career man, Major Brodie may have been as susceptible to his bride's sexual allure and mesmerizing charms as his predecessors. But he was no pushover when it came to handling the couple's finances and personal property. He was a strong man, and his reputed refusal to go along with his wife's demands was a surefire formula for serious trouble in the marriage.

Jill wasn't a woman who could live with her wings clipped and a crimp put on her high-flying ways. That wasn't her style, and any effort to restrict her freedom wasn't something she would put up with for long. It amounted to a declaration of war. She had her own business and other interests, and many other personal affairs were still centered half a continent away in New Orleans and even more exotic locales.

Back home in California, the honey in Jill's relationship with the marine officer rapidly turned to acid, corroding feelings, sensibilities, and emotions. Unhappy with the role of military wife, and blocked from getting her way, Jill packed up her sons and cleared out of Southern California.

Jill and the boys returned to New Orleans, the city of voracious mosquitoes, persistent mildew, distinctive colors, aromas, and tastes—and just enough of the hint of madness, brash dreams and opportunity about it to be irresistible. It was her childhood home, and it was perfect for her. She settled with her boys into a temporary domicile in the 9800 block of Joel Street in Harahan. A separate town of about 11,000 people in Jefferson Parish, Harahan is just below Metairie and it bulges snugly into one of the loops of the north bank of the Mississippi. It is a working-class town where rusty tugboats and fishing skiffs are tied to the piers and docks.

The new address would merely prove to be a stopping-off place where she parked the boys for awhile. A handy baby-sitter was nearby: their grandmother. And Jill's lawyer friend was no longer a half-continent away. The law offices of DiRosa & DiRosa, at 812 Pere Marquette Building, were a fast twenty-minute drive from Harahan. The sturdy old brick structure, only one block off Canal Street, New Orleans' main shopping thoroughfare, was about fifteen floors high, and in those days before the construction boom of the 1980s and 1990s it was one of a handful of buildings that dominated the skyline. It was a modern landmark.

FOUR

Louis

When Jill left California she was ready to embark on imaginatively challenging ventures and to hammer strong new links into her long, ongoing relationship with Louis DiRosa.

In some ways, the wealthy forty-seven-year-old lawyer was the perfect partner for her. He was knowledgeable, with legal and political savvy that could be invaluable to someone with Jill's hungry obsession for wealth.

He had already helped smooth her passage through some fretful times, and it wasn't easy keeping up with the legal and personal needs of a woman like Jill. Some of her enterprises were as quixotically off-the-wall as they were ingenious.

She hadn't lived very long with Brodie, certainly nowhere near the six years she spent with Clark Coit. But actions she took after returning to her hometown indicated the ill-fated union had lasted long enough for her to produce another son.

Jill claimed she was pregnant when she left California, and at 2 AM, on October 18, 1974, gave birth to a boy at 864 Roosevelt Place in New Orleans. She lived in Apartment B, and it appeared that delivery of her fourth son was a home birth.

The child was named Thadius John Brodie, according to a certificate of live birth authenticated by the Louisiana State Registrar. Boxes on the certificate for identification of the birth attendant by profession were checked off both for "MD" and "Other." A box to indicate the presence of a midwife was left blank. The name "T. Kisla" was signed in the space for the signature of the attendant. It was a name that would show up in different variations at other time's in the "mother's" adventuresome life.

Neither Brodie, nor it appears anyone else, ever saw Thadius. There was a good reason for that. There never was a Thadius John Brodie born at the New Orleans apartment building. The entire affair was a hoax.

DiRosa was having personal problems of his own by that time. His marriage of more than twenty-five years was crumbling.

Louis Anthony DiRosa and Marie Buffa were married on September 8, 1948, at the altar of the St. Louis Cathedral in the French Quarter. The stately basilica is one of the oldest active cathedrals in America and easily the most famous structure in New Orleans. For nearly two centuries, the famous as well as the little-known have attended mass and worshipped together at the cathedral and its predecessor.

Constructed on Chartres Street in 1849 after its predecessor was razed, the famous old cathedral faces St. Anthony's Square, where high-spirited Creole dandies, wealthy gentlemen, and military officers at one time fought bloody duels with *colche-mordes* (sword canes) or pistols over sloe-eyed New Orleans belles and matters of honor.

In more recent times the one-time *Place d' Armes,* or military parade ground, is better noted for the amateur and professional artists who sketch, paint, and peddle their work there; for peanut vendors; leftover hippies; beggars; lovers; casual passersby; and office workers on lunch breaks who share its simple enjoyments.

The wedding in the historic cathedral was an auspicious beginning for the couple's life together, and while Louis was busy building a successful career, Marie was providing him with a handsome family of two boys and two girls spaced nearly fifteen years between the first and the last. Claire Frances was born on November 29, 1950; Denise Marie on December 2, 1953; Louis Anthony DiRosa Jr., on October 18, 1956; and Daniel Anthony on March 20, 1963.

The family home was on Robert E. Lee Boulevard, in a suitably genteel and upscale neighborhood in the far north area of the city, only a few blocks from the scoop-shaped shoreline of Lake Pontchartrain. Through his successful law practice and other investments, DiRosa was able to provide well for his family, presenting them with a nice home and good educations for the children. As 1974 was drawing to a close he had accumulated community property valued at nearly $2 million and was earning about $300,000 annually, according to information in legal documents.

The documents were part of a divorce petition filed on December 6, by his wife. Marie accused her husband in the action of adultery, mental harassment, and abandonment. And she pointed her finger squarely at Jill as the other woman involved in the breakup of the marriage.

Marie claimed her husband and Jill had been carrying on an adulterous affair for roughly four years, and they used aliases at times to help cover up their activities and behavior. According to the documents filed in Civil District Court for the Parish of Orleans, Louis used the alias "Ladd DiRosa" and Jill used the name "Sandra Kelly."

If the allegations about a long-running affair were

true, the romance spanned the last, rocky years of Jill's marriage to Clark, her adoption by Edwin Bruce Johansen, her marriage to Brodie, and the years since her return to greater New Orleans. Jill was already carrying on her dalliance with the lawyer while she was leaving her husband and children behind in Houston to take off on business trips, and when Clark was murdered, if the time frame outlined in the divorce petition was correct.

Marie Buffa DiRosa didn't simply manufacture the information to back up her allegations out of thin air. She hired a private detective to check into the activities of her husband and the stunning woman who was spending so much time with him in business dealings and other activities the suspicious homemaker believed to be of a much more personal nature.

The choice of a private investigator was a good one, even though it could hardly have been further from the classic image of a crusty, hard-smoking, hard-drinking, woman-chasing gumshoe. She was no Mike Hammer.

Glenda Imburgia was a middle-aged, matronly woman, a real-life Jessica Fletcher with more meat on her bones. Her ordinary appearance was perfect cover for her profession. She was also bulldog tenacious, a quiet, serious professional who paid attention to detail and understood the most basic requirement of the job, one recognized by any sleuth worth his or her salt: legwork pays off. She searched through courthouse records, examined business dealings, looked through old newspaper files—and knocked on doors.

One of the doors she knocked on was at B. B. and Ginny McCurdy's house in Sharpstown. She talked with them at their home on two different occasions before she extracted enough information to satisfy her. One time she brought her mother along with her from New Orleans, and the women took the McCurdy's out to dinner. The PI told the couple she was working for Marie and trying to pin down how much family money DiRosa had invested in real estate or other business projects he and Jill were involved in. She also wanted to know how much money Jill had contributed to the joint ventures, and how much she received from Clark's Tenneco-related benefits.

One day after the private investigator had already spent months tracking Jill and DiRosa's movements and purchase of properties through Texas, Louisiana, and California, McCurdy telephoned her in New Orleans. The PI's mother answered the telephone and broke the bad news. Her daughter had died. But a good portion of her investigative work was reflected in documents filed with her client's divorce suit.

DiRosa was served with the divorce papers at his law offices in the Pere Marquette Building and retained attorney Sydney J. Parlongue to represent him. His wife was represented by another prominent attorney, J. Harrison Henderson III. Neither side in the domestic dispute was willing to simply roll over and give in.

Marie claimed her husband lived with Jill at a home in the 2100 block of Cleary Street in Metairie from January 7, 1971 through October 1974. At the end of October they reputedly moved to an apartment in the 3800 block of Dumaine, and an apartment at 864 Roosevelt Place, both in New Orleans. The apartment at Roosevelt Place was the location of Thadius's reputed birth. Both properties were owned by the Tower Advertising Agency, in which Jill was an incorporator and the majority stockholder.

The petition also claimed Jill was still married to Clark, but that was an error. At the time the divorce was filed, the Tenneco engineer had been dead more than two-and-a-half years.

Jill eventually bought a bundle of properties around

New Orleans. In documents identifying her as the widow of William C. Coit Jr., Jill took out a $255,000 mortgage on nineteen lots known as the Mid-City Baptist Church property on June 1, 1973.

A couple of months before buying the church property she had arranged to have herself named as the natural tutrix of her three boys, a legal maneuver that expanded her powers over the normal responsibilities of guardianship for her minor sons and their estates. At the time of the appointment in the Twenty-fourth Judicial District Court in Jefferson Parish, the total property said to be owned by the boys was appraised at a measly $4,666.66.

Peering at the legal strategem from the outside, it appears to be a curious action to take. But the hidden motivations and Machiavellian finagling that lurked behind Jill's surface behavior were seldom easy to figure out.

The divorce was quickly settled at a hearing on March 10, 1975. It was barely three weeks short of the third anniversary of Clark's death. After considering the pleadings and evidence offered by both parties and listening to the arguments of their attorneys, Judge Henry J. Roberts found for the plaintiff. He granted a divorce to Mrs. DiRosa and continued a previously-issued preliminary injunction, blocking her former husband or anyone acting with him or on his behalf from selling or otherwise disposing of or tieing up any of the community property. It was a broad-ranging order that applied to real estate, stocks, bonds, bank accounts, partnership interests, and other property they shared ownership in.

Exceptions were made for some personal and office bank accounts at several New Orleans banks for DiRosa and some personal accounts in the name of his ex-wife. The law practice remained with Louis.

Mrs. DiRosa was given custody of their last remaining minor child, Daniel Anthony, with visitation rights granted to his father. The newly-divorced lawyer was ordered to pay permanent monthly alimony of $250 to his ex-wife, and $750 per month in child support. The $1,000 total was to be paid in increments of $500 each on the first and the fifteenth of each month. DiRosa was also ordered to make mortgage payments, and to pay taxes, insurance, and electricity bills on the family home, as well as school tuition for Daniel.

Although the divorce itself was quickly settled, the contest over related matters dragged on for months, becoming a nasty marathon of accusations and denials.

Louis had taken a good shot in court, and the acrimony wasn't over yet, but the way was clear for the next act in the business and romantic saga he was playing out with Jill. On October 11, 1976, eighteen months after Marie obtained her divorce, Louis and Jill slipped off to Mississippi to tie the knot.

When she was a little girl, Jill may or may not have dreamed of marrying in the majestic St. Louis Cathedral, but it's unlikely she even considered that for her union with the lawyer. The Cathedral was for white dresses and at least the appearance of virginal brides, and Jill hadn't qualified at any of her weddings.

Temperatures in Louisiana were hovering in the high sixties, and the banana leaves and the ginger lilies were just beginning to turn brown when the couple drove northwest past Baton Rouge, then continued on through the plantation country and on across the Mississippi state line to Wilkinson County. There, in the quiet town of Woodville in the middle of nowhere, they repeated their vows in front of the Reverend O. B. Beverly. The ceremony was simple, as they tended to be at Jill's weddings. The bride gave her age as thirty-three. The groom was fifty.

Unsurprisingly for a couple who were so familiar with the workings of the courts, divorces, and such weighty matters as alimony and property rights, they signed a prenuptial agreement before repeating their "till-death-do-us-parts." The pact waived the Louisiana community-property laws and declared their property to be separately owned.

DiRosa knew his way around the divorce courts because it was his business to know, and he had recent personal experience as well. But Jill was no babe in the woods when it came to the marriage game either. She had logged in more experience than most brides and divorcees, and she knew how to protect her financial interests.

Her proximity and intimate relationship to the experienced lawyer was also adding to her knowledge of how to use the legal system to her advantage. She was alert, attentive, and eager to learn, and she acquired a smattering of knowledge about some of the convolutions and ambiguities that are such puzzling aspects of the law to most.

It was just enough knowledge to smooth the way for some of her business deals—or to get her into a peck of trouble if she became too ambitious and made a misstep. But Jill understood that her spouse was the lawyer in the family.

Looking back on the marriage years later, Nancy Reed, her longtime friend in North Manchester, observed: "She was attracted to men who could teach her lots about life." Nancy was impressed by the two of Jill's several husbands she had met, and thought they were nice, interesting people.

Jill helped arrange for her former high-school friend to move to New Orleans for awhile, and the young woman from North Manchester worked for Louis while she lived in the Crescent City.

When the tugboat captain's daughter drove home with her new husband after the wedding in Mississippi, she probably felt that she had at last acquired the credentials to move into a strata of New Orleans society where she had belonged all along. It was a world of personal prestige, power, money, and all the trappings of flash and luxury that go with it.

She wasn't a woman who got terribly excited about fixing a dinner at home, and she loved to eat out. New Orleans was perfect for that and offered nights of fine dining in a city where it may well be argued that its unique culinary arts are surpassed nowhere in the world, not even in Paris. Fine restaurants with world-renowned chefs, and smaller, more intimate eateries that were off the beaten path offered gourmet specialties with everything from Creole favorites like *crawfish étouffée* and gumbo to blackened redfish and rich desserts of pecan pie. There was always shrimp, prepared in a variety of manners, of course, and other fresh seafood appetizers of raw oysters, clams, and scallops.

Jill bought and wore exciting clothes and exquisite jewelry, drove sleek and powerful automobiles, and rubbed shoulders with male and female companions whose social skills were finely polished. Jill may not have vaulted all the way to the top of New Orleans society, and she and her husband weren't about to pull up stakes and leave Louisiana for a Palm Beach mansion, but she was living an exciting life. And she was accumulating more knowledge and wealth with every marriage. She was on the fast track. Doors of opportunity previously closed to her were opening, and she wasn't shy about continuing to pound at those that were still closed. The sky was the limit.

On September 19, 1977, almost exactly eleven months after the quiet Mississippi wedding, Jill and Louis married again. The reason? Jill loved wedding ceremonies. This time the early evening nuptials were performed in marshy St. Bernard Parish which curls under Lake Borgne at the southeastern edge of the Crescent City. The vows were repeated in the town of

Chalmette before Michael D. Roig, a justice of the peace. The bride's name on the marriage certificate was listed as Jill Billiot (Coit.)

The bride listed the address in the 3800 block of Dumaine Street, as her home. The groom listed 864 Roosevelt place as his domicile. Jill also identified the birthplace of her mother as Louisiana, rather than Indiana, and indicated on the license that she had completed four years of college. Her husband stated on the form that he had "5 +" years of college.

Jill indicated it was her second marriage, and that her previous union had ended in death. DiRosa also indicated it was his second marriage, and his first marriage ended in divorce.

Chalmette is best known as the site where advancing British troops were slaughtered by a rag-tag army of American frontiersmen including Tennessee sharpshooters led by General Andrew Jackson and a corps of ragged Baratarian pirates headed by swashbuckling buccaneer Jean Lafitte during the Battle of New Orleans. Tragically, the bloody confrontation occurred a few days after a peace treaty was signed between the American and British governments, officially ending the War of 1812. But because of the primitive system of communications at that time, the combatants didn't learn the war had ended until after the battle.

It's doubtful that Jill and her husband wasted any thoughts that night on the role of Chalmette in America's military or political history. They were concerned with more personal struggles and challenges. And, in fact, when they repeated their vows for the second time, their own history together was already rapidly nearing an end.

Less than four months later, according to court documents filed by the groom, the couple separated. Jill had kept busy buying up valuable property almost to the last minute, and a few weeks before the separation she took out a $100,000 mortgage and purchased another.

On February 1, 1978, however, she left behind her lawyer husband, the enticing business opportunities, and the sultry, moist heat that produces ugly tempers and prickly red blotches on the skin. Once more she headed north to Indiana, and the bleak, frozen, midwinter farm country of Wabash County. Her friend, Nancy, had already returned home, and Jill had other close ties there, as well.

FIVE

Eldon

Although Jill may have slipped relatively quietly into North Manchester when she was a teenager, she played out a complete reversal when she returned to the bucolic farm community ten years later. She blew back into town with all the subtlety of a hand grenade with the pin pulled out. And she didn't try to get her old job back at the book bindery.

By most local standards the former North Manchester High School dropout had metamorphosed into an accomplished woman of the world; an exotic and sexually-magnetic siren who had crisscrossed half the country and carried a passport stamped with the names of glamorous foreign locales (in those days) like Port-au-Prince in Haiti and Tegucigalpa, Honduras.

But she was a single mother with three sons, and she behaved like she was serious about putting down some strong new roots in the close-knit little community. She told friends she wanted to raise her boys in a safer, more wholesome environment than New Orleans.

Jill backed up her words by buying a farm a few miles northwest of town and began putting together a menagerie of animals there for the boys. She planted a garden, harvested the crops, and canned and froze the fresh produce. She also proved that she could put together an impressive meal. She was a fantastic cook, according to her friend Nancy.

Once she was back home, Jill renewed and cemented old friendships and made new ones. She was generous, and frequently surprised people she liked or wished to impress with fine gifts. She was charming, a great storyteller who had wonderful tales to spin about her travels, experiences, and husbands. An exciting air of mystery seemed somehow to always cling to her.

At the time, she was between husbands—sort of. During the winter of 1977 to 1978, when she swept back into North Manchester, she was still legally married to DiRosa, although divorce proceedings were already filed.

But she wasn't a woman willing to settle for being without a special man in her life for very long. As old-timers in Indiana say, the flamboyant, effervescent beauty with the exquisite café-au-lait complexion was the kind of woman whose smoldering gaze could make a man's eyeballs sizzle.

She had barely swept back onto the scene in North Manchester with her boys, her flashy, expensive jewelry, and her snazzy red classic T-Bird before she attracted the eye and earnest attention of one of the community's most eligible bachelors.

Eldon Duane Metzger was a highly respected local farmer and businessman who had managed to hold onto his bachelorhood for thirty-seven years before his path crossed with Jill's. Various branches of the extensive Metzger family in Wabash County and other nearby northern Indiana communities had produced lawyers, teachers, doctors, nurses, secretaries, truck drivers, and practitioners of a host of other professions. The Metzgers sprung from solid, taciturn German Baptist stock, and when Eldon brought Jill along to family get-togethers, she livened up the normally-subdued, proper affairs.

Metzger was best known in North Manchester for his dual professions as an auctioneer and realtor. The Metzger Auction & Realty Company was a fixture in North Manchester. And just about every weekend when the weather was good, and often when it wasn't so good, Metzger could be tracked down in front of a local home in town or a Wabash County barnyard auctioneering household goods, farm equipment, real estate, and animals.

Metzger Realty helped her purchase a store building in Laketon, another little settlement of about 500 people a few miles southwest of North Manchester. It was known locally as Mary's Sundries and was a popular local hangout. Jill turned it into a luncheonette. Years later she dropped the luncheonette idea, and opened a noodle factory in the building. The boys helped their mother with the noodle-making, she said. Local residents remembered the noodle venture differently, however, and claim that except for being involved in a real estate transaction for the building, she had almost nothing to do with the business.

She was working hard to build up new businesses, however, and she was also occupied with more personal matters—building a relationship with the new man in her life.

Jill had the rare ability to spot vulnerabilities in a man, and she focused in on their weaknesses like a hungry cheetah surveying a herd of wildebeest. Men were her prey, and when she was on a blood-scent she didn't deviate from her target. She was a sultry temptress who could addle male minds with her sexual charisma, serve as a charming dinner companion, or chat knowledgeably about sports cars, guns, or business.

On March 14, 1978, Jill and the auctioneer drove across the Ohio line to the Allen County seat of Lima and filed an application in the probate division of the common pleas court for a marriage license. The bride identified herself to the license clerk as Jill Coit-Johansen, and stated that her union with Metzger would be her first marriage. Spaces on the form for listing of prior marriages and minor children were left blank. Her birth date was listed as June 11, 1943, her birthplace as Iberia, Louisiana, and her profession as secretary. In the blanks on the form for the name of her father and the maiden name of her mother, she stated they were Edwin Johansen and Mary Taney.

Metzger entered his birth date as July 14, 1940, his birthplace as Wabash County, Indiana, and his occupation as "farming." He identified his parents as Orville E. Metzger and the former Ellen Niccum. Curiously, both the prospective bride and groom gave their residence as Route 4, Manchester, in Jacob County, Kentucky. The tiny Cumberland mountain settlement of 1,800 people in the Bluegrass State is more than three hundred miles from North Manchester, in the Daniel Boone National Forest near the tri-state border with Tennessee and Virginia. And it is in Clay County. Manchester is adjacent to Jackson County, but there is no Jacob County in Kentucky.

Such minor inconsistencies in the filling out of personal details on legal documents weren't anything new when Jill was involved. The couple drove back to North Manchester to wait out the next few days until they could be married. A week later they returned to the old courthouse in Lima for the ceremony. Each of them signed their names—his as "Eldon D. Metzger" and hers as "Jill C. Johansen"—under a statement certifying that they were legally free to marry, according to Ohio laws. The statement read: "That neither of the said parties is an habitual drunkard, imbecile, or insane, and is not under the influence of any intoxicating liquor or narcotic drug, that neither has syphilis which is communicable or likely to become so and they have complied with the Ohio serological test. Said parties are not nearer of kin than second cousins, and there is no legal impediment to their marriage."

In the state of Ohio, as in other states, a former marriage that has not yet been legally dissolved constitutes a legal impediment to a new marriage.

But Common Pleas Court Judge Richard D. Heeter was obviously unaware that the bride was still married to a husband in New Orleans, and he performed the civil ceremony. This time when the couple drove back to Indiana, they returned as bride and groom. Jill's marriage to Metzger marked the second time she had committed bigamy.

She didn't get around to making an effort to officially cut her conjugal ties to DiRosa until she had already been married to Metzger for nearly eight months. In November she and DiRosa boarded flights to Port-au-Prince to obtain a Haitian divorce. The process required little more than Jill appearing before a civil court official on November 4 with a French and English translator and signing a one-page statement signifying she and her husband were incompatible and wished to be divorced.

The statement dissolving the fourteen-month union two days later specifically referred to the marriage on September 19, 1977 in St. Bernard Parish. The wife's name on the document was entered as Mrs. Jill J. Coit-DiRosa, and her domicile was entered as 864 Roosevelt Place, Apartment B, New Orleans. Her husband's domicile was listed as 812 Pere Marquette Building, New Orleans. It was the address of his law office.

The civil court functionary also ruled, "that the lady has the right to use again her former married name: COIT."

When the divorced couple left Haiti and flew back

to the United States, nothing had been entered on record in Port-au-Prince about Jill's marriage to DiRosa in Mississippi or about her latest marriage to Metzger.

The auctioneer got along well enough with Jill's boys, but she had other priorities that sometimes conflicted with her role as a mother. In her wanderings around the country while she flitted from husband to husband, the boys were a necessary burden. If she didn't exactly operate according to the old saying, "out of sight, out of mind," she sometimes came close. At least once she fixed up the basement of her home, so her sons could live downstairs most of the time, out of the way and out of sight of adults.

"It was always a different person, a different man," her youngest son, William III recalled years later. "She just . . . kept us in a little closet."

Jill was a busy woman, and she had to have help raising the boys and with her housekeeping. She liked the Old Order Amish and hired some of the plain, unassuming young women to help out with the homemaking. At one time she also arranged for a woman who was a Central American refugee to live with her and take care of the house. When the housekeeper worried about a child she left behind, Jill brought the youngster to live with them in Indiana.

It was that kind of generous behavior that endeared Jill to her friends in Indiana. Jill was a woman who seemed never to forget a card or a present for the anniversary or birthday of a friend. She worked hard at being a friend. Even then, though, some of her friends had second thoughts about her motivations for some of the things she did.

Nancy Reed later recalled in an interview with the hometown newspaper that Jill was the sharpest businesswoman she ever met. She was constantly "wheeling and dealing" and striving to get ahead. Reed said there was always a sense, however, that Jill wasn't being completely upfront. "She had so many stories, she had been so many places, done so many things, that after awhile you couldn't keep up and didn't ask all the questions that came to mind, because you knew you wouldn't get answers."

When the younger boys became old enough, she arranged for their education away from home in boarding schools or military academies. She squeezed every dime she could get out of the trust estates left by her former in-laws, the Coits, with pleas for money she said was needed to pay for the boys' educations.

Seth grew up closer to his mother than his younger brothers did, and as they gradually drew away from her, he seemed to grow closer. When he was thirteen, about the time his mother married Metzger, he began helping out at the office of a Manchester veterinarian. He held onto the job for several years, and as he grew older he also obtained experience in farming.

By the time he was twenty-one he was working in the little farming town of Nappanee at the edge of the Amish and Mennonite country in nearby Elkhart County at Holiday Rambler as an insulator and roof assembler.

Soon after their mother settled again in Wabash County, the two younger boys were enrolled at the Culver Military Academies, roughly fifty miles west of North Manchester along the north shore of Lake Maxinkuckee.

Maxinkuckee is the second largest natural lake in Indiana. The town of Culver, a popular summer resort of about 1,600 year-round residents, curls around the northwest shoreline where bathers congregate at a fine public beach during the warm summer months. But the Marshall County locale is best known nationally for CMA, the Culver Military Academies—Culver Military Academy, the Culver Girls Academy, and the Culver Summer Camps. Established in 1894 as the

Culver Military Academy for boys only, the expanded program now draws both male and female students to the 1,500-acre lakeside campus from throughout the country and from foreign nations as far away as the Republic of Korea, Thailand, India, Japan, Israel, Slovenia, France, and Spain for its fine prep-school educational opportunities and summer camping activities. About twenty percent of the student body is from foreign countries.

Students at the tradition-steeped institution can train for private pilot ratings at Fleet Field, the academy's own twin-runway airfield; learn sailing skills aboard the *R. H. Ledbetter,* a three-masted sailing ship or smaller watercraft; or become an accomplished equestrian and polo player, along with mastering traditional academics. Culver has the largest equestrian school in the United States, and since 1897 has been home to the Black Horse Troop that has ridden at ten presidential inaugurations beginning with the presidency of Woodrow Wilson, and his vice-president, North Manchester's famous son, Thomas Marshall. The troop led the inaugural parade for President Jimmy Carter.

Costs of obtaining an education at Culver are not cheap. By the beginning of the 1994 school year, the total for basic tuition and board at CMA and CGA was $16,950. Hefty additional charges are tacked on for special programs such as pilot instruction, the Black Horse Troop, and the sister program for girls, "equitation" (horsemanship).

But Jill's sons were enrolled at one of the premier prep schools in the nation, with alumni who made names for themselves in everything from politics, business, and the media to the entertainment industry and the military. Michael Huffington, US Congressman then an unsuccessful US Senate candidate from California; Will Van Rogers Jr., movie actor, congressman,

Battle of the Bulge tank commander, and son of famous humorist Will Rogers Sr.; actor Hal Holbrook; New York Yankees owner George Steinbrenner; and Pulitzer-Prize winning producer and director Joshua Logan are a few of the better-known graduates.

While her boys were at CMA being looked after by someone else or looking after themselves, Jill kept busy pursuing her quest for wealth. She collected and hoarded expensive toys, baubles, and easily-negotiable possessions like the T-Bird and diamonds. She stashed South African gold Krugerrands into three and four-foot lengths of two-inch metal pipe then sealed them by capping the ends. The valuable coins were a perfect fit.

"She was money mad, money mad," says McCurdy. A few years after Jill arrived back in Wabash County she had approximately $100,000 invested in certificates of deposit, and $150,000 in cash in addition to diamonds and gold and silver coins in her safety-deposit box.

She bought a used 1976 Mercedes to drive when she wasn't tooling around in the T-Bird, and added a Lincoln, two Porsches, a U-Haul truck and an Airstream trailer to her growing fleet of vehicles.

She also scanned legal advertisements in the *News-Journal,* the *Plain Dealer* in Wabash and in other area newspapers, and checked at the courthouses for tax-sale properties she could invest in. Other people's failures and disappointments turned into her opportunities and accomplishments. Eventually she acquired a house in North Manchester, two houses in Wabash, two farms, including one spread that was fifty acres, and approximately thirty pieces of tax-sale property in northern Indiana. She owned other pieces of real estate in Louisiana and Texas, including an $8,000 property in Austin.

Most of the properties were purchased under Tower

Advertising or other corporate names. Seth moved into the North Manchester house, which was purchased under the Nei Mar Corporation A few years later she made him an equal partner in the corporation.

Jill was a natural saleswoman and entrepreneur. She had a keen eye and ear for business and the personal charisma of a successful evangelist. She was also a devoted collector of licenses, diplomas, and certificates of accomplishment. She was credential-driven, and licenses and similiar documents were essential elements of her freedom and mobility. With the right license she could go almost anywhere and do almost anything.

If she wasn't out somewhere buying properties, she was attending night school or some other class in order to equip herself with new skills or hone old ones to a greater degree of proficiency. One of the schools she attended was sponsored by State Farm Insurance to train its agents.

While Jill was attending the school she shared a motel room with another woman. One evening after returning from classes Jill walked into the room and dumped the contents of her purse on her bed. Her roommate was shocked when a little pearl-handled pistol tumbled out onto the bedspread.

"What are you doing with that pistol?" the woman gasped.

Jill stared at her as if she was insane for asking such a question.

"You mean you don't have a pistol?" she asked. "Every woman should have a gun. How are you going to defend yourself?"

Jill's companion found herself apologizing for not carrying a gun and trying to hide her embarrassment. She had grown up in a small town where the streets were safe, and private homes were secure sanctuaries. Jill was from New Orleans, a big and violent city where people locked their doors at night and were as likely as not to barricade their windows with metal bars.

The way Jill explained it, packing a gun in her purse made a lot of sense. She had a way of turning things around, so that her eccentricities seemed suddenly not so curious anymore and anyone who didn't share them appeared to be the one who was out of step.

One of her girlfriends from her high-school days in North Manchester was visiting at her house once when Jill opened a dresser drawer. It was crammed full of handguns.

The same year Jill was licensed as a State Farm agent, she obtained a real-estate license, an auctioneer license, a nursery-dealer's license, and a health-food license. She began attending school to obtain a travel-agent's license but dropped out. Her health failed her, she explained.

In 1981 she took a trip to North Carolina where she got herself a gun license. She used the name Terri Kisla, a variation of "T. Kisla," the name used for the doctor or paramedic on the bogus birth certificate for Thadius Brodie. Jill also bought a tract of tax-sale property while she was in North Carolina.

Back home she ran ads in the *News-Journal* encouraging insurance shoppers to: "See me for car, home, life, health, and business insurance." A photograph run with the advertisement showed Jill's hair pulled away from her face and piled high in a bun. Large circular earrings dangled from her ears, and she was wearing a business-suit jacket with a tasteful high-necked blouse and a knotted scarf. Jill ran the busy agency from a yellow house on West Street, just off the main drag.

She was a hard worker, and a decade later she was receiving monthly checks from the company for more than $1,600 in residuals from policies she sold during her brief career in insurance. Jill often opened the doors at six-thirty in the morning to take care of business with factory workers before they checked in at their jobs. It wasn't at all unusual for her to stay on the job until seven or eight o'clock at night.

Eventually, during her travels around the country she collected driver's licenses from more than a dozen states, usually in one of her married names. She acquired a North Carolina driver's license, however, in the name of Jill Theressa Kisla. She also obtained an Alaskan voter-registration card.

Jill lived in some of the states where she acquired driver's licenses, such as Louisiana, Indiana, and Texas for years. In others—Arizona, California, Georgia, Kentucky, New York, New Mexico, and North Carolina—she stayed for only a few weeks or for a few months.

If Jill is to be believed, however, after she settled down in rural North Manchester tending to her duties as homemaker, mother, and businesswoman, a painful tragedy intruded on her busy life. She claimed to have given birth to another baby, and it died.

When stories first began circulating around town that Jill was pregnant and Eldon was going to become a father, it was considered good news. Jill's boys were growing up, and townspeople who knew the couple speculated that it would be about the best thing that could happen to the marriage to have a new baby in the house. At the time she was living in a farmhouse west of town, and she fixed up one of the rooms as a nursery. She showed the nursery off to her friend Nancy, along with baby clothes for the anticipated newcomer.

Jill, it seemed, was a woman who didn't gain much weight, even in an advanced state of pregnancy. She explained to her friend she never showed.

When the time came for the baby to arrive, how-

ever, Jill was out of town. She returned after a few
weeks without the baby, and quickly resumed her normal routine looking as slim and feisty as ever. When
people began asking questions, she explained the baby
was afflicted with serious congenital defects and had
to stay behind in a hospital incubator. One day when
Worth Weller, the local newspaper publisher, ran into
Metzger on the street, the newshound told the auctioneer how sorry he was to hear the tragic news about
the baby.

"He just gave me a blank look," Weller recalled
later.

According to Weller, a few days later his weekly
newspaper, the *News-Journal* ran an obituary for
Tinley Metzger, who it appeared had died in a hospital
halfway across the country without ever drawing a
breath in Indiana.

It was true that Jill had been back in New Orleans
again, but she didn't go there to have a baby. She was
still involved in legal wrangling involving DiRosa and
his former wife, Marie. Jill was in New Orleans to provide a deposition, a legal term for testimony or a statement given under oath outside a courtroom.

Some of the questions asked at the December 14,
1978, confrontation were merely curious, others were
exceedingly odd. "Have you used the name Jean or
Gene Remington?," she was asked. "Are you related
to the Rockefeller family?," and "Are you presently
living with Elton Metsker?" The auctioneer's first and
last name were spelled phoenetically by the court reporter.

Her attorney, Harry R. Cabral, Jr., refused to permit her to answer the questions, claiming Marie was
merely attempting to humiliate his client. However,
according to the records, she did state that she was not
married at that time and was currently living in Princeton, Indiana. Princeton is more than 200 miles catty-

cornered across the state from North Manchester, and the town of approximately 9,000 is in Gibson County near Evansville. Jill did not say anything about how she happened to settle so far from her more usual haunts in the northeastern area of the state. Another smaller Indiana town named Pierceton is only a few miles from North Manchester in adjoining Kosciusko County, however, leaving the question open that her statement may have been misunderstood during transcribing of the deposition tape.

Jill also didn't say anything during the deposition hearing about being pregnant with or giving birth to the auctioneer's child. The Metzger baby was another phantom, like Thadius, as difficult to grasp and pin down as the putative mother.

Early in 1979, Marie Buffa-DiRosa filed a lawsuit against Jill and her New Orleans lawyer, Cabral, accusing them of defamation of character. Cabral represented Jill in the divorce suit between DiRosa and Marie. Curiously, among the information filed with the suit, three separate Social Security numbers were listed for Jill.

The first Mrs. DiRosa sought a total of $300,000 from the two defendants for humiliation and mental suffering allegedly caused by a petition for injunction that Cabral filed in the Orleans Parish courts accusing her of making threats against the lives of Jill and her children. Cabral asked the court to issue an order prohibiting Marie from interfering with Jill Coit-DiRosa or her family in any matter whatsoever.

Through her attorney, Marie denied threatening or harassing Jill and contended the allegations were made in order to damage her character and reputation. She claimed the petition exposed her to "disrepute and ridicule and has lowered her in the opinion of her friends and family by picturing her as a jealous

wife who would go to any extreme to cause harm to
Jill Coit-DiRosa . . ."

In filing the petition for injunction, Cabral "acted
recklessly, maliciously, and in wanton disregard of the
truth," it was claimed in the lawsuit. Breaking down
the requested judgment, Maric's lawyers asked for
$100,000 for injury to her reputation in the eyes of her
friends, $100,000 for injury to her reputation in the
eyes of her relatives, and $100,000 for injury due to
embarrassment and mental anguish caused by filing of
the injunction petition.

The Jefferson Parish-based lawyer and Jill apparently avoided any serious damage from Marie
DiRosa's spirited defense of her character. At her request, the suit was dismissed in August, less than four
months after it was filed.

Seth was a teenager while Jill was coping with phantom pregnancies, depositions, and a Haitian divorce,
and he was experiencing some troubles of his own. He
was named in a paternity suit filed in the Kosciusko
County Courthouse in neighboring Warsaw.

Jill was undaunted by all the fuss about babies. She
was on a roll, frenetically collecting licenses, educational credits, and properties. She was obsessed with
money and all its trappings, and was constantly scheming, plotting and mapping out new ways to accumulate
more wealth. In 1980 she bought a three-year-old
Porsche.

She also managed an amicable breakup with her
husband and took up with another local man. He was
the grown son of a well-to-do Wabash County farmer,
and they were involved with each other after Jill
moved out of her husband's farm home and into a
historic home near North Manchester's downtown
area. But Jill didn't invest too much of her time on the
farmer's son before that relationship, like her marriage to the auctioneer, ended.

Other business and romantic interests were already developing a few miles west of North Manchester in an area of small farming communities that were very much like those in Wabash.

Wabash County is known for its scenic namesake river that winds southwesterly to Terre Haute where it dips almost due south and defines Indiana's western border with Illinois until it flows into the Ohio River at the tri-state juncture with Kentucky.

Jill was busily shuttling between North Manchester and Marshall County, where the best-known body of water is the 1,854-acre spring-fed Lake Maxinkuckee. The town of Culver and the Culver Military Academies are located on it's shores.

SIX

Carl

"I had some of the best training that the world has to give. . . . I think in terms of mental and emotional toughness, was the Marine Corps. If you're gonna lead marines you need to be more than just physically tough. You have to be mentally and emotionally tough. And I was prepared for that. But I wasn't prepared for the likes of her."

Carl Victor Steely,
Interview with author

The pace in Culver, Indiana, was slow, and the people were friendly.

A huge chunk of the local economy was geared to visitors attracted to the academies and to vacationers who settled into rental cottages and boarding houses or motels to take advantage of the recreational activities provided by the lake. For generations, Maxinkuckee's cool waters have offered opportunities to swim, fish, boat, water-ski, or simply sunbathe and shake off the pressures of the workaday world for awhile.

Little more than a half-century ago, in the days before electricity transformed refrigeration, harvesting of lake ice was still a major commercial wintertime undertaking. One year shortly after the turn of the century, robust ice-gangs harvested an incredible 40,000 tons of ice from Maxinkuckee. Some of the workmen were paid in gold from a local bank for their frigid labors.

Historians agree the lake's name is a Potawatomi Indian word, but translators have never quite settled on the exact meaning. Some have translated "Maxinkuckee" to mean "clear waters." Others believe "peaceful waters" is the correct translation, and still others say "high land and good water" is the proper meaning.

Civil War general Lew Wallace, a native Hoosier, wrote part of his epic historical novel, *Ben Hur*, at a popular Culver lakeside hostelry, Allegheny House. Broadway director and composer Joshua Logan attended elementary school in Culver, and Buffalo Bill and World War I General John J. "Blackjack" Pershing, who later chased Pancho Villa, visited the resort community. The Potawatomi were long gone by those days, broken in spirit and decimated in numbers after being sent off in 1838 to a reservation in Kansas in a forced march that became known as the "Trail of Tears."

The attention of modern citizens of the town is focused on happier events, and each July back to back weekend celebrations, the Culver Lakefest, and the Corn Roast and Firemen's Festival draw huge crowds of people from surrounding communities to the small town.

But when Jill wheeled into the postcard-pretty little lakeside town to check on her two younger sons at Culver Military Academy she wasn't looking for festivals, good neighbors, or a picturesque new home.

New surroundings meant new business opportunities. And if the timing and situation were right, they might also lead to a new romance and a pliable new man in her life.

Carl Victor Steely was the commandant at CMA, and he was just the kind of man she needed to fill the recent void in her life. Except for one glaring deficiency, a lack of property or ready cash, he was excellent husband material.

A tall, spare, ramrod-straight man with glasses, penetrating blue eyes, and thinning hair cut military-close and doorknob-smooth, Steely had recently undergone some dreadful personal and financial reverses. He was at a low point economically. He had gone through a painful divorce and had to close down a flying school he operated in Florida with several partners that left him deeply in debt.

But he had a responsible job at CMA, and as Jill quickly learned when she glided into his life, he was an only child who anticipated a hefty inheritance when his aged mother in Kentucky died.

After lonely months of bachelorhood, the commandant suddenly found himself making the dating scene once more, strolling the lush, heavily-wooded academy campus, sharing long drives around Marshall County in a sporty red T-Bird, and dining out with a delightfully entertaining and lovely companion. Culver residents became used to seeing them holding hands as they pedalled twin 10-speed bicycles side-by-side along the tree-lined streets of the resort town.

Jill was cultured and intelligent. She told the commandant she was a graduate of the exclusive Newcomb College, an all-girls' school with a campus that adjoins that of Tulane University in New Orleans. It was there, while she was studying drama at Newcomb, that she met her late husband, "W. C.," she said. Jill had taken long ago to calling her late husband by his initials; there was something classy about it. Jill, of course, had attended Tulane, not Newcomb.

At first, there were long, serious discussions about her sons. She was concerned one of the boys wasn't doing well enough with his studies and needed additional help. But the conversations quickly became more intimate and turned to personal interests they shared like horseback riding, sports cars, traveling, flying, and skiing.

Steely was an athletic man and a licensed pilot. He bicycled, rode motorcycles, and perhaps most importantly, was an avid skier. Skiing was a sport Jill also shared a healthy interest in. During winter breaks around the Christmas and New Year's holidays, Steely liked to board an airliner and fly to Colorado to spend a few days or a week on the slopes of one of the ski resorts clustered in the Rocky Mountains. About the only major ski resort in the state he had missed was Steamboat Springs, a picturesque community of about 6,000 people nestled in the fertile Yampa Valley a drive of only an hour or so from the Wyoming state line. He was determined to try out the slopes there at the first opportunity.

But one of the most appealing characteristics to Steely about the sexy woman he was squiring around Culver, was her ability to discuss the Bible so knowledgeably and with such insight. The CMA commandant was a former Southern Baptist minister who had once pastored his own church in Kentucky about twenty miles up and across the Ohio river from Cincinnatti. Jill told him that she too was raised as a Southern Baptist, and she could match him word for word and thought for thought when it came to quoting verses of the Bible or analyzing parables and lessons. They began attending church services together.

"That's what really drew us together," he says.

The son of Arthur Dilman Steely, a family doctor in Kentucky, and Thelma Christine Steely, a homemaker, the lanky young man felt a sincere calling for the ministry. He enjoyed his work, but he was troubled that he was too young and didn't have the experience to counsel members of his tiny flock about such intimate matters as problems with their marriages and other troubles.

"I realized, in the ministry, I was trying to counsel people about their problems, and I really led a very sheltered life . . . I really didn't understand people's problems."

He decided a good way to gain experience, while seeing the world, was to join the Marine Corps. As far as matters of personal safety were concerned, Steely's timing was fortunate. The Korean War was winding down, and the the US military wasn't yet bogged down in the war in southeast Asia. Steely began his brief military career as a second lieutenant, serving at the US Marine Base at Quantico, Virginia, before he was given a duty assignment to Camp Fuji, the US Marine Corps Base at the foot of Mount Fuji in Japan. He wound up his four-year Marine Corps enlistment at the Parris Island Marine Corps Recruit Depot just outside Beaufort, South Carolina.

Older, more experienced, and presumably wiser, after his stint in the marines Steely shifted gears and entered what he now calls "the ministry of education." A former marine friend he knew at Parris Island told him about an opening on the faculty of the Florida Military School in Deland, a few miles inland from Daytona Beach.

Steely stayed there for seven years. He also got together with some business acquaintances and formed the Piper Acceptance Corporation. The group established a flying school at nearby Sanford on Lake Monroe and the St. John River. Initially, they also sold airplanes but eventually decided to concentrate on teaching other people to fly. It was more profitable.

Things began turning sour at the flying school, about the time a new federal statute was passed permitting the Drug Enforcement Administration and other law enforcement agencies to seize cash, real estate, and other property including cars, boats, and airplanes purchased with drug profits or used in drug trafficking. As the DEA cracked down on smugglers in the Miami area, some of the drug-runners began to move their operations further north. Steely says he and his partners realized they had almost no protection against the possibility that one of their instructors might use one of their aircraft to make a drug run. Students or pilots who rented their aircraft could also bring the law down on them, and they could lose their small fleet of Pipers and everything they owned. They wouldn't even be able to get insurance.

Then they learned that one of their pilots may have already been involved in drug-running, Steely says. According to the forfeiture law, the government doesn't have to prove that the owner is a criminal, only that the property was used in commission of a crime or bought with crime-generated funds. Steely and his partners reluctantly decided to fold their business.

In 1966 when a job opportunity became available at CMA he left the Florida Military School and moved to Culver. He was an energetic man, and while attending to his duties at CMA, he added to his collection of degrees by earning a Masters in Business Administration from the University of Notre Dame. The Notre Dame campus is a thirty-five-mile drive northeast of Culver.

Less than a week into the new year, on January 6, 1983, the couple were married on the campus inside the stately Culver Memorial Chapel. CMA Chaplain David R. Pitt conducted the ceremony. It was a typically frigid northern Indiana midwinter day, and a few hundred yards outside the chapel, the bulky figures of hardy fishermen dotted the lake where they huddled over holes chopped in the ice and angled for fat crappie, yellow perch, bluegill, and an occasional catfish or pike.

Jill may have still been married to two or three men at that time. Many aspects of her intricate life are murky, and a decade later private investigators, legal authorities, and journalists were still trying to sort them out. There was difficulty locating any records showing she and Metzger had divorced, and the auctioneer was keeping a tight lip on the subject although he eventually told a local reporter his marriage was dissolved.

But there was no question the Haitian divorce from DiRosa was invalid. She was committing bigamy for the third time, and may have been married simultaneously to three men.

Jill and DiRosa still hadn't gotten around to obtaining a legal US divorce that would stand up in the American courts. Less than a month before she and Steely stood together at the altar in the academy chapel, a judge in the Civil District Court, Parish of Orleans, declared the Haitian divorce to be invalid.

The pre-marital agreement signed before the weddings in Mississippi and in St. Bernard Parish appeared to be at the heart of the belated legal move initiated by DiRosa. The New Orleans lawyer filed a petition for declaratory judgement to invalidate the divorce. He stated that he and Jill were both residents of the United States and travelled to Haiti for the sole purpose of obtaining a divorce. Consequently it should be declared invalid, and the prior marriage recognized, DiRosa stated. He asked that the pre-marital contract waiving community assets and providing instead for institution of separate property rights be confirmed by the court.

On December 14, 1982, Judge Henry J. Roberts Jr., issued an order complying with the request. Jill, who was named defendant in the action, once again wound up apparently married to two husbands at the same time—DiRosa and Metzger. Three weeks later she added Steely to the roster.

DiRosa didn't obtain an American divorce from Jill until the summer of 1985. He represented himself in the proceeding filed in the Civil District Court, Parish of Orleans. At that time Jill had been married to Steely more than two years, and may have still been married to Metzger as well.

Nevertheless, a few weeks after the ceremony on the Culver campus, the bride and groom visited Carl's mother in Louisville and reaffirmed their marriage by again repeating their vows in a church. This time they were taken with the Reverend Carmen Sharp officiating.

The marriage, followed by the reaffirmation, marked a break from the tradition Jill had established of out-of-town rituals conducted quickly and quietly. For her initial marriage to Steely, however, she didn't even bother slipping off to another state to obtain a license. They drove fourteen miles to the Marshall County Courthouse in Plymouth for their license. Judge Michael D. Cook waived the usual waiting period for the couple.

On the application for marriage license, both the bride and the groom listed a post-office box at Culver Military Academy as their address. Jill named her three sons, Jonathan Seth and the two Williams, as dependent children. There was no mention of Thadius, or of a child born to her while she was living with Metzger.

Steely had experienced his own problems, including the 1982 divorce from his wife of ten years, Jody Hollowell MacGregor-Steely. His earlier union produced four children. The three girls and a boy were scattered around the South, two in Florida and one each in Virginia and Georgia. Jill stated that her last marriage ended in the death of her husband. She also indicated her parents were living in Texas.

Steely gave the date of his birth as September 8, 1930, and his birthplace as Kentucky. Jill listed her birthday as June 11, 1944. It was the same date used for her marriage to Ihnen. But it was one year later than on documents for her previous marriages to DiRosa and Metzger and three years earlier than the date provided when she married Brodie. Her birthplace was given as Louisiana, and she signed her name as Jill Coit.

There was no mention of Metzger, DiRosa, or any of her other previous husbands, except for the late engineer in Houston, whose last name she was still using.

Jill hadn't cut all her ties to Wabash County, and for several months she continued making the roughly forty-five-mile drive between the two communities several times a week to take care of her varied business interests in North Manchester.

New crops were already springing green and sturdy from the rich loam of Wabash County, and farmers were in their fields on tractors breaking up the soil to prepare it for planting when she reported to the North Manchester Police Department that she had been assaulted and robbed at knifepoint in her State Farm Insurance Office.

Armed robbery is not a crime that commonly shows up on the police blotter in the quiet farming community. Petty thefts, public intoxication, occasional minor hell-raising by exuberant teenagers after a big game, and physical violence or threats between spouses are more likely to be logged as offenses. North Manchester even has an occasional murder; but armed robbery? No! Nevertheless, despite the local rarity of such a serious crime, when hometown journalist Worth Weller made his routine police-beat check there was nothing on the blotter to tip him off to the reported robbery.

Weller and the *News-Journal* didn't know anything about the report of a major felony occurring on West street, a five-minute walk from their offices, until they read about it in a competing newspaper. The *Plain Dealer* in nearby Wabash ran a story about the robbery report.

Weller and his wife were near Jill's age, and they had a friendly relationship. Like the State Farm slogan says, Jill was a "good neighbor," and she had bought gifts for the Weller children. The small-town journalist was embarrassed and outraged. He stormed across the street and down the block to confront the police chief and find out how he was scooped and what was going on. The local police were usually cooperative and as open as law enforcement ethics and good sense would allow, but they were strangely reticent to talk about the report.

According to Jill's account, she was working late at her offices on May 23, 1983, when a man telephoned and said he wanted to buy some life insurance. She had withdrawn $1,600 from the nearby Francis Slocum State Bank earlier that day to buy a graduation present for one of her sons, and still had the money with her when the stranger showed up about seven PM.

Preparing to fill out the paperwork, she asked who would be making the payments for the insurance. At that time the customer pulled out a knife and growled, "You are."

Jill reported that he took the $1,600, forced her to slip a ring off her finger and give it to him, then threw her on her back, kicked her several times, and tied her up. After freeing herself from the rope, she was driven to the Wabash County Hospital where she was treated for a bump on the head and a bruised rib. Jill told police she had never seen the man before, and didn't recognize the name he used. It was assumed the name was an alias.

Weller left the police headquarters with the firm impression that the local lawmen were so uncharacteristically quiet about the case because they were suspicious about the legitimacy of the report. A decade later the current police chief, who was a patrolman when the report was filed, still didn't want to talk about it.

The *News-Journal* ran the story in its May 30 edition. Although it appeared near the top of the front page with the headline "Suspect At Large After Armed Robbery," it was about as short as it could be: two paragraphs of one sentence each. Police Chief Buddy Hittmansperger was quoted as saying the robber was known to police but hadn't yet been located. That was the end of the news coverage of the chilling downtown knifepoint stickup.

Curiously, however, at some time after the reputed armed robbery, the incident was somehow transposed into a rape when Jill discussed it with acquaintances. One of her closest female friends visited to comfort her while she was in bed recovering from what the insurance agent described as a violent sexual assault. Years later the incident would be referred to in court by two attorneys as a reputed rape rather than as a robbery.

Jill's trauma over the dreadful assault was ultimately eased with monthly disability payments from State Farm and from Social Security, based on her reported head injury. Characteristically, even years later State Farm authorities were close-mouthed about the incident. Claim records are confidential, they pointed out.

In Culver, Jill's life with her new husband was proceeding in more orderly, less traumatic fashion. But an exact rundown on the intimate details of the married life of the one-time Kentucky preacher and the fast-stepping Southern belle depends on whose recollections are tapped.

In legal documents filed at the courthouse in Plymouth, Jill claims that from the beginning the couple had a platonic relationship. Her descripton of the marriage indicates it was purely a business deal that included her agreement to advance her husband thousands of dollars in interest-free loans over a period of years to bridge the gap between his earnings and his expenditures.

Jill says it didn't bother her that Carl was broke, "because he was a Christian and [that] he would never take from me. After all," she added, "he told me he was a former Baptist minister."

According to her account, she wanted him to help her youngest son. At that time Steely was in debt and living by himself in a $75-per-month room at the Culver Inn on the Academy campus. He was still saddled with payments stemming from his flying-school venture. And his only personal possessions were a sofa and his clothing. Even the vehicle he was driving, "an old beat up green car, about a 1976 Chevy," belonged to his mother, she claimed. By contrast, Jill was a woman of considerable means.

Consequently, in return for his assistance with her son she agreed to help him live the lifestyle expected of a senior member of the CMA faculty. Steely earned roughly $30,000 annually at the Academy, but his income was eventually expanded by another approximate $2,000 from nearby Ancilla College where he began teaching geology and other courses part-time in the late 1980s.

The worth of Jill's possessions and income from the properties she owned, stock earnings, her work in real estate and insurance sales and other earnings amounted to considerably more. One of her farms in Wabash county brought in about $600 per month. Her income also included combined disability payments totalling approximately $1,200 per month from Social Security and State Farm for a brain injury reputedly suffered during the reported robbery/rape in North Manchester. The Social Security payment was $520.

Residuals from past insurance sales boosted her monthly income by almost $1,000 more, so her total checks from State Farm alone amounted to $1,644. The disability payments from both sources were tax free.

The money reportedly borrowed from Carl's new wife was to be paid back within six months of the time his mother died and he came into his inheritance. The old woman's estate was expected to be worth in the neighborhood of $400,000. As part of the agreement, Jill said she expected Carl to provide her with dental and medical insurance, and after he obtained his inheritance to loan her money if she needed it.

A document Jill identified as a promissory note dated December 31, 1983 and carrying signatures with the names of herself and her husband indicates she loaned him or paid out money for his bills and other expenses amounting to $30,000. Another note dated on December 20, 1984 was for $40,000 she claimed was advanced to Steely during the second year of their marriage.

But Steely claims the marriage was much more than a loveless, business deal. It was a normal romantic marriage, in which sexual relations played a traditional role. He says that he and Jill were husband and wife in every way. He also denied signing a special pact outlining proposed living arrangements and signing the promissory notes.

Steely was aware that Jill had a partial hysterectomy when William Clark III was born or shortly thereafter and could not have any more children. There were never any female sanitary items around the house, and if she had the need for such things she wouldn't have made a secret of it, he says. She wasn't shy about matters of that type.

She did keep several handguns around the house, however. Jill hadn't broken off her love affair with guns, and her husband was aware that she carried a small pistol in her purse. As a former marine, he was familiar with firearms, and her affection for guns didn't bother him at all. He was proud of her knowledge of weapons, and pleased that she knew how to use them.

Steely recalls that Jill told him one time soon after their marriage that she was afraid of Charles Coit because he believed she murdered his brother. Don't ever answer a knock or a ring at the door by simply opening it up; always make sure you know first who's outside, she cautioned him. "He's after me." Steely had never met Charles Coit, but he knew he was an Episcopal priest. It seemed difficult to believe he was such a threatening or violent man that Jill would be afraid of him.

The commandant's new wife was full of surprises. Just about a week short of their first wedding anniversary, the couple flew to Port-au-Prince and obtained a quickie Haitian divorce. The papers were signed and the divorce was granted on December 29, 1983 and validated by a government functionary in front of a French and English translator. Jill stated that "an incompatibility of temperament" existed between her spouse and herself. She claimed they had separated the previous June.

Civil Registrar Emeran Cineas added once again, as another Haitian bureaucrat had done five years earlier: ". . . the lady has the right to use again her maiden name: COIT."

According to Steely, Jill explained the paper divorce was necessary for tax purposes. The couple returned to Culver from their brief trip to the Caribbean in time to celebrate the New Year, and carried on their married lives just as they had before the divorce. Looking back on the curious proceeding a few years later, Steely, described the Haiti trip as a honeymoon.

Despite, or perhaps because of the perplexing quirks in her behavior, Jill was an exciting and entertaining woman to be married to. Steely was impressed by her keen business sense, and he loved her humor and her energy. She was an exciting woman of the world, who told wonderful stories, and could concoct dramatic epics from the most miniscule incidents.

She also confided that her late husband, W. C., was chairman of the board at Tenneco, Carl later recalled. Furthermore, her lawyer husband from New Orleans was a federal judge. It's true today that DiRosa eventually moved up to the bench. But when he made the move, it was as an elected member of the civil district court, a position that falls far short of the responsibilities and prestige that goes with appointment to a seat on the federal bench.

The couple settled into a large tree-shaded two-story house at 203 Lakeshore Drive in Culver, a casual ten-minute walk from the public beach. Neatly-tended flower beds that bloomed with peonies, Indiana's state flower, and other brightly colored blossoms, sprouted in the back yard and decorated the approaches to the house. Jill bought the attractive neo-colonial style home in June for approximately $70,000 with proceeds from the sale of her house in North Manchester. Ownership was listed under the Nei Mar Corporation.

They also upgraded the diverse fleet of vehicles Jill had brought to the marriage. In 1984 she traded in her 1977 Porsche on a rugged new utility vehicle, a Toyota 4-Runner. They bought their own U-Haul truck, an Airstream Trailer, and spent about $7,700 at a dealership in South Bend to have a new transmission and new engine installed in Jill's 1976 Mercedes.

The couple jointly purchased a forty-acre parcel of North Carolina mountain property worth more than $20,000. Jill was the sole owner of another property there valued at more than $5,000. She also continued to scan area newspapers for tax sales and occasionally submitted a bid but didn't make any additional local real estate purchases. While she was in North Carolina she also obtained a driver license, using the name, "Jill Theressa Kisla." She gave her birthday as June 11, 1946, and signed the license in her distinctive straight-up-and-down script.

Tower Advertising was already registered in Indiana, and she used the company for her earlier tax sale purchases. But she also formed a new corporation, Coit International, and plunged into a couple of challenging businesses in the lakeside community. One was a cab company. A woman acquaintance who lived at the Academy came up with the idea for the venture, and they went into the business as equal partners, according to Jill. The taxi service was established exclusively for transporting students and families at CMA to and from area airports, usually either to the Plymouth Municipal Airport or thirty-five miles to the Michiana Regional Airport in South Bend. The South Bend airport is the closest facility to Culver that was served by commercial airlines.

When her partner moved to Turkey, Jill brought Seth in to operate the taxi business, she says. He had left Holiday Rambler at Nappanee and was employed for a year at the Dollar General store in Plymouth, spent a few months teaching water safety to summer school students at CMA, and worked at a lumber yard before going on the payroll at Culver Taxi.

Jill was the sole owner of the other business she opened. The Culver Bed and Breakfast was operated out of her home, and she set it up exlusively for Academy-connected guests. She claims she started the bed-and-breakfast because friends of her husband were taking advantage of their hospitality for frequent overnight stays, and she decided she might as well put things on a paying basis. The inn was listed in a booklet published by the Marshall County Convention and Tourism Commission, and included in other material recommending accommodations for visitors to the area.

Jill's darkly-handsome oldest son also pitched in and assumed a key role in operation of the bed-and-breakfast. Seth kept in good physical condition, and he was constructed like a body builder, with big shoulders, a barrel chest and heavily-muscled upper arms. He moved into the house, where he cooked, baked, and functioned as the general manager. Jill and Seth were close, and he became somewhat of a confidant for her.

The other boys, who spent most of their time in prep school, didn't form the same strong emotional ties with their mother. It was difficult to become firmly attached for very long to any of the men in their mother's life, either. There was such a parade of them. The boys looked at her husbands, the various men she was involved with, simply as their mother's friends, according to Jill's youngest son, Billy, years later. It seemed there was always a different man around.

For awhile Seth attended Vincennes University a couple of hundred miles downstate from Culver. The two-year college is in the historic city where British forces surrendered Fort Vincennes to George Rogers Clark in 1779 during the Revolutionary War. The school has a strong agriculture and pre-veterinary program, but Seth obtained an associate degree in business in 1987. Later he returned to Northern Indiana and enrolled in courses at Ancilla College where Carl taught part time. Jill also attended some general business courses at the independent two-year community college and took additional classes at Indiana University Extension Campus in South Bend. Her youngest son, William Clark III, was shipped off to upper Michigan to complete his prep-school education.

"Jill is a very bright woman, very bright. She's an entrepreneur who likes to start businesses, get things going, and then move on to something else," Steely recalled.

The prep-school educator's personal and professional financial fortunes weren't improving, and a few years after the marriage he moved from the position of commandant to a job as a dean. Later he became assistant director of admissions. But he also formed a corporation of his own.

Despite the setback, the couple continued to live their affluent lifestyle. Jill was no longer as enthusiastic about cooking as she had been when she first returned to North Manchester, and her husband didn't have an opportunity to sample any Cajun or south Louisiana dishes whipped up in their own kitchen. Although she could still put together a tasty basic meal if it was necessary, they usually dined out, sampling the menus at some of the finer restaurants in Marshall County or in nearby Starke, Pulaski, and St. Joseph counties. South Bend was only about a fast hour's drive away.

They continued to maintain the fleet of cars. Jill dressed in flashy and expensive clothes. During the long summer vacation period at the Academy, the couple took the opportunity to make frequent trips around the United States and out of the country together. "We skied the world," Carl later recalled.

During their travels they collected passport stamps from Curaçao, Argentina, Ecuador, Australia, New Zealand, Luxembourg, and Switzerland. Jill browsed in some of Europe's toniest shops. But she also bought two fur coats on separate trips to Zurich from a used-clothing store that one of her sons discovered. One of the furs cost $140 and the other $107, in American money.

Closer to home, Steely made frequent trips with his wife to North Manchester and other locations in Wabash County where she had property. The prep-school educator was impressed with the friendship that seemed to still exist between Jill and Metzger. He later remarked to a news reporter that they seemed to be better friends after their divorce than they were before. Jill said she divorced her husband in North Manchester and Steely believed her. But like many things related to Jill's life and associations, locating records of her divorce from Metzger was difficult to do.

Two days before Christmas 1985, Thelma Steely died. She left an estate valued at $151,000, far less than half the amount her son and his wife had anticipated. There would be enough to repay the $70,000 worth of promissory notes, with some to spare. But it was already December, and it would be several weeks, perhaps months, before the estate was finally settled. A week after his mother's death, according to documents on file at the Marshall County Courthouse, Carl signed another $50,000 promissory note with his wife. The authenticity of the documents would be seriously questioned.

The elderly widow also left Carl antique furniture, including a cherry canopy pencil-post bed, a Queen Anne swing-leg game table, and a mahogany Martha Washington chair, as well as other personal property. Many of the old woman's antiques were sold to a dealer in Louisville for a total of $14,795.

After the death of Steely's mother in Kentucky, the intricate personal and business dealings of the couple in Culver became even more elaborately complicated than before. They plunged into a baffling maze of legal complexities.

With the easing of Carl's financial difficulties after his mother's death, the couple apparently settled whatever financial accounts that existed between them. Jill wrote "paid in full" across the documents purported to be promissory notes from her husband. Remaining funds from the estate were deposited in a Teachers Credit Union account that he shared with Jill.

Carl also dug $22,000 from his pocketbook and presented his wife with a 1988 Suburban as a birthday present, according to Jill. That marked only the second time during the more than six years of their relationship up to that time that he had given her a gift, she says. The first present was a pair of cloth earrings, according to her account. On August 8, a couple of months after her birthday, the couple flew to Las Vegas, obtained another marriage license and were wed once again. This time they exchanged vows in one of the glitter city's quickie wedding chapels.

Steely recalls the ceremony as merely a "reaffirmation" of their earlier vows, a practice many couples share on dates that are important to them such as five or ten, twenty-five and fifty year anniversaries. But few of those couples, if any, bother with a new marriage license. Carl and his two-time bride obtained a Nevada license at the Clark County Courthouse in Las Vegas.

The license contained true, false, and a confusing mix of information put together from various marriages and other important events and players in Jill's busy life. The bride gave her name as Jill Johansen-Coit, and indicated her father was Edwin Johansen and her mother's maiden name was Juanita Engleman. She said she married once before, and the union ended in 1972 with a Haitian divorce. In a space under

her name asking for "her address," she indicated her
home was in Harvey, Louisiana. Her birthday was
listed as 6-11-1944 and her age as forty-four.

A couple of curious entries also appeared among
information on the document provided for the
groom's background. In the space set aside to indicate
the number of marriages, "1st" was typed in. And in
the space set aside under Steely's name for listing of
the city or town where he lived, the words "Liberty,
Texas" appeared. Liberty is an east Texas town of
about 8,000 people along US Route 90 midway between Houston and Beaumont.

Reflecting on his life with Jill, Steely says he believes the marriage, or marriages, began to go bad after she lost her temper one time in front of him and
one of her boys. She tried to enlist him in a scheme to
kill her brother, because Marc had informed William
III that he was old enough to handle his trust himself,
Steely says. Jill was furious at the prospect of losing
control over the money.

He says he chuckled when Jill brought up the subject of murder. "We thought she was just having a little temper tantrum or something," he says.

"I think her past caught up with her when her
brother blew the whistle on her to her younger son
. . . and she knew I was going to find out about it,
and that's when she began conniving against me. Because there was none of that during most of our marriage. She was married to me the longest of anybody.
And I really think that we got along well. Until the last
year, when things fell apart." The marriage lasted nine
years, including the final two years when they no
longer lived together.

But when Jill brought up the subject of murder, he
figured she was merely joking or overreacting. She was
a natural-born comedienne who was outlandishly dramatic and exaggerated everything. Jill talked at differ-

ent times to her husband about studying drama at Newcomb College, and he was used to outrageous outbursts or behavior that might alarm someone who didn't know her as well as he did.

It appears more likely, however, that the tangled financial maneuvers between the entrepreneur and the educator had more to do with their final parting of the ways.

The storm clouds began to form after Steely suggested to Jill they take a trip to Steamboat Springs to ski and find a house to settle down in. Early in 1990 he was fifty-nine years old and rapidly nearing the age when he was looking forward to going into semi-retirement, relaxing and catching up on his skiing. It was early spring and the snow on the slopes was excellent.

One of Jill's knees was hurting her, so while Carl skied, she looked for a place to live. She found the Oak Street B&B, which, depending on how the main house was partitioned, could be set up with more than a dozen rental units. She was also nearing the half-century mark, and after giving birth to three children and developing some health problems, she was receptive to the idea. Running a bed-and-breakfast in the popular resort town seemed to fit perfectly into the plan. It appeared the timing might be especially good because the resort was catching on with affluent skiers from Japan.

Jill has a different version, however, of how she came to set her sights on going into business as an innkeeper in Steamboat Springs. She claims it was all her idea, and her husband was dead set against it.

The story is still being sorted out, but certain facts are known. Jill began to marshal her financial resources to meet a $230,000 purchase price on the inn.

She sold a farm in North Manchester; cashed an IRA for about $19,000; withdrew her $15,000 retirement fund; cashed $15,000 in certificates of deposit

from the Bippus State Bank in the hamlet of Bippus a
few miles south of North Manchester; and at last sold
most of the shares of Tenneco stock she inherited as
part of Clark's estate. The stock had appreciated considerably during the eighteen years she held onto it
and brought in $46,581 to apply to purchase of the
business in Steamboat Springs.

Steely also reportedly provided $47,000 toward the
purchase price. He sold off $30,000 worth of Exxon
stock his mother had left him, and withdrew money
from an IRA and his retirement fund. Jill says it was a
loan, and she signed a promissory note to repay the
money. She swapped him a tax-sale property in return
for an agreement to make the loan interest-free for
five years, she added. If the money was not repaid by
June 15, 1995, he would become owner of her tax-sale
properties in Indiana, Louisiana, and Austin, Texas.
She bought the Austin property in 1974 for $8,000.

Her husband co-signed a note on another loan of
more than $70,000 using the combination home and
bed-and-breakfast as collateral. In return for the favor,
she wrote him a $3,000 check on the new account set
up for the Oak Street Bed & Breakfast, she says.

He stayed at the resort only a week before catching
a flight back to the Midwest in order to finish up the
current school term running through April and May.
Later he would have to prepare for the new class reg-
istering at the academies for the fall school term. According to his account, they agreed he would remain
at the academies for one more term before retiring
and joining her in Steamboat Springs. His salary would
come in handy getting their new business started. Jill
stayed behind to complete details of the purchase, do
some redecorating, and make other changes in the
B&B.

Jill sold the bed-and-breakfast in Culver for
$120,000 to Conley B. Phiffer, Jr., and his wife, Mary

Jane, acquaintances she and Carl knew from the church they attended. Earlier, the same couple had taken over the taxi operation.

Since the house was sold and Carl had a new school term coming up at CMA, he moved out of the bed-and-breakfast over the Labor Day weekend and into an apartment. He never considered applying for a leave of absence. Borrowing a Suburban from friends, he made several trips back and forth with his clothes and other possessions. The furniture and most of his wife's personal property were loaded into a truck and sent to her in Steamboat Springs.

When he left Jill in Steamboat Springs it marked the beginning of the end of their connubial life, however. Their comfortable union seemed to spoil virtually overnight, souring like fresh milk left unattended on a back porch. Carl says Jill began talking about him hanging onto his job at the school for a year, not for merely one more semester. And when he tried telephoning her in Steamboat Springs, she was never available for the calls.

In early summer, after the end of the school term, he flew to Denver, then caught a commuter flight to the Steamboat Springs Airport on Elk River Road. His reunion with Jill was disappointing. Among other things, he learned he wasn't even named as a co-owner of the bed-and-breakfast. Seth and his mother were the co-owners. The vibrations were all bad, and a few days after arriving in the resort community, Steely packed up his clothes and returned to the Midwest, alone.

The seven-year marriage was suddenly slipping away in a morass of bitter accusations of scheming, cheating, thieving, and betrayal. Steely found himself in one of the few legal fights of his life. On August 7, 1990, he filed a petition for divorce at the Marshall County Courthouse in nearby Plymouth. In the petition his wife was referred to simply as "Jill Steely," with no mention of a middle name, married name, or any of the other names she had been known by during the past quarter of a century.

They had been separated since July 12 and the marriage was irretrievably broken, Steely asserted. Significantly, he also stated: ". . . the parties have acquired real and personal property subject to division." Steely was represented by attorney Peter L. Rockaway, a partner in the Plymouth law firm of Rockaway and Shorter-Pifer.

A few weeks later Jill cross-filed, asking through her attorney for a decree of divorce from the Marshall Circuit Court, a decree distributing marital assets, restoration of her pre-marital surname of Coit, costs of the suit, and any other relief the court considered to be just. The petitioner was identified as "Jill Coit-Steely." She concurred with her estranged husband's assessment of the marriage, and stated it had irretrievably broken down. That was one of the few things they agreed on anymore. Jill was represented by attorney John C. Hamilton of Doran, Blackmond, Ready, Hamilton & Williams in South Bend.

Although the legal action surrounding the divorce was played out in the Marshall County Circuit Court, it ultimately involved lawyers, witnesses, or depositions from South Bend, Culver, Steamboat Springs, and Plymouth. The court was showered with a flurry of interrogatories, affidavits, writs, motions, and other legal papers that fell like confetti at a wedding.

Nevertheless, teams of judges and lawyers worked for two years to sort out the tangled marital and business affairs of the feuding couple. It was a nasty divorce, filled with incredible amounts of acrimony, spite, and bizarre accusations.

Obviously, falling in love with Jill was an experience that was fraught with dangers. But each of the combatants, the much-married entrepreneur, as well as the prep-school educator, had grasped a tiger by the tail. Once Steely slipped the gloves off, he was a formidable and determined fighter. Neither of them dared to let go.

Jill depicted Carl as a miserably impoverished fortune hunter, who preyed on her because she was a wealthy woman. "His first wife tried to warn me, but I would not believe her, that he was only marrying me for money," she complained. "When I look at how much money we went through during the years we were in contact, I realize she was right. His promise to me that he would never try to take any of my property sure was a lie."

According to Jill's calculations, she contributed about $41,000 to the couple's living expenses, and her husband contributed approximately $15,000 during the first year of their marriage.

The following year, 1984, she contributed about $66,000 to their expenses. "Carl's directed deposit was $626 every two weeks," she said. She computed the amount: "$1,252 × 12 = $15,024. If you take out the $200 per month he had to pay every month for his bad-debt loan, that reduces his contribution to $12,614 for the year."

In 1985, Jill's initial estimate of her contribution was $74,000, with her husband pitching in only $18,000. Running through the arithmetic in more detail, however, she dropped the amount he contributed to an even more anemic $14,760.

In 1986, the first year after her husband's mother died and his financial situation eased somewhat, she came up with $68,000 for their expenses. Jill said Carl's take-home pay from his primary employer was about $19,000 that year but he had probably begun his part-time teaching at Ancilla and his new source of income was enough to offset the monthly cost of paying off his old debt.

Jill claimed they signed a ten-year living-arrangement agreement prior to their marriage. She produced a document to back up the assertion.

According to the pact, she says she agreed to buy a house in Culver within one year for them to live in and attend social functions with him together, so long as he contributed $200 per week. He could also use her cars if he helped maintain them. Whether or not they married, Jill agreed to behave in public as if they were. But there was to be an understanding that he was not to expect her to submit to sexual relations, and he would not claim any interest in her cars, stocks, or other property she already owned or acquired in the future, even if they later decided to marry.

She also produced a document dated May 1, 1990, to back up her insistence that her husband was never a part owner or would-be partner in the bed-and-breakfast in Steamboat Springs. The document stated:

"I, Carl V. Steely, acknowledge the fact that I have no interest in the property Jill Coit is intending to buy in Steamboat Springs, Colorado. I have advised her against the purchase and want no part of it. I think it will not succeed. I do not want to be liable for any debts she might incur. I have never, except for one in North Carolina, been a partner to her purchases, a forty-acre track (sic) we bought together. She is disabled and I do not feel that even with her son being a partner, this enterprise will be successful."

Jill continued pecking away at her husband's story and his reputation. She accused him of taking a hoard of loose diamonds that were squirrelled away in a storage container in the attic of the Culver house and of digging up and making off with gold and silver coins in an ammunition box that was buried in a crawl space. Carl responded that he never saw the treasure after his wife left town. At the beginning of the marriage there was approximately $10,000 worth of diamonds and thousands of dollars' worth of gold and silver coins as well, he said.

Jill also claimed she had a pair of phony identification documents he overlooked in a dresser drawer with his passport, a sweater, and some underwear when he left their Steamboat Springs home for the last time. In turn, she accused him of keeping her tax-sale and other business and banking records when he loaded the truck with her belongings to be transported to Colorado. He also reputedly kept her keys to safety deposit boxes at the Bippus State Bank and in the NorCen bank in Culver.

Carl said in an interrogatory that Jill had their income-tax records. And he clawed back at his estranged wife with all the feisty ferocity of a cornered possum, targeting her with a flurry of hurtful accusations of his own.

In remarks independent of the bitterly-contested divorce suit, he indicated he believed his wife twice attempted to kill him or to have him murdered.

One morning she didn't leave for her college class as she usually did. Instead she stuck around the house and made coffee for him, according to his account. A short time later while he was teaching his first-period class at the Academy, he passed out as he was standing at the blackboard and struck his head. Tests run a few days later were inconclusive, he said.

Another time he was pedaling along the street on his bicycle, his long, lanky form looking like Ichabod Crane with a crew cut, when a motorist tried to run him down. Since that time he has told more than one person he believes he is lucky to be alive. Jill labeled the intimations or accusations of attempted murder as absurd.

In documents filed as part of the divorce suit, Steely

branded the promissory notes as bogus. She used photocopies of his signature to forge the documents, he claimed. "This came as no surprise to me because on previous occasions she thought that she was very clever in cutting and taping documents to make them read as she wanted," he said.

Steely said he believed the house in Culver, as well as the new business in Steamboat Springs were titled jointly in the names of himself and of his wife, ". . . but I am finding that is not correct." And in statements outside the court suit, he said he was surprised when he learned he wasn't listed as a part owner and that Seth was listed as Jill's partner. He also claimed an equitable interest in the remaining house in Wabash because of repairs he said were financed in part with his income. He contributed to repairs on the Oak Street Bed & Breakfast as well, according to his account.

Steely accused his absent wife of receiving monthly disability payments based on bogus claims of a head injury received in a feigned accident. In a statement labeled "Wife's proposed findings and conclusions," that was submitted to the court, Jill responded through her attorney:

"Carl acknowledged on the basis of his allegation of Jill's engagement in a campaign of fraud of having been both a witness to, and participant in, Jill's alleged misconduct, including his presence with her at Rush Presbyterian Hospital where, according to Carl, her fraudulent endeavor was pursued with apparent success. Carl also acknowledged having received some of the benefits of the alleged fraud in the form of Jill's ongoing disability payments."

The statement was couched in classic legal language, but it sounded as if her lawyer was saying she didn't do it, or at least no one had yet proven she did it. But if she did do it, her accuser himself was up to his ears in the fraud. It was the kind of statement that is made in American courtrooms every day.

A bit further along in the document, Hamilton remarked that it was "more probable than not that Jill did suffer a disabling injury in 1983," and asked that Carl be made liable for her support in the event that at some future date the disability left her unable to support herself.

A representative from the State Farm Insurance Company headquarters in Bloomington, Illinois, eventually filed a handwritten request with the circuit court clerk asking for a complete transcript of the divorce case. The transcript was provided to the company, as requested. A State Farm investigator also talked with Steely. Jill had collected a small fortune in disability payments related to her reputed injury while she was representing the company in North Manchester.

Hamilton took a swipe at Steely for reputedly painting himself as someone who didn't know much about business and was unsophisticated in financial matters. The attorney pointed out in the "proposed findings" that the educator had several college degrees, including a Master of Business Administration, and had once established his own corporation in Florida that apparently included issuance of stock.

If Jill's husband was indeed trying to give a false impression that he was a naive babe in the woods when it came to business dealings, she was playing a bit of the same game: Jill Coit-Steely an innocent girl who had hardly any education and was being taken to the cleaners by a conniving man.

Steely complains it took years to drag her into court, and when his attorneys finally got her there, she tried to get the judge's sympathy by saying she had never graduated from college. "Whatever she thinks is going to get the desired effect, that's what she's gonna say." Whenever she was caught in inconsistencies, she sim-

ply backpedaled out of it, and she did it gracefully.
"She was really good at backpedaling, and you know,
making you laugh," he says.

Considering all the years she had devoted to study
on college campuses, attending the State Farm school,
gathering licenses, buying up real estate, and her myriad other business dealings, it seemed difficult to believe she would err so fundamentally as to execute
promissory notes with her husband for loans involving
tens of thousands of dollars and not bother to have
the documents witnessed.

She was also apparently very good at winning delays
in the proceedings. One time when she was supposed
to fly to Indiana for an appearance in the divorce proceeding, she claimed she suffered a "seizure" at the
airport in Denver, Steely reported. "Throughout the
seven years of our marriage Jill talked at length about
how easy it was for her to 'beat the system' in this way
by faking a medical disability."

In a final argument, Rockaway claimed his client entered the marriage trusting that "we shall be open and
loving and share everything." He also scoffed at the
crude pre-nuptial agreement Jill claimed she and Carl
entered into prior to their marriage.

". . . this woman is far too clever not to have had a
legitimate pre-nuptial agreement drawn up if she
wanted one. Instead she wants us to believe that these
two people looking forward to marriage in several
days are signing a document that says one is a poor
wretch who is divorced, living in a one-room motel
unit with debt and no money whereas the other one
will build up his image by buying a house, etc.," the
lawyer declared. "I suspect that this document was
written somewhere in October 1991, and not in January of 1983."

Rockaway made similar observations about the
promissory notes. "This is patently an attempt to jus-

tify Jill in her grabbing her husband's inheritance so that she can then say that he was paying her back the debt he owed her," he asserted. "It has the same ring of falsity as does her other exhibit that supposedly Carl was against buying the Colorado property and that this was strictly her business endeavor."

The small-town divorce lawyer's argument was sprinkled with colorful remarks like: ". . . no Johnny-come-lately to manipulating money," "This is a cunning mind at work," "There is no need for this Byzantine cloak-and-dagger stuff," and "he didn't know that his wife had secrets which the heart is not prone to disclose." Rockaway has a definite flair for the dramatic, a knack with words that would have made great sound bites for television, if the electronic media had been covering the divorce trial.

He requested the court award his client a money judgment of about $130,000. "It's not much to ask for a man reaching the end of his working life," Rockaway added in what for him was couched in rather plebian language. In a note to Hamilton, the Plymouth lawyer stated his client had left the couple's financial matters to his wife to handle and consequently didn't know how all of the funds were expended.

"Apparently a lot of the moneys were moved in and out of different banks—foreign corporations were utilized, etc.," he wrote.

Tracing some of the couple's expenditures during the ill-fated marriage, Steely said his wife bought new cars for each of her sons. And despite Jill's claims she didn't continue to buy tax-sale properties during their marriage, he said she drew from their Teachers Credit Union account to make new purchases. The withdrawals included at least $20,000 for tax-sale investments in Colorado, he said.

Asked on an interrogatory if he contended his remarriage to Jill in Las Vegas either didn't happen or was invalid, Steely said he didn't know what the legalities were. "I have assumed that Jill and I have been continuously married since the date of our first marriage, and that any terminations in that were only for purposes of tax necessity, which she had indicated," he said.

The contest played out over nearly eighteen months before Judge Cook at last brought it to a conclusion. He was the same judge who waived the waiting period prior to the marriage nearly nine years earlier. Jill flew back to Indiana, and Carl drove the fourteen miles along the narrow, winding, bumpy asphalt trail that is State Road 17, for the hearing in Plymouth.

The slate-gray, early winter skies outside were overcast and a brisk wind was whipping through the bare black branches of the maples and oaks that dotted the lawn of the Marshall County Courthouse when the estranged couple and their lawyers assembled before the judge for the final time.

Judge Cook ordered the marriage dissolved. He further decreed that the respondent's premarital name, Jill Coit, be reinstated. It wasn't the first time, nor the last, that she would regain her late husband's name.

It was December 23, 1991, the sixth anniversary of Thelma Christine Steely's death. It was also just under eight years since Jill and Carl obtained their paper divorce in Haiti. But the Plymouth judge's decree was no paperwork quickie or exercise in voodoo law; this time the divorce was for real, as legitimate and binding as it can be. Both parties wanted it that way. They were serious about a permanent parting.

Judge Cook observed that the former man and wife had agreed in most part about how their property should be distributed.

"The actual financial circumstances of the respondent (Jill) are not fully understood by the Court, inasmuch as a total accounting of the respondent's assets was not made available to the Court," he added.

Considering the convoluted nature of Jill's business dealings and financial affairs, it was an observation that would be difficult for almost anyone familiar with them to disagree with. It sounded like an understatement.

The jurist observed that during the marriage Jill contributed a disproportionately large amount to their financial upkeep, and that they both lived "a rather extravagent lifestyle" in view of the modest income of the petitioner (Steely). Judge Cook declared, however, that he did not believe notes and documents submitted as evidence were valid.

He also noted the conflicting accounts concerning the whereabouts and ultimate fate of the diamonds and coins left at the house in Culver. Jill claimed Carl made off with them. He said he never saw them again after she left Culver for Colorado. The judge left it at that, without adding any remarks of his own about which one of the accounts he may have found more believable. Carl's accusations about Jill's disability claim were handled in the same manner.

"The Petitioner (Carl) also contends that the Respondent's (Jill) disability is the result of a feigned accident and brain injury and that he in fact, has participated in that deception." If there were to be any follow-up investigation related to Jill's disability claim, it wasn't a problem that would be sorted out in Judge Cook's court.

Cook did point out however, that Jill acknowledged she owed her husband $47,000, and that Steely was asking for $130,000 from her as the balance due him from his mother's inheritance. The CMA faculty member acknowledged expenditure of $35,000 from the inheritance while supporting his and Jill's lifestyle.

Consequently, the judge ordered that the Oak Street Bed & Breakfast, the house in Culver (already sold), the tax-sale properties in Louisiana and Texas, in Wabash County, Indiana, and the remaining tract in North Carolina were all Jill's and that Steely would have no further claim on them. Additionally, the vehicles, including the Thunderbird, Mercedes, Suburban, Toyota 4-Runner, U-Haul Truck, the Airstream trailer, a computer worth about $600, and diamonds and gold and silver coins that were her pre-marital property went to Jill. The Porsches and the Lincoln had already been disposed of, and the other vehicles were in Colorado. The Suburban had been sold to Seth, and even the T-Bird was mortgaged, Jill claimed.

Steely wound up with a laptop computer worth about $900, a VCR worth an estimated $300, personal property such as his clothing, and ski and motorcycle equipment, along with diamonds and gold and silver coins as his share of the personal property. No estimate of the value on the gems or valuable coins was given for either Jill or Steely.

Perhaps the Marshall County jurist's most significant decision in regard to splitting up the couple's assets, was an order that Jill pay her ex-husband $100,000. He specified that the payment was to be made on or before January 1, to prevent a lien from being placed on her real estate. Jill had barely one week to come up with the money.

For one of the first times in her adult life, she was suddenly facing a critical money crunch. With the whopping judgment favoring her ex-husband, piled on top of debts she had already incurred to finance purchase and renovation of the bed-and-breakfast in Colorado, she was seriously overextended financially. Everything she had built up could come tumbling rap-

Jill Coit being escorted into the Routt County Courthouse in Steamboat Springs for a hearing. This was shortly after her return from Greeley. (*John F. Russell*, Steamboat Pilot)

Michael O. Backus, Jill's co-defendant, being escorted into the Routt County Courthouse for a hearing with Jill. (*John F. Russell,* Steamboat Pilot)

Jill and husband Gerald "Gerry" W. Boggs at the social event of the season, the annual Ski Ball in Steamboat Springs in December 1980. (*John F. Russell,* Steamboat Pilot)

The alpine home of Gerry Boggs on the day his body was discovered inside. (*John F. Russell,* Steamboat Pilot)

Childhood photo of William Clark Coit II (taken about 1931), Jill's first husband to be shot to death with a .22-caliber pistol. Clark grew up in Gates Mills, Ohio, a well-to-do suburb of Cleveland. (*Reverend Charles Coit*)

Jill with William Clark Coit II (*right*), and his brother, Reverend Charles Coit, during a trip to meet the family in Gates Mills, Ohio at Thanksgiving, 1965. This was while she was still married to college student Steven Moore, and shortly after the birth of her oldest son. A few weeks later, she and Clark married in what was her first bigamous marriage. (*Reverend Charles Coit*)

Jill with her three sons: Seth, the oldest, to her right; middle son William Andrew, to her left; and William Clark III in the foreground. (*Reverend Charles Coit*)

William Clark Coit with his mother, Anna Dix Coit, and his and Jill's youngest son, William Clark Coit III, during a visit in 1967. (*Reverend Charles Coit*)

From left to right: Jill and her oldest son, Seth; the middle son, William Andrew, who everyone said was his father's double; and the youngest, William Clark Coit III. (*Author's collection*)

William Clark Coit II on one of the pipeline projects he engineered for Tenneco. (*Reverend Charles Coit*)

Jill's first bed and breakfast in Culver, Indiana. Photo taken in the summer of 1994, when it was under new ownership. (*Author's collection*)

Below: The Oak Street Bed & Breakfast on the corner of 7th and Oak Streets in Steamboat Springs, one block from the town's main street, and one block from Boggs Hardware Store. (*Author's collection*) *Right:* Brochure from the Oak Street Bed & Breakfast.

Oak Street
Bed & Breakfast

corner of Oak & 7th

Telephone & Fax
(303) 870-0484

Features:

Downtown Location
Private Baths
Cable Television & VCR
1 and 2 Bedroom Suites
On City Bus Route

Rates include a savory breakfast with
homemade breads, meats, eggs, fresh fruit,
and more.

We hope you will visit us soon

Julie & Seth Coit   Jill Coit

P.O. Box 772434 • Steamboat Springs • CO • 80477

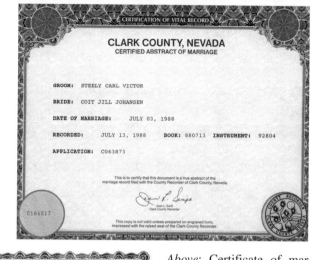

CERTIFICATION OF VITAL RECORD

CLARK COUNTY, NEVADA
CERTIFIED ABSTRACT OF MARRIAGE

GROOM: STEELY CARL VICTOR

BRIDE: COIT JILL JOHANSEN

DATE OF MARRIAGE: JULY 03, 1988

RECORDED: JULY 13, 1988 BOOK: 880713 INSTRUMENT: 92804

APPLICATION: C063873

This is to certify that this document is a true abstract of the marriage record filed with the County Recorder of Clark County, Nevada.

Joan L. Swift
Clark County Recorder

C164517

This copy is not valid unless prepared on engraved form, impressed with the raised seal of the Clark County Recorder.

ANY ALTERATION OR ERASURE VOIDS THIS CERTIFICATE

Above: Certificate of marriage for Jill Coit and Carl Victor Steely. *Left*: Marriage license and certificate of marriage for Jill Coit Steely and Gerald Boggs. *Below*: Birth certificate for Jill's first "phantom" baby, Thadius Brodie.

Evidence from the trial, including a picture of Gerry Boggs as he was found slumped on his utility room floor after the murder. (*Author's collection*)

idly down, and the thought of starting all over again had to be a frightening prospect.

Jill was in a pressure situation with a potential for disaster that neither Judge Cook nor the attorneys appearing before him could have foreseen.

SEVEN

Gerry

"I sleep with them, I marry them, okay? I could just sleep around."

Jill Lonita Coit
Deposition, January 30, 1993

There was a new man in Jill's life! She met him while she was fixing up her new business, before her breakup with Steely, and months before the divorce.

When Jill assumed ownership of the Oak Street Bed & Breakfast, she launched herself into the enterprise with her usual energy and enthusiasm.

Once her husband was back in Culver she worked quickly to wind up the paperwork finalizing the sale, so she could turn her full attention to renovating and redecorating the B&B to meet her own specifications of what it should look like.

Seth tagged along with her and apparently invested somewhere between $53,000 and $106,000, most of it from his trust fund, to become a partner. Different versions were eventually given of exactly how much of his money went into the B&B.

They shared the work as well as the financing. Jill cooked, cleaned, handled the books, and ran the office, making reservations and welcoming guests. Seth mowed lawns, did most of the repairs and handled the day-to-day maintenance. Neither mother nor son were lazy.

The business partnership between them was a business decision that Steely bitterly complained he had been unaware of.

"I didn't even know my name wasn't on the paperwork when the trouble started," he says.

In Steamboat Springs, Jill was busy launching the new business. The B & B at the corner of Oak and Seventh Streets occupies a large lot with a string of single story wooden motel guest units painted brown and arranged in an L-shape. A two-story brown, wood-frame house constructed at the intersection of the streets, which sits back across the driveway and parking spaces from the center of the "L" has five additional guest rooms in the upstairs area.

Across an alley behind the ground-floor L-shaped units, there was also a small house and four additional parking spaces that were included in the purchase. Jill and her son rented the house to tenants.

A small single-story wooden building at the side of the main house in the motel complex was set up as the dining room, where guests were served a varied menu of breakfasts featuring selections from eggs cooked to order, with bacon, sausage, and ham, to delectable French toast or pancakes and hot or cold cereals. Guests were provided with endless pots of steaming coffee, fruit juice, and a selection of fresh breads and rolls, jams, and jellies and fruit—everything served family style at place settings arranged with linen napkins.

But Jill's taste perhaps was most obvious in her decoration of the guest rooms. They were small, snug, and cozy. Perhaps above all, they were decorated with a feminine appreciation for design and comfort.

The one-bedroom units were dominated by huge, high brass beds that sat in the middle of the rooms, made up with thick, fluffy comforters with bright floral patterns. Pillows were almost big enough to serve as beds themselves. Another patterned quilt used as a wall hanging covered one side of the rooms. A large cradle-shaped wicker basket on the floor filled with fluffy towels and washcloths decorated with bright floral patterns to match the decor of the room, brass-based lamps and a couple of small tables—one accommodating a television set—comprised the remainder of the furnishings. Narrow walkways surrounded the bed on three sides, and a tiny bathroom about the size of an average closet accounted for the remainder of the space.

The low ceilings were barely high enough to accommodate a six-footer without bending his head, but rather than being a negative aspect, they merely added to the cozy atmosphere of the rooms. They conserved heat and made it easy to imagine returning from a cold winter day on the slopes, and burrowing into the warmth and snug security of the little bungalows. Crisp white lace curtains were hung at the windows, and a couple of healthy green plants completed the decorating motif.

Inside the house, the living room was sparsely furnished with antiques, including a few pieces retained from the estate of the late Thelma Steely. The brightly-polished hardwood floors and stairway bannisters were stained or varnished in their natural color to show the grain. A fireplace was built into one wall. The upstairs accommodations were also small, and a hallway bathroom was set up to be shared by the guests in two of the rooms. There were also a few two-bedroom units.

With all the renovations, Jill and her son were able to offer guests rooms ranging from $90 to $125 nightly during the ski season. The location, a few minutes' walk from the shops, restaurants and taprooms along Lincoln Avenue and the side streets, was prime. Jill fixed up one of the upstairs units in the house for herself.

Seth and his girlfriend, Julie A. English, lived in one of the apartments in the L-shaped units. Another unit was set aside as a laundry room, leaving eight for rentals. Julie was an industrious and solidly-built young woman from Georgia who skied and enjoyed bicycling, gardening, and other outdoor activities. She also liked to travel, and she worked for awhile as a cashier at the Hard Rock Cafe in London, England, and as a travel coordinator and receptionist for a firm in Melbourne, Australia.

Seth began to look into the possibilities of adding a 500-square-foot greenhouse with dormer windows and French doors onto the central building, making preliminary enquiries with a builder and discussing city-zoning requirements with an attorney. He also talked about putting in a hot tub and spiffing up the driveway.

But the renovating and redecorating didn't occur overnight or without a lot of hard work, and Jill found herself making regular buying trips around the corner to the Boggs Hardware store.

Boggs Hardware is a downtown landmark in Steamboat Springs. It is one of the oldest family-owned businesses in the resort town. And it occupies the ground floor of a two-story, red-brick building at 730 Lincoln Avenue, facing on the north side of the main drag, which is also US Route 40 and defines the little resort town's six or seven-block-long central business district. Longtime residents refer to the structure simply, as the "Boggs Building."

Surrounded by restaurants, taprooms, curio and souvenir stores, and T-shirt and ski shops that cater heavily to the tourist trade, Boggs Hardware was only a few minutes from the B & B. It was a trip Jill made frequently, and more often than not, of all the busy clerks and salesmen she was waited on, she was most often served by one of the co-owners, Gerald William Boggs. Family members and almost everyone else called him Gerry.

In 1989 when Jill bought the B & B, Gerry was a tall and husky lifetime bachelor a few days away from his forty-eighth birthday. He had rapidly balding dark hair, wore a heavy but neatly trimmed mustache and dark-framed glasses. He and his younger brother, Douglas W. Boggs, were the children of William Harold Boggs, who started the business in Steamboat Springs in 1939. A half-century later ownership had passed to the two sons and to another partner, Bob McCullough.

The Boggs brothers were native Coloradoans, but the oldest son was born in Burlington in Kit Carson County a few miles west of the Kansas border. At about the time WWII broke out in Europe, the family moved further west across the Front Range of the Rockies to Steamboat Springs in the fertile Yampa Valley. It was a nice place to live for a young family, with parents who were independent, hardy, and energetic enough to thrive in and endure the fierce winters.

Even in those early days, the vibrant little community already had a reputation as a resort town, although it is also the center of commerce for scores of other families who make their living as ranchers, farmers, miners, or railroaders. Many of the people who drove into Steamboat Springs to shop lived in other even smaller towns nearby.

But Steamboat Springs was the commercial center. And it has always drawn tourists. As recently as the early nineteenth century, nomadic Indians still made annual treks to the valley to live off the local bounty, while soaking in the profusion of hot sulphur springs that bubble up throughout the area. They believed the springs were sacred and the Great Spirit lived below them, hidden deep in the earth.

The Indians found the springs rejuvenating and visited them when they were exhausted, ill, or after battles with their enemies. Most of the visitors were bands of Arapaho or northern Utes, mountain Indians who pursued deer and elk in the high timber country and fiercely defended their Rocky Mountain domain against occasional hunting or war parties from Shoshone, Cheyenne, Kiowa and other neighboring tribes. The Arapaho and Utes clashed frequently over the lush hunting ground.

Most of the Utes who visited the roughly 150 natural mineral springs in what is now Routt County during the summer belonged to the Yamparika, or Yampa, band. Related Utes called them root-eaters, because of their fondness for the succulent carrot-like yampa root that was as much a part of their diet as wild game. They dressed in buckskin decorated with feathers and beads and lived during the deadly cold winters in teepees made of buffalo hide.

The tribal name of a group of their smaller, more primitive and weaker Piute cousins, the Uintahs, which fished and foraged farther west in the sun-parched desert plateau near Great Salt Lake, was eventually adapted to coin a name for the state of Utah.

The most memorable of the thermal springs once visited by the Yampa Utes is Black Sulphur Spring. It was the churning roar of the unique spring that led to the community's current name. According to early storytellers, French trappers made their way into the valley in the mid-1800's when they heard the sound of chugging, and assumed the noise was caused by an approaching steamboat. The mountain men were wrong. The noise was made by Colorado's only geyser, chugging and gushing water into the air.

If the trappers had been in the area awhile longer and paid closer attention, they would have realized there was no way a steamboat could have negotiated the swift-moving shallow water of the rocky Yampa River at that point. Although there may have been periods of heavy snow-melt or other conditions a century ago when the river swelled, even then it's still highly unlikely that anything with a deeper draft than a raft or a canoe could have safely skimmed over the rocks and boulders. Cold and clean, with deep pools scattered here and there, it was near perfect for breeding trout, but it wasn't a stream that was formed to handle commerce or passenger boats.

Hot springs still bubble from the earth in the settlement today, but the geyser and chugging are long gone. The underground foundation was disturbed when the railroad was constructed through the valley. There are still more natural springs in the immediate area than any other location in the world, however. And residents share their habitat with a surprising variety of wild animals that have survived the encroachment of civilization. Mule deer show up in back yards, foxes raid chickenhouses and spook dogs, raccoons pilfer cat food from pet dishes, and rare bald eagles still occasionally screech overhead.

It wasn't long before people realized the potential of winter sports for tourist revenue, and skiing became an important local business as well as an avocation. In the meantime, world competitors were developing on the slopes as males and females trained and vied in everything from cross-country and downhill skiing to slalom and jumping.

By the time Jill and Seth bought the Oak Street Bed & Breakfast, the even smaller town of Vail surrounded by the White River National Forest miles to the south, was the Rocky Mountain ski resort of choice for most of Hollywood's celebrities for winter vacationing. But buoyed by the attraction of Mount Werner, which peaks at 10,585 feet and is named after a legendary family of world and Olympic skiers, Steamboat is becoming more popular every year. Storm Peak and Sunshine Peak are only 300 feet lower than the crest of Mount Werner, and with Thunderhead Peak, Christie Peak, and Rendezvous Saddle, they offer a glistening white powder crisscross of ski slopes and trails for everyone from beginners to world class competitors.

Winter tourists begin showing up in full force with the first deep snowfall to ski, snowmobile, dogsled, hunt, and take advantage of other winter sports. Steamboat's resort hotels, motels, bed-and-breakfasts, and condominiums fill up with visitors, and the winter resort comes into its own as "Ski City USA." The population of the town of 5,000 nearly doubles.

Gerry spent his formative years there, and returned to live out his life as an adult. He graduated from the local high school in 1959, then matriculated to the University of Colorado. He majored in political science, with a minor in Russian language.

Graduating in 1964, he enlisted in the Army and successfully applied for military-intelligence training. By the fall of 1965 he was in Vietnam as a member of the First Cavalry Division and helped set up the huge base at An Khe in the central highlands. He was assigned to a helicopter unit. After completing his one-year tour of duty he returned to Steamboat Springs for a thirty-day furlough, then went back to Vietnam as a volunteer for a second tour. He was awarded a Bronze Star for his service, and in 1967 was given an honorable discharge.

Although he joined the family business, his adventurous life didn't end after returning home from the military service. He took advantage of a government program to learn to fly and eventually qualified to pilot multi-engine aircraft. And he became an excellent scuba diver and undersea and outdoor photographer, using his vacation time to travel to Pacific Ocean diving locations at least once or twice a year.

Like so many of his Rocky Mountain neighbors, he was a devoted outdoorsman. But he was also careful to make time for the academic and intellectual side of his personality and was an avid reader. He continued to take classes at the University of Colorado, served as a museum tour guide, and became a very good amateur archeologist and anthropologist.

He had a special fondness for mind-games, cryptograms, and anything that challenged the intellect. He liked movies and was a regular patron at local theaters, the Chief Plaza III across Lincoln Avenue from the hardware store, and the Times Square Cinema among the shops and restaurants scattered at the foot of Mount Werner. He frequently rented videos to watch at home, as well.

Gerry also loved children, showering the offspring of family and friends with attention and presents. He was "Uncle Gerry" to many youngsters, and became the godfather of the son of his business partner, Bob McCullough. He was a regular visitor at the McCullough home and on Christmas and birthdays, children could count on "Uncle Gerry" to show up with an armload of presents. He was a caring and loyal friend, and McCullough's wife once remarked to her husband that if anything ever happened to him she knew she would have Gerry to lean on.

His friends were devoted to him, as he was to them. But if there was one thing he had missed out on in his busy life it was heavy dating experience or serious relationships with women. He was simply too busy, or too shy, to chase after them.

He was the kind of man Jill was especially successful with. And he looked like excellent husband material. He owned his own $90,000 home, earned a good sal-

ary of $2,500 a month with take-home pay of about
$1,900, and had no large debts.

She could hardly have been more charming during
their brief encounters at Boggs Hardware. According
to Jill, she eventually spent nearly $19,000 at the store
during her renovation project at the B&B. Her relationship with the quiet bachelor didn't progress beyond small talk over her purchases at the store,
however, until a warm day in the late spring or early
summer of 1990—Jill was later unable to remember
more exactly—when they chanced on one another outside the City Market Food & Pharmacy in Central
Park Plaza at the edge of town. Gerry was with his
father when they stopped in the parking lot to chat
about her T-Bird. It was warm and she had removed
the top.

The sports car was perfectly cared for and it was
shining like new. Gerry remarked that he would love
to drive it. He invited her out to dinner.

As Jill later recalled the incident, she told him that
if he wanted to take her T-Bird for a spin it was okay
with her. Later she dropped off a note for him at the
hardware store. It was typewritten in cursive style on a
word processor and, although her name was typed on
the note, typical of her, it wasn't signed. By Jill's own
admission, her handwriting was atrocious and she
typed almost all of her written communications on a
word processor, usually in cursive letters. And
throughout her relationship with the Steamboat
Springs merchant, she began his first name with a "J"
rather than a "G."

Gerry took her out, and he drove the T-Bird. He
headed west on Route 40 past the Yampa Valley Regional Airport to a little restaurant in the town of
Hayden, which developed after the railroad arrived as
a cattle-shipping center for surrounding ranches.

After their first date, the couple got together a cou-

ple of times a week, usually driving somewhere for
dinner dates or simply meeting for lunch at the Para-
dise Grill and Saloon, the Fifth Street Cafe, Anderson
& Friends Good Earth Restaurant, or some other
eatery near the hardware store. The people who live
and visit in Steamboat Springs tend to be active and
outdoorsy, and tourists are lured during the more tem-
perate seasons with a variety of festivals and other
events. Although snow sports and attractions are what
Steamboat Springs is most famous for, they are far
from the only game in town.

Jill and Gerry, like their neighbors, had year-round
local entertainment choices. June featured marathon
footraces, a music festival, the Yampa River Festival,
and the Western Weekend with a huge chili-cooking
contest, cowboy poetry reading, a rodeo, and an Old
West gunfighter competition. On the Fourth of July,
children and adults joined in a downtown parade
along Lincoln Avenue. There was Cowboy Roundup
Days for rodeo fans, the Summer Jubilee, and the dramatic and colorful Rainbow Week featuring a "hot-air
balloon rodeo." A softball tournament and more ro-
deos were offered for entertainment in August. In
September there was Motorcycle Week to look forward to; they could view the annual Vintage Auto
Race and *Concours d'Elegance,* or enjoy the Vintage
Aircraft Fly-in.

But Jill and Gerry shared more personal pleasures,
as well. They were both avid bibliophiles and they
talked about books they had read and collected. One
day she surprised him with a present of a Nordic-
Track, which was set up in an area of the house used
as an exercise room. She had a stationary exercise bike
which also wound up in the room, alongside weight-
lifting devices and other workout equipment. Jill believed in keeping fit, and in addition to her lifelong
avoidance of smoking and drinking, exercise was an

important part of her healthy lifestyle. She and Gerry sometimes rode a tandem bicycle around the neighborhood. It was Jill's.

By the time of the Christmas holidays, Jill had virtually moved out of her upstairs quarters at the bed-and-breakfast and into Gerry's home at 870 West Hillside Court, on a steep ridge overlooking the town. Early the next year, Jill and Gerry slipped off to Boulder and obtained a marriage license. It was April Fools' Day.

Three days later they were quietly married in a private civil ceremony in Steamboat Springs by a municipal court judge. The bride had told her groom she was married twice before: to William Clark Coit, and to Carl V. Steely. She was once-widowed, and once-divorced.

She gave her name on the application as Jill Coit-Steely, and indicated that she was divorced in 1983 in Haiti. Her birthday was entered on the form as June 11, 1944, and her place of birth as New Orleans. She used a post-office box number for her current address. The groom indicated his father was William Harold Boggs and his mother was Edith (Parke) Bullock, who was deceased. The elder Boggs had been married to his wife, Sylvia, for years.

There were no formal wedding announcements, and no photos of the happy couple in *The Steamboat Pilot*. Their friends and relatives learned about the marriage a few at a time. No fuss, no muss. Jill liked it that way, and Gerry was agreeable. He was a private man who had never sought out attention. Seth, his mother's faithful confidant and shadow, didn't even attend. Gerry's brother and sister-in-law, Jan, joined the newly-married couple in celebrating the wedding with a big feed at the Old West Steakhouse a few blocks down Lincoln Avenue from the store.

Months later, the bride complained that two weeks

after the wedding her new husband went off by himself on a scuba diving trip to Belize when he should have been with her on their honeymoon. He told her he couldn't spend two weeks in a confined area with one person, she said. So she cancelled out and her husband went on the Central American scuba-diving adventure by himself.

The lifelong bachelor probably never should have gotten married in the first place, Jill groused. She married him for his intellect. Most of the eligible men in Steamboat Springs were ski bums, she explained.

Despite the irritation of the separate honeymoon, even if Jill's version of the odd event is indeed true, the first months of the marriage were nearly idyllic. The energetic couple took weekend trips and occasional longer journeys together around Colorado or nearby states, usually staying in bed-and-breakfasts. Operators of many of the hostelries banded together to swap complimentary rooms and meals, and the couple took advantage of the cost-saving opportunity to travel.

About the time Gerry went off on his diving trip, an insurance claim was filed for major water damage at the house. The loss was eventually estimated at more than $17,400. Jill blamed the incident on Gerry. He insisted on remodeling his garage just about the time the season's heavy snowfalls were about to begin, she said. Even though he had been warned about the bad timing, he undertook the project for her so there would be room to park her car in the garage alongside his Jeep. Another version of exactly why Gerry was remodeling the garage would be told later.

The claim, nevertheless, included damage to the drywalls, replacement of carpet from the upstairs hallway, bedroom, bath, and stairs, and major remodeling. Georgia A. Taylor, one of the few woman acquaintances in Steamboat Springs that Jill sometimes lunched with, was the claims adjuster. According to Jill, Seth pitched in to help out with the repair work, putting in more than thirty hours and charging for only a fraction of his time.

Jill drove all the way to Denver to shop and save money on appliances for the house. She bought a black leather sofa for the living room, replaced kitchenware, and shored up the supply of towels and linens. Even before the water damage occurred, Gerry's house was sparsely furnished with a combination of treasured longtime possessions and cast-offs passed on to him by friends or relatives. He lived bachelor style. His new wife enjoyed upgrading things and giving the home a feminine touch.

Despite the damage, Jill moved most of the rest of her possessions into her husband's house, and assumed the role of the new Mrs. Boggs. She already knew her father-in-law, William, and his wife, Sylvia; her brother-in-law and his wife, Jan. She met nieces and nephews and cousins; and she met the Boggs family attorney, Vance E. Halvorson.

She later recalled that shortly after Gerry introduced them, the lawyer soberly advised her that she was now a Boggs and should conduct herself as a Boggs. The implication was clear: her new role carried important obligations and responsbilities.

Now that he was married to Jill, Gerry had less time for private hours of reading, playing intellectual games, and poking around with hobbies like archeology and anthropology. For the first time, he attended the annual ski ball sponsored by the Steamboat Springs Winter Sports Club. It was the central event of the local social season. During all his years of living in the resort town, Gerry had never attended a major social event, and a photographer for the local newspaper, the *Steamboat Pilot,* snapped a picture of the prominent retailer, gussied up in a handsome, dark suit with his beautiful wife on his arm. Dressed in the suit and tie, Gerry looked more stiff and uncomfortable than entertained. But Jill, wearing her hair cut Audrey Hepburn-close, with dangling oval earrings and a white formal gown, was smiling and radiant as she walked into the glittering ballroom at the Sheraton Steamboat Resort with her husband.

When Jill's middle son, William Andrew, got married, Gerry traveled with Jill to Jackson, Mississippi, to attend the nuptials. Andrew and his bride, Lynn, settled in Denver.

Gerry met Jill's parents, Henry and "Nita" Billiot at the wedding. The first thing Mrs. Billiot asked her new son-in-law was about his religious beliefs. It was a surprising question, and he was a bit taken aback.

"I'm sort of a Heinz Fifty-seven variety-type religion," he replied. Gerry wasn't a regular churchgoer and religion wasn't a big part of his life, but he was tolerant of the beliefs of others including some non-Christian traditions. Judging by the query, he figured Mrs. Billiot to be a woman of strong religious faith. The question was obviously important to her.

William Clark III also married. The youngest son and his wife eventually settled in Manhattan Beach, California, where he assumed a management position overseeing the operation of three stores for a national retail chain. When Gerry's niece married, Jill attended the wedding with him, and some of the out-of-town guests stayed at the bed-and-breakfast. Suddenly, Gerry's days and nights were filled with social events and family activities, many of them organized or arranged by his bride.

As they always had, cars continued to play an important role in Jill's life. She loved them and she loved driving. She also resumed her zealous pursuit of education. Jill signed up for college classes at two schools in Greeley, the town laid out and settled east of the

Rocky Mountains at the confluence of the South Platte and Cache LaPoudre rivers more than a century earlier.

She took psychology, education, and Asian history classes at the University of Northern Colorado, and geography and US history classes at Aims Community College. Jill attended UNC full-time during the summer and fall terms in 1991, and eventually continued through the fall term of 1992 and the spring term of 1993. She was especially interested in acquiring the proper education and credentials to counsel people who were suicidal. She was combining studies at two schools so she could graduate more quickly, and told people back in Steamboat Springs she was working for a master's degree.

For most people perhaps, regularly making the grueling two-hundred-fifty-mile round-trip jaunts over the Continental Divide between Steamboat Springs and Greeley might be a prospect that was more discouraging than attractive for a successful businesswoman and homemaker who was already in late middle age. But Jill wasn't intimidated, and she easily found accommodations in Greeley where she could stay during the week. She and her husband took turns driving to visit with each other on alternating weekends. One weekend he drove to Greeley or some other town where they could stay together at a bed-and-breakfast, and the next weekend she did the driving. Often their get-togethers were a hundred miles or more from either Steamboat Springs or Greeley. They went wherever they had a complimentary room, and they had an opportunity to visit areas of the state they hadn't seen or spent much time in before.

At that time, Gerry owned a 1984 Toyota Jeep and a 1976 Toyota 4-Runner he had bought from his niece, Carlynn Taylor. Gerry usually drove the Jeep, and he fretted that it wasn't good for the 4-Runner to sit around idle, so Jill borrowed it for some of her trips.

One weekend he borrowed Jill's Mercedes to drive to Evergreen, just outside the southwest edge of Denver to stay with her at a bed-and-breakfast. He picked up the car from Jill's son, who had some diesel-mechanic training. Seth checked the oil and drove the car to a gas station where he filled the tank before turning it over to Gerry. Before his stepfather drove away in the car, Seth explained a few basics about its operation, such as how to gas it up, and how to buckle the seat belts. He cautioned that if motor oil was added, Gerry should use diesel.

Nevertheless, when Gerry was still miles from Evergreen the oil pressure trouble light flicked on. By the time he got to the bed-and-breakfast the engine was ruined. Seth drove down the next day in the Suburban with a mechanic and they hauled the car back to Four Star Repair in Steamboat Springs. Jill was upset, and let her husband know she blamed him for the expensive repair.

Gerry offered to pay for the repairs, but according to his later account, Jill refused. She planned to pawn the damaged car off on Carl Steely as part of her settlement with him. Jill denied she had any such intent. "I think it's a joke because Carl would not accept a broken-engine car," she scoffed.

The vehicle was the same car taken to a South Bend Mercedes dealer to replace the engine and transmission a couple of years earlier. Estimates for replacing the engine once again varied from $5,000 to $7,000, depending on who was making the calculations and whether or not a junkyard Mercedes could be found and cannibalized for the expensive part. The *Blue Book* value was only $2,800. A professional insurance adjuster eventually appraised the total value of the Mercedes at much less than that: $1,001.23.

Although Jill had a way of making a mountain out of a molehill, it appeared at the time that the bad luck with the Mercedes had caused only a minor glitch in the happiness of the marriage. She had another, more positive and happier revelation to spring on the couple's acquaintances and friends.

Jill was either forty-six or forty-seven—depending on which year of birth, 1943 or 1944, is correct—when she began confiding to various people in Steamboat Springs that she was pregnant with Gerry's baby. She told Georgia Taylor, and she told William and Sylvia Boggs. The prospective parents made an appointment with a local obstetrician-gynecologist, and discussed home birthing and the possibility of home delivery. But Jill never returned to the doctor for follow-up prenatal care.

Gerry was ecstatic. His heart was set on becoming a parent, and he especially wanted a little girl that he could raise and spoil. He even picked a name for their child: Lara. Jill disclosed to close friends of the couple that she underwent an ultrasound, which confirmed the baby was a girl.

Gerry's friends in Steamboat Springs and elsewhere were thrilled at the news and happy for the couple. Barbara Smith, who had known Gerry since 1968, later recalled how excited he was about his impending fatherhood. He laughed and joked, and they decided to set up a college fund so Lara could attend Harvard. Gerry was obsessed with his daughter and speculated endlessly about how she would be raised and about her future.

He had the Boggs family attorney draw up a new will for him naming Jill and their unborn child as beneficiaries of his estate. Gerry explained to Halvorson that his wife also planned to have her lawyer, Bruce Jarchow, draft a new will for her.

The Thanine (Thane) Gillilands, a couple from the western Denver suburb of Westminster, who were especially close and longtime friends of Gerry, gave the expectant parents a crib, a stroller, and clothing left by their own little girl who had died. They were gifts from the heart, and Gerry appreciated their importance and special meaning to his friends. Mrs. Gilliland helped Jill shop for other baby clothes.

The expectant parents kept busy preparing for the arrival of the child.

Gerry had a $19,500 addition built onto his house for the baby. He bought books and audiotapes on child rearing and a car-seat baby carrier, and he promised he would arrange to pick up a high chair at the store, where he got a discount. Children's books, including copies of *Grimm's Fairy Tales, If I Ran The Circus, Aesop's Fables, Sneches* and *Six By Seuss,* were collected, along with video movies: *Treasure of the Lost Lamp, The Jungle Book,* and *Fantasia.* A stuffed animal collection was started for the baby, with a large pink panther and a small dinosaur. Gerry was even given a card signed, "To Daddy, from Lara."

Jill came home with armloads of baby clothes. "I bought gobs of clothes. . . . Everywhere I went. Any time there was a sale. I'm basically cheap. I bought lots of clothes," she later recalled. Jill watched for sales at stores like Steamboat Kids and bought little girl baby clothes from infancy up to the age of four.

She explained she was seeing a doctor in Greeley to monitor the health of herself and the baby. But when Gerry asked who the doctor was, she was evasive. Eventually she gave him the name of a doctor at a womens' clinic. The birth was expected in September, but the due date was eventually set back by several weeks.

Nonetheless, Jill inquired at a Steamboat Springs dentist's office about making an appointment for a checkup after Lara cut her baby teeth. And she talked to a hairdresser about making an appointment to have the infant's hair done. Lara was still apparently months away from making her appearance, but her mother was arranging a busy schedule for her. Nothing about her future welfare was being neglected.

Jill was gone from Steamboat Springs for weeks at a time, attending classes and hitting the books in Greeley or taking care of business affairs. It worried her husband terribly. He was concerned about his pregnant wife being away on her own so much and doing all that driving over treacherous mountain roads while she was carrying their baby. The child was the only thing he talked about when he telephoned or visited with his friends the Gillilands.

Despite his suspicions about Jill's curious pregnancy and odd behavior, he asked his friend, Gilliland, for a professional opinion: Was Jill really pregnant? Gilliland was a Certified Physician's Assistant (PAC). He was a highly-trained medical journeyman who was professionally and legally qualified to perform many, although not all, of the functions of a physician. Gerry cast him in multiple roles and at various times he was asked to be doctor and medical advisor, father confessor, and most important of all perhaps, trusted friend.

At that time, according to Jill, her pregnancy was in the seventh month. On the rare occasions lately when Gerry saw her, she didn't look pregnant to him, but he didn't trust his own observations. Although his brother and sister-in-law had a couple of children, and he was a godfather to another child, he hadn't spent much time around pregnant women. He wasn't quite sure how they behaved, or if a woman could carry a baby at that late stage without showing more physical signs than Jill was exhibiting. She was supposedly in her third trimester.

She wore bulky clothes, but that wasn't unusual for anyone, man or woman, pregnant or not, who lived in the Rocky Mountain ski community during the late fall or early winter season. Jill was still pert, still full of energy, and looked as healthy as a whole-grain muffin.

Gilliland told his friend the only thing he could, considering the circumstances. Jill had dropped in for a visit with the Gillilands the previous week, but Thane hadn't examined her. He said he simply didn't know.

Gerry's chum didn't let matters drop at that, however. He telephoned the clinic in Greeley and asked for the doctor Jill had named as her obstretrician. No one there had been monitoring a pregnancy for Jill Boggs.

While Jill was replaying the old phantom baby game with her prominent Steamboat Springs husband, pressure was building on her from the divorce court judgment in Plymouth, Indiana. She owed Steely $100,000, and the deadline set by Judge Cook had long ago come and gone. Steely wanted his money. But coming up with the purchase price of the Oak Street Bed & Breakfast, costs of renovations and other expenses, had depleted most of her ready cash and other negotiables and plunged her deep into debt for loans from banks, family members, personal acquaintances, and ex-husbands.

In North Manchester, Metzger had indicated he would help out with a $50,000 loan. She was counting on an acquaintance in Mississippi, R. L. Goodwin, to provide more money. And the First National Bank of Steamboat Springs agreed to float a $50,000 loan to Jill and Seth.

Just about the time it looked as if she was about to work herself out of her financial morass, Steely filed a suit against her for $250,000. She and Seth were anxious to build the greenhouse and make other improvements at the bed-and-breakfast. But she was suddenly back in the soup, plunged even deeper than before into a money mess and left with hardly any room for necessary financial maneuvering.

She had tapped just about every possible source of loans she could think of, and she was still dreadfully short of money. Jill advertised the bed-and-breakfast for sale. An ad in the *Steamboat Pilot* on April 11, 1991 announced: "OAK STREET BED & BREAKFAST. Recently renovated, nine-unit plus five-bedroom house, charming antique decor in this turnkey operation." No price was quoted.

Another ad in a giveaway real estate publication, however, pitched the B&B for $750,000. This time the copy specified a total of thirteen "professionally-decorated" rooms, one less than the newspaper listing indicated. A later ad in a different real estate booklet listed the "charming B&B located in the heart of Old Town" for $650,000. The ad carried a picture of the inn, and also stipulated thirteen rooms.

Jill also went to her new husband for help. She said she needed to borrow $100,000.

As later recounted by Jill in depositions, Gerry agreed to take out a loan from the Yampa Valley National Bank in Hayden where his brother was a member of the board of directors. Then he would pass the money on to her, in return for a personal note or deed of trust on the bed-and-breakfast. Jill signed over a partial deed of trust and settled back to wait for the loan.

Seth also recalled discussing the loan with his mother's husband a couple of times—once during Burger Night at the Old Town Pub & Restaurant and another time during Taco Night at the Old West Steakhouse. "Gerry Boggs mentioned it to me that he was going to help us out," Seth remembered, "because I was really stressed out about it. Gerry was going to help us out. Loan us $100,000."

Like so much about Jill's life and business affairs,

explanations and surface appearances don't always tell the whole story about what was really going on, however. For one thing, Gerry firmly denied in depositions that he ever agreed to try to use his brother's influence in any way to obtain a loan from Yampa Valley National. He also denied talking with Seth at the restaurants and telling him he was going to loan the young man and his mother $100,000.

Gerry provided a startling different version of Jill's motivations for signing over the deed of trust to him. She explained she wanted to give him the deed of trust in order to protect the Oak Street Bed & Breakfast for their child, he said. Jill didn't want Carl Steely coming to town and seizing the business to satisfy the whopping financial judgment ordered by the Indiana court.

That version of the affair sounds especially believable in view of the fact that Jill never got the $100,000 loan Gerry supposedly promised to arrange for her.

Jill may have been concerned by the threat to the financial bulwark she had built for herself. But neither that nor baby Lara slowed the pace of her frenetic life. While all the talk and commotion was going on about the mysterious new member of the Boggs family, other more ominous matters that Jill and her husband were initially unaware of were already set in motion that were about to shatter her latest masquerades. Ghosts from her past were lurking just offstage, and were about to make their appearance.

The Boggs brothers were close, and Douglas was troubled by ugly suspicions about the real background and character of the perplexing woman who had charmed his longtime bachelor brother. All the mystery and intrigue over the baby simply didn't make any sense, and other aspects of Jill's behavior were troubling. She was pestering him to help her out financially, and there seemed to be reason to believe that both Gerry's welfare and that of the hardware store could be damaged.

The concern mushroomed after Carl Steely traveled back to Steamboat Springs to ski and to talk with the local lawyer who was working with him to collect the divorce judgment from Jill. Attorney William C. Hibbard was also a skier, and the two men spent some time together on the slopes, mixing business with pleasure. Hibbard reportedly told Douglas Boggs that Jill's husband was in town and he wanted to settle up matters with his wife. He was planning to file a lawsuit against her. The news was a bombshell. Douglas is said to have told his brother about the planned lawsuit —and that Jill was still married to a man in Indiana.

She was furious when she heard the story. Hibbard's office was on Oak Street only a couple of blocks from the Bed & Breakfast, and she stormed inside to read the riot act. She was outraged because Gerry's brother learned about the impending suit. "I went in and told Bill Hibbard, number one, he shouldn't be putting my business on the street before he did something," she later explained.

Among other things, she was also angry because some of Hibbard's business associates or clients sometimes stayed at the B&B, and he had agreed to represent Carl. She considered the combination of the two to constitute a betrayal.

But the cat was out of the bag. Douglas Boggs talked by telephone with Steely. The Indiana educator had some hair-curling stories to tell about his onetime helpmate.

Douglas Boggs hired a private investigator from Denver to check into the life of the merry widow and divorcee who had breezed into town and married his brother after a whirlwind courtship. Judy Prier-Lewis had been a close friend of Gerry's for twenty years and a private investigator for more than half that time. She turned to the task at hand with quiet determination. It didn't take long to confirm that her friend, the brother of her client, was married to a bigamist.

As the investigation broadened the industrious PI learned that the new Mrs. Boggs had many other secrets hidden in her background. When the investigation turned for help to Houston, the private detective called on Stan Lewis Associates, a firm headed by a fellow sleuth in the Bayou City area. The two Lewis's were no relation through either blood or marriage, but she had done work for him in the past. Stan Lewis, his colleagues, and Judy Prier-Lewis quickly collected an alarming package of information.

Jill Boggs was a woman who had been married to four different men before tying the knot with Gerry. It would still be awhile before Gerry learned she was wed to almost twice that number of men before she charmed her way into his life. A deposition was eventually filed in Routt County Circuit Court stating: "Four of the prior marriages overlapped and were either bigamous or polygamous."

The investigators ultimately inspected court records, records of property sales, interviewed a string of men and women, and conducted surveillances. They determined Jill had used a fistful of names, including aliases that had no connection to the surnames of her various husbands. Perhaps most disturbing of all, one of her husbands had died in an unsolved shooting nearly twenty years earlier that occurred only twenty days after she filed for divorce. And despite police efforts to question her in the baffling case, she had avoided all personal contact with homicide investigators.

Gerry was crushed when he learned that his wife was still married to Carl Steely. Jill said she was merely confused about her marital status, and had made an honest mistake. She had believed she was divorced.

Jill went to a Greeley attorney, Elizabeth Strobel, and explained her problem, or at least part of it. She applied for declaration of invalidity of her marriage to Gerry, a legal ruling and terminology that amounted to an annulment. He was agreeable to permitting Jill to handle the matter with an out-of-town lawyer, and in an out-of-town court. He hadn't done anything wrong, but it was embarrassing none the less, and he could see no reason to make the marriage muddle a public affair in Steamboat Springs. He didn't even tell his family lawyer, until the annulment procedure was already a done deal.

The settlement was affirmed by the Logan County District Court in Sterling, more than one hundred miles northeast of Greeley on December 3. It wasn't likely that a snoopy reporter from either Steamboat Springs or from Greeley would hear about it, and if a Sterling journalist stumbled onto the file he or she would have no interest in the case. There wasn't much chance anyone outside the courtroom knew either Jill or Gerry or cared if they had obtained an annulment. The town and the court in the far northeast corner of Colorado less than an hour drive from the Nebraska state line was about as isolated from Steamboat Springs and Boggs Hardware as it could be.

A decree of invalidity of marriage was issued by Judge Steven E. Shinn. The jurist noted the couple believed at the time of their marriage that Jill's previous union to Steely was already dissolved. When she attempted to obtain a copy of her decree of dissolution of marriage from the Indiana educator, however, she learned that it hadn't yet been issued. She was still married to him.

"It is therefore ordered, adjudged, and decreed that the marriage of the parites in this matter is void, *ab initio,* and the Court declares this marriage to be invalid," he wrote.

The judge observed that the couple indicated they hadn't incurred any joint debts during the union, and agreed they had no joint marital property. Jill had indicated she was a student at the University of Northern Colorado, and was self employed as an owner of the Oak Street Bed & Breakfast. She listed monthly earnings of $2,000, including $1,500 in take-home pay. Her total income listed on the previous year's federal income tax was approximately $24,000. She also indicated on an affidavit of financial affairs supplied to the judge, ownership of a single vehicle, the 1984 Toyota 4-Runner.

In an accompanying document in a space referring to custody of minor children, she declared that no children were born of the marriage. There were no references on the paper to the possibility that she was pregnant.

The matter of the annulment was handled quietly by the couple. Jill appeared at the final hearing with her attorney. Gerry didn't make the long, exhausting drive across the front range for the hearing. The mess wasn't the kind of personal Boggs family business that would lend special luster to their reputation in the community. After the annulment was concluded, they continued their rather odd relationship and living arrangements for awhile. They told the judge they planned to remarry once the legalities of her relationship to Steely were finally sorted out.

Jill's sordid marital background had been exposed, however, and the handwriting was on the wall. In early December she packed up some of her clothes, cosmetics, and a few other small personal possessions and stormed out of Gerry's house for good. They had locked in a nasty quarrel that Jill claimed was sparked when Gerry's brother tipped off his parents about the annulment.

Gerry spent Christmas Day with Douglas and the

rest of the Boggs family. He didn't know where Jill was or who she spent the holiday with, but he couldn't turn off the worry—because she had advised him three days earlier that he was a new father.

She talked to him by telephone and told him she had given birth to their daughter in Denver, alone and unattended at about eleven o'clock, Saturday night, December 21. She was at her son William Andrew's home, but claimed she convinced him and his wife to go ahead with plans for a holiday visit with Lynn's family in Mississippi. Gerry never saw his daughter; Jill never brought the baby home to show to him.

He became more despondent than ever, and Gilliland's concern for his old friend mounted. He tried to talk Gerry into consulting a friend of his who was a psychiatrist. But Gerry was a proud man who was used to dealing with his own problems and had always been able to work his way out of whatever troubles were bothering him. He turned his thumbs down on the proposal.

Sometimes when he was especially desperate to get away from all the trouble for a while, he drove to the Gilliland home to stay over the weekend. He was embarrassed, frustrated, and so depressed he could barely function. Gerry fretted about Jill, about Lara, and about the effect his troubles were having on his parents and on the family business.

He was unsure of himself. His eyes were hollow, his hands shook, and he had been making mistakes at the store. He had trouble sleeping, his memory was shot, and it was beginning to look like he would never be able to work his way out of the mess he was in.

Gilliland suggested a couple of more times that he seek professional psychiatric help, but Gerry stuck to his guns. His troubles were something he would have to work out for himself. One time Gilliland talked with Douglas Boggs about arranging to have the troubled man hospitalized, but the discussion concluded with a decision to wait awhile longer.

As Gerry's frustration and torment increased, Jill continued living life to the fullest, with the seemingly limitless energy she had possessed since childhood. Neither the baby, nor any of her mounting troubles seemed to slow her down. She was Gerry's nemesis, and she pestered him by telephone at the house on Hillside Court, until he told her not to call him anymore.

"Don't call me. Call my lawyer," he snapped.

Seth helped his mother remove more of her possessions from the house. Gerry wasn't at home. He had packed her things and dragged them into the garage near the door where she could pick them up without moving any further inside. She and Seth loaded two cars, then came back for a second trip to pick up books and a few other things they hadn't had room for the first time around. Jill had a big collection of books. Seth wanted to take his mother's stationary bike, but it was locked in the exercise room.

She still owned the U-Haul, but it was being used for storage and it would have taken too long to unload. Jill wasn't at all pleased, and her son also complained that Gerry apparently tossed everything down the stairs into the basement, before moving them into the garage.

In an angry note, she complained to Gerry's lawyer that her ex-husband deliberately destroyed her things. "Did you advise him to trash my possessions?" she demanded. She charged that Gerry scratched her oak furniture and tossed breakable items into boxes with other effects to deliberately cause breakage. He was hanging onto her good china, twenty-four-karat gold-rimmed goblets and purple wine glasses, and she simply wouldn't stand for it, she warned.

She identified a long list of items she wanted returned, that included everything from five skillets and a coin ring to a Nikon camera, a gold bracelet, and a leather notebook she had planned to give Gerry for Christmas. Their relationship didn't survive until the holiday, she said, so she wanted the notebook back.

"He is trying to force me to be mean and do something nasty so that he can retaliate."

Halvorson countered the accusations by declaring his client hadn't intentionally or accidentally damaged any property of Jill's that was left at the house. If any damage occurred, he indicated, it was her own fault because she deliberately left possessions there so she could remove them in dribs and drabs in order to provide an excuse for continuing to pester Gerry.

"Mr. Boggs does not wish to retain personal effects of hers to the extent they have been left behind by her, but he doesn't want her coming and going for her stuff on a repetitive basis," the lawyer declared.

Jill fussed over everything. Nothing, it appeared, was too petty to pester Gerry and the lawyers with. She complained about the damaged Mercedes, but eventually agreed Gerry had offered to have it repaired and the offer was repeatedly refused. And Gerry claimed through his lawyer the engine was defective before he drove it, and Jill knew it. So she assumed the risk of the car being further damaged when she decided to drive it and to allow Gerry to drive it in a defective condition.

One day while Gerry was away from home, someone took the hand-held electronic garage door opener from his Jeep and used it to get inside the house. The intruder left a business card on his pillow so he would know someone had been there. Months later when a lawyer asked Jill about the incident, she denied having anything to do with it. She had no idea who might have done such a thing. It was an absolute mystery.

Regardless of whoever was responsible for the incident, it was part of a pattern of harassment that Gerry was subjected to for months. There seemed to be little question that Jill had a hand in most, if not all, of the dirty work.

As for Gerry, he could never completely relax. Just when he was about to take a deep breath, and try to convince himself he could see the light at the end of the tunnel, something new happened to upset him. He had taken over financial responsibility for the investigation, and eventually paid an estimated $6,000 in PI and lawyer fees while tracking his former wife's trail of deceit and connubial flim-flam through Indiana, Texas, and Colorado.

He even enlisted the help of another Plymouth lawyer, Roy D. Burbrink, to collect information from court records and from witnesses in Indiana. Metzger was one of the witnesses called to the law offices of Stevens, Travis, Fortin, Lukinbill and Burbrink in the center of the Indiana town's business district to give a deposition.

After the year-end holidays, Jill resumed her classes in Greeley, moving into a two-story house she bought. And the storytelling about the baby and other aspects of her life with Gerry turned extremely ugly.

She continued to commute between Greeley and Steamboat Springs, and when she was back in the Routt County resort town she spread false stories that Gerry was a closet homosexual. He managed to keep his guilty secret all those years because he traveled to other towns when he felt the urge for intimate male companionship, she asserted.

Jill was a passionate letter writer. The letters were almost always undated, and when they were inspected months after composition it was difficult to tell when they were really written. But they were convenient building blocks that always backed up her version of the relationship between herself and Gerry. Like the dental and hairdressing appointments for Lara and the stories about the pregnancy and birth, they provided ammunition for whatever Jill felt at the time would throw the most suspicion on Gerry and cast her in the best light.

She seemed at times to be operating as if she had taken to heart an old Indiana farm axiom, "If you toss enough fresh manure against a barn door, some of it's bound to stick." She flung a lot of verbal cow flops.

In an undated letter she addressed to Gerry, Jill berated him for drinking too much one time while they were soaking in a hot tub. She criticized him for what she said was his inability to love and be a friend to people. She referred in the note and in other statements to what she claimed was a traumatic event in his childhood when he was sexually abused by a male teacher. She accused him of belittling her because she was half American Indian, because she was Southern, and treating her as if she were stupid. She was maintaining a 3.5 grade-point average, while carrying at least twenty-one hours each semester, she defended.

In one letter, Jill was angry because he had wanted her to go to San Francisco with him for "one last fling," she wrote. "Are you nuts?" Elsewhere in the angry missive, Jill complained she paid for his flight with her credit card, and he expected to use her paid hotel accommodations as well. (During their last days together she purchased a two-for-one airline ticket, permitting one passenger to pay and her companion to fly free. But they broke up before the scheduled date of the trip.)

Despite her claim in one letter that she was sensitive because of her cultural heritage, Jill was showing about as much compassion and understanding for her ex-husband's feelings as a Lucrezia Borgia.

In another earlier note apparently written while they were still together, Jill complained he refused to have sex with her and used sex as a weapon. Because of her classes they were only able to see each other on weekends, and even then he wouldn't touch her. Jill demanded to know if it was because he thought she was ugly.

Perhaps the most bizarre letter of all, however, was addressed to her husband's attorney, Halvorson, at his office suite. This time there was a postmark with a date: Humble, Texas, January 6, 1992. Humble is a little town about the same size as Steamboat Springs, just outside the north edge of Houston. The letter was a ten-page diatribe aimed at convincing him she had given birth to a baby and was caring for it.

She apologized for choosing Gerry as the father of her child, but accepted the blame on herself. She claimed she got pregnant before they were married. She said she made him deny the pregnancy to his friends, because that was the question they all asked immediately after the marriage. At first, she also denied the pregnancy.

She concluded that the whole marriage was based on a lie. But, despite all the efforts at a cover-up, Jill said, "I still ended up giving birth to an illiagamatee [sic] child."

The long letter was generally composed with good sentence structure and proper grammar, but she made a few glaring spelling errors such as her trouble with "illegitimate." Another word she had a surprising bit of trouble with, considering her unique marital history, was "marrying." She spelled it "marring"—and perhaps that was closer to the truth than the traditional spelling.

Jill rambled on about what she claimed was her parents' opposition to the possibility of giving Gerry joint custody of Lara. She claimed he never wanted a child, but she desperately wanted a little girl—and should have gone to a sperm bank instead of depending on a husband who didn't love her and was a reluctant dad.

She promised to never file a paternity suit or seek child support. She promised not to try and get in touch with the elder Boggs couple even though she had already told them they could visit with their new grandchild. She referred to them as "Mother and Father Boggs."

Repeating her accusation that Gerry kicked her out of the house, she claimed he told her to go to the bed-and-breakfast where Seth could take care of her until the baby was born. He wanted the child born at Routt Memorial Hospital in Steamboat Springs, but she insisted on returning to Greeley for the birth even though the due date was only about a week away.

Jill said Gerry may have been feeling a little guilty the morning after their titanic squabble because he helped her load some clothing for herself and the baby in her car before she started the long, arduous drive to Greeley. He even offered to permit her to stay at the house until she gave birth. She was uncomfortable and her back was killing her, but she gamely declined the last-minute offer of a reprieve. She also refused to ask her son to take care of her.

Jill said when she got to Greeley she became frightened because it was the semester break and her student neighbors were gone. So she drove to her son Andrew's house in Denver. But he and his wife, Lynn, left for a visit to Mississippi, after she assured them that if she needed help she could call Gerry.

He telephoned her the next morning and screamed and threatened that if she refused to go to a doctor with him and his friend, Thane, he wouldn't continue supporting her through her troubles with Carl, and he wouldn't recognize the baby as his, according to the account.

Jill was drawing a tragic picture of a woman

hounded by a cold and vicious man who drove her from his house only days before she was to give birth. She worried that she would be arrested for bigamy and Lara would wind up with a child protective-services agency. And she fussed and fretted because he told people he wasn't even sure she was pregnant.

How could he wonder about that when her breasts had swollen from size 34D to 34EE, and her belly had grown about ten inches, she asked the lawyer in apparent amazement? Gerry had rubbed her back and gone through false labor with her; and then had the gall to say that maybe she wasn't pregnant, that she was just getting fat.

Jill wrote about her lonely ordeal delivering Lara by herself at her son's house about twelve hours after suffering through the abusive telephone call. It was an easy delivery; the baby practically dropped out, she said.

Lara had Gerry's temper, and yelled so loud for her one o'clock breast feeding a couple of hours later that one of the neighbors across the hall asked her whose baby was squalling.

After noting that she had expended her "emotional enema," Jill wrote, "so I leave you alone." Then she typed four more pages.

According to Jill, her real friends, who knew her character, were lining up in her support.

She claimed her lawyer in New Orleans whom she didn't name but identified as a "personal friend," told her to forget about Gerry. She didn't need the emotional stress and financial drain of another fight with someone, in addition to her ongoing legal troubles with Steely.

Her banker, who also was unnamed, also reputedly assured her she was a good person, a good mother, and a sound businesswoman.

She returned to Culver to see her friends there and

seek out their moral support. They advised her to forget about Gerry and about Steamboat Springs.

Only her clergyman told her it was her own fault for getting herself into the mess, and if she was sincere when she took her vows she was married "until death do us part." Jill noted she was concerned about her daughter's religious upbringing because Gerry believed as much in Buddha, which she spelled "Buda," as much as he believed in Jesus. He believed equally in all gods.

Jill also couldn't resist taking a few more potshots at Gerry's sexuality, claiming he was homosexual and married her only to provide cover for his secret life.

She also claimed he had what she described with typical college-classroom psychobabble as "a seasonal affective [sic] disorder," that made him depressed and negative. He didn't want to be around people.

Jill told the lawyer she could be contacted at the address in Humble for about a week. (She was staying with a relative.) She didn't know where she and little Lara would be after that. The lawyer had been around the legal merry-go-round for a few years and had talked to Jill a few times. If he believed there was anything to her story about little Lara, it didn't show.

In early December a bulletin from the Steamboat Springs Evangelical Free Church which Jill attended made hazy reference to problems in her personal life. Under a column titled "Prayer Concerns," the first listing asked the congregation to: "Pray for our family of the week, Gerald Boggs." Other prayer pleas printed on the same missive were made for a family that had lost two girls to a traffic accident and for the success of a church remodeling project.

Jill told people in Steamboat Springs and other Colorado communities, including an acquaintance in Boulder, that Gerry kicked her out of their house a few days before Christmas. Lara was her little girl by

Gerry Boggs, but he refused to recognize her as his, she explained to the hairdresser. Lara was never brought into the shop for the appointment, however.

According to some reports, Jill showed up in Steamboat Springs at least once with a warmly-bundled-up baby. It was little Lara, she claimed. After the probe of Jill's background and activities, investigator Judy Prier-Lewis arrived at a different theory about the infant that was shown around: the would-be mom paid someone to borrow a baby. Reporter Joanna Dodder of the *Steamboat Pilot,* speculated in a private discussion that she suspected the baby may have been a bundled up doll.

The terrible stories Jill was spreading about Gerry could be extremely damaging to someone who had been such an important part of the local business community for so long. The Boggs name, after all, was etched in the stone of one of the oldest and most impressive buildings in the very heart of the town's downtown shopping area.

Gerry was devastated by what was happening to him, embarrassed for his family, and troubled by the nagging possibility, dim though it was, that Jill really had given birth to a daughter. He served two tours in Vietnam and acquitted himself with integrity and courage. But he had never dealt with someone like Jill and what appeared to be her hateful determination to ruin him and drag his family name through the mud.

The former Mrs. Boggs actually seemed to gather new vigor and energy from the marathon bickering. She was growing stronger and more cantankerous all the time. But the vicious wrangle was taking a dreadfully savage toll on her onetime husband's self-confidence and emotions. He wanted it settled and over with.

"At the time I believed there was no child, and yet every time Jill came to Steamboat she would go around telling people that she had given birth and that I kicked her and the child out of my home," he said in a deposition. "And needless to say, this upset me greatly, and I guess maybe that since hope springs eternal, I thought, well maybe she did have a child."

Intellectually, Gerry found it hard to believe there was really a baby, but emotionally he still wasn't sure. He was being cruelly whipsawed by his emotions, suspicions, and doubts. He talked a few times by telephone with Steely, and the Indiana educator assured him Jill had undergone a hysterectomy. It didn't seem likely she could give birth to a baby, no matter how much she might wish to. Gerry observed that she had shown a baby, or what appeared to be a baby, around town, and even if she had adopted a baby, he would feel a responsibility.

"She really knows how to pull my chain," he groaned. At other times he walked around, or stood shaking his head and muttering to himself, "What a fool! What a fool!"

Now working at Gerry's request, his friend Judy Prier-Lewis beat the bushes in three states looking for a baby no one really expected her to find. She tracked Jill in Colorado, Indiana, and Texas. Jill had drifted back to the Lone Star State and was shuttling between the Houston area and Greeley.

The investigator checked with one of Jill's ex-husbands in Indiana, and asked if he thought the Billiots might be taking care of the baby. He didn't. By that time, Henry Billiot was living in the little farming and onetime glass-manufacturing community of Greentown just outside the east edge of Kokomo. Judy Prier-Lewis passed the information on to Gerry, and he telephoned his former in-laws to ask if they had the baby. He talked to both parents.

"Did Jill have a child by me?" he asked. They seemed to be taken completely by surprise. They said they didn't know of any new grandchild. Jill hadn't given birth to another baby.

Gerry was satisfied he had been told the truth. "I felt if anybody on the face of the earth wouldn't lie to me about this it would be her parents," he remarked.

At last his depression and uncertainty turned to anger. He had been lied to, made a fool of, and almost driven into a mental hospital. He was still worried that his former wife might find some awful new way to revenge herself on him by hurting his parents, but he decided it was time to strike back. He revoked the will he had prepared the previous year naming Jill and their expected child as beneficiaries.

And when Jill got word to him she wanted the deed of trust returned, Gerry refused to meekly hand it over. He was determined to hold onto it until he was absolutely convinced he was not the father of a daughter Jill had hidden away somewhere. It was his most important bargaining chip.

"I find out she had been married numerous times and didn't tell me about it. She had been pregnant and not had this child, and things of this nature certainly led me to believe that I was not going to sign any document and give it to her," Gerry reflected. "I think she knew perfectly well she was still married when we got married, when she married me. For reasons like that, I was not going to give her a signed document and let her walk off with it except in the presence of my attorney."

The deed of trust was a powerful lever, the key element in Gerry's defensive arsenal. Jill wasn't a person who could stand for things to remain static in her life, especially anything related to her financial affairs. Money and property were to be used to make more money. But almost everything she owned, in real estate, other solid material goods, and on paper, was tied up in the Oak Street Bed & Breakfast. Gerry had her in a bind, and financial institutions wouldn't consider taking new mortgages or liens on the bed-and-breakfast until the property was free and clear of the deed of trust.

Although Gerry had never provided the actual cash for the $100,000 loan to her, he had a legal document that said he did. And as long as he held onto it, he had a financial stranglehold on Jill. Seth's investment was tied up as well.

Gerry wasn't a cheat, and he didn't want Jill's money or Seth's. There were other considerations he insisted she meet, however, before releasing his hold over her finances. And he wanted everything spelled out in firm, indisputable legal terms before he budged. It wasn't a matter that Jill could any longer settle with idle verbal promises or softly uttered pillow talk.

When Gerry at last dug his heels in Jill responded with a new torrent of anger and abuse. She telephoned him so often at his house that he began taping the calls. Jill did most of the talking, but when he had a chance to get a word in he assured her he was willing to return the deed of trust once he knew for an absolute certainty there was no baby.

Jill filed a civil suit in the District Court of Routt County for return of the deed of trust and to settle other elements of the dispute. Seth was a co-plaintiff with his mother in the civil action over the deed. Jill was represented by attorneys Randall W. Klauzer and J. Richard Tremaine. The offices of their law firm, Klauzer & Tremaine were on Lincoln Avenue.

Gerry struck back by filing a counterclaim. In the document prepared by his attorney, he accused Jill of false representation, infliction of emotional distress, defamation, extreme and outrageous conduct, and asked for an unspecified amount of damages.

The defendant in the suit was named as "Jill Steely aka Jill Coit aka Jill Coit-Steely," but referred to in the body of the document by the first of the names, Jill Steely. She was no longer referred to as Boggs, the name she had proudly laid claim to for such a short time. Once more, Jill and a man she had married found themselves and their lawyers in a nasty court fight.

Through his attorney, Gerry stated that Jill was living at an unknown location in Texas and was planning to remove a material portion of her property in Routt County in order to make it unavailable to her creditors.

On a more personal level, he accused her of lying to him about being a single woman available for marriage and of later lying about being pregnant and giving birth to a daughter he had conceived. He complained he had justifiably relied on her word, with the result being that he suffered damage and loss in time expended, effort, and money preparing for the birth of the daughter who never was.

He asserted that she told him and others he was not a good father to the child and caused him great shame, distress, and a baker's list of other emotional damages and embarrassments.

Supporting the charge of defamation, he declared: "That since January 1992 to the present, Steely (Jill) has told numerous parties that Steely had a baby by Boggs and that Boggs disowned Steely and the baby. She and the baby had been thrown out by Boggs and ordered out of town and/or words to similar effect which gave the listener the understanding that Boggs was a bad and neglectful father . . ."

It was a mouthful, and it was couched in a typically awkward run-on sentence, but the message was clear. Jill was a baldfaced liar, who had been going around badmouthing Gerry. She was depicting him to friends and acquaintances as a rotten father who disowned his own infant daughter and threw his pregnant wife out

of his house. Gerry invested considerable time and
money in lawyers, investigators, and travel expenses in
order to determine if he was, indeed, the father of a
child, it was added.

He asked in the countersuit for a decree from the
court stating that no child was born of the relationship
between Gerry and Jill, as well as an order for a cash
award.

Halvorson charged $140 an hour as his normal rate
for services. Meeting his fee could translate into a
whopping amount of sales of paint, nails, tools, and
plumbing supplies at the hardware store. He put in a
lot of hours working to sort out the legal morass his
friend and client had gotten himself into.

Even before the suits were filed, the lawyers set to
work exchanging a busy dither of telephone calls and
legal papers—letters, proposed agreements, releases,
drafts, and suggestions for a non-disturbance pact. At
one point during the summer of 1992, Klauzer wrote
to Halvorson and pointed out Jill was in Alaska, and
he would deal with the issue of the non-disturbance
agreement as soon as he could. She bought some real
estate and picked up an Alaskan voter registration
there.

On the subject of the non-disturbance agreement,
Klauzer said he planned to modify the proposal to
make it "somewhat more bilateral in its application."
Gerry wanted Jill to leave him alone.

He insisted she promise to no longer use the Boggs
name. She was to confirm either that no child was
born as a result of their union, or if a child was indeed
born, that she would provide visitation, (in a more formal version, she was to acknowledge she never became pregnant by Gerry, nor had a child by him). She
was to refrain from contacting him in person, by telephone, mail, or through members of his family, in any
manner except through his lawyer. She was to agree

that she, her heirs, or anyone representing her had no claims against him for money, property, support or inheritance. Finally, each of them would agree not to disturb the tranquility of the other, and agree not to enter the other's residential or business properties.

The non-disturbance pact was central to obtaining the release of the deed of trust. It was Gerry's position that one agreement was linked inextricably to the other.

Klauzer didn't see it that way. He argued to Halvorson that the issues weren't related. If the question of a child was truly an issue for Gerry, then that problem was a matter to be worked out by the Logan County District Court which handled the annulment, which he referred to in proper legal terms as the "invalidity action."

"This issue is clear-cut. I cannot in good faith agree that they should be interrelated," he wrote. Klauzer repeated his earlier request, that Halvorson send him a signed release for the deed of trust. Jill's lawyer probably wasn't at all shocked, when Gerry's lawyer failed to comply with the request. Halvorson wrote in part in his reply:

> "I further find it amazing that you have failed to confirm that there is a baby yet you assert that we can bring paternity proceedings. If paternity proceedings are appropriate, they are customarily brought by the mother and she has not done so to date. Indeed, such is one more fact which convinces us that there was no baby and any claims to the contrary were deceitful and outrageous."

He also assured his legal adversary that Gerry preferred to minimize or avoid the stress and expense of litigation by reaching an amicable solution to the dispute with Jill.

The wish expressed in Halvorson's letter to reach an amicable solution without resorting to litigation wasn't to be realized. A few weeks later the lawyers broke off their efforts to settle matter by mutual agreement and filed the lawsuits.

Accompanied by her lawyer, Jill went to Halvorson's offices in the Norwest Bank Building at 320 Lincoln Avenue early in January 1993 where she and Seth were scheduled to answer questions in depositions. A couple of weeks earlier, in the middle of December, Jill drove over the Continental Divide from Greeley to meet with her lawyer in Steamboat Springs and prepare for the proceeding. She stayed overnight, then made the exhausting return trip.

Seth was the first to be interrogated.

At the very beginning of the session, just after Seth was sworn in, he was asked what he did at the bed-and-breakfast. "I do everything," he replied.

"You do everything? What is the nature of the duties you perform?"

"Cleaning toilets and fix breakfast."

Taking Seth's deposition was a trying process that was made even more difficult by Jill's frequent interruptions. From time to time she broke into her son's testimony to prompt him or to make remarks including: "He didn't understand what you mean, Vance," "What does litigation mean?" and "That was a guess, Vance. We were estimating it."

Halvorson finally became fed up and asked Tremaine to keep his client quiet until it was her turn to talk. If that couldn't be done, he was going to ask Jill to leave. Tremaine apologetically agreed that he understood the other attorney's position. Jill quieted down, squinting and furrowing her eyebrows occasionally, but managed to hold her peace throughout most of the remainder of the process.

Significantly, when Seth was asked if he had siblings

and what their names were, he replied that he had two. "Andy and Billy."

"Do you happen to know whether or not your mother became pregnant during the course of her relationship with Gerry Boggs?" Halvorson asked.

"She's too mature to be doing something like that," Seth replied. "No. No."

"Okay, she didn't," Halvorson acquiesced. "And how do you know that?"

"Because I think they usually swell at the belly." Seth could respond to certain questions in a manner as disconcertingly neutralizing or peevish as his mother.

Seth indicated he and his mother never discussed the possibility of her having children with Gerry, and she never said anything to him to make him believe she was pregnant during the period she was with Gerry. "She has not had a child since 1968," he said.

Although the lawyer didn't go into the matter of the earlier phantom children, Seth's statement would indicate there was no Thadius Brodie and no Tinley Metzger—as well as no Lara Boggs. Jill's only children were Seth and the two Williams.

At one point when Halvorson was trying to learn the name of the girl in Indiana who filed the paternity suit against Seth, he pleaded that he was having trouble understanding some of the questions because of his dyslexia. His difficulties were audio-visual, and he sometimes had trouble with big words or round-about questions. "Just go right to it," he suggested.

At another time when Halvorson was discussing possible fears that Steely would try and attach the Oak Street B&B to satisfy the court judgment in Plymouth, he asked if Seth had employed a lawyer.

"For my mental . . . ?"

"Pardon?" Halvorson appeared surprised at the answer, but he didn't follow up on the possible implications. Instead, Seth quickly recovered and explained in an obvious reference to Klauzer and Tremaine that they had. "Richard and Randy." The local lawyer team had represented him and his mother in their business matters as long as they had known them.

Seth painted Gerry as a man who could be cruel and made his mother cry and said she used her money to meet the couple's expenses. "My mom would spend money, Gerry would not." He said their relationship was erratic. "Gerry has a different beat, a different drummer, a different attitude towards women. Up and down. Cold!" Seth didn't know his mother's friends. It wasn't his business who they were. He had other things to do, he said.

The husky young man conceded he didn't attend his mother's wedding when she married Gerry. Halvorson asked if he approved of Gerry.

"My mom's a big girl. She can do what she wants," he said. But he agreed he didn't like the way his mother was treated by the hardware store owner.

Continuing to respond to the lawyer's questions, Seth indicated he didn't want to sell the bed and breakfast. He had gotten to understand the business and to be comfortable with it, and he liked it. "I have people drive by and wave at me," he said. "So I'm pretty happy where I'm at."

Seth agreed the business may have been listed for sale at one time since he and his mother bought it; he wasn't sure. But he didn't want to sell it, and in fact he had bought his mother's interest. Halvorson wanted to know how much he paid for Jill's share of the inn, but Seth couldn't provide him with an exact figure. He explained that she just took whatever she needed.

"Whatever she needs?" Halvorson asked in what appeared to be understandable surprise.

"Uh-huh!" Seth agreed.

"What was the amount that you have agreed that she needed?"

"She just—I just let her take whatever she wants," Seth repeated.

It was a curious, and it would seem, a dangerously sloppy way to operate a business. It was especially strange for someone who was such an experienced businesswoman as Jill, and Halvorson asked if she took money out of the till on a regular or on an occasional basis. Seth said he wasn't sure. He didn't keep track.

When it was his mother's turn to testify, she announced she wasn't going to cooperate and stalked out. Halvorson later asked the court to order her to repay his client's attorney fees for the lost time, and to force her to submit to the deposition.

Jill had a way about her of delaying the legal process when it was time to give depositions.

When Jill finally gave her deposition about three weeks later, it was a tedious and trying process. As Halvorson struggled to pin down specific information, Jill bobbed and weaved, pleading for an opportunity to check her records at some other time or cited problems with her memory. Her affliction with dyslexia made it difficult for her to keep numbers in her head, she explained.

Obtaining a clear picture of her financial arrangements concerning the Oak Street Bed & Breakfast was especially difficult and trying. Jill agreed she got a $47,000 loan from Carl, but said it wasn't recorded. Some of the amounts she borrowed were recorded and some were not.

Halvorson observed she had said she got $135,000 from the First National Bank and $50,000 from Eldon Metzger. "It was [$60,000]," she corrected him on the Metzger loan.

"Well, that's true. Then why does this say [$50,000]

here?" the lawyer asked, pointing the sum out on a list.

"I don't know. But it was [$60,000]," she insisted.

"And Henry Billiot, $20,000?" Halvorson asked, as he consulted the same list. "I think it was $35,000."

"It was [$35,000]," she responded.

Later in the deposition process, Jill said she gave her father the T-Bird in return for the money he turned over to her. It was worth $35,000 in the condition it was in, she said. "To me it was worth a million."

Halvorson wanted to know about other loans.

"Jules English," he queried. "It says $20,000?"

"Okay, don't touch it. Don't correct it. I'm sorry . . ." Jill stammered.

"What was that loan?"

"I don't know. I'll have to check the record," she replied. Jill was having as much trouble keeping the amounts of her loans straight as she would later have explaining the dates of marriages and divorces with her husbands. It was all very confusing. Even the names of her creditors were turning out to be sources of confusion.

Halvorson said he assumed "Jules English" referred to Julie English, the maiden name of Seth's wife. It wasn't. He didn't even have the gender right. Jules and Julie were two different people, Jill said.

"Oh, this is somebody else?," Halvorson asked.

"Yes, sir."

"Okay. Jules English. Who is Jules English?"

"A male," Jill replied.

"Pardon?" The deposition wasn't going as smoothly as it might have. Jill seemed determined to make the lawyer work for his information and wasn't giving anything up easily.

"It's a male. It's not a female," she said. If the lawyer wanted information, he was going to have to squeeze it out of her. Jill may or may not have been able to give a precise definition of obfuscation, but she knew how the process worked. She was expert at slowing down a line of questioning.

She agreed again in response to another question, that Jules English was a male, not a female. "Then tell me, what is your relationship to Jules English?" Halvorson persisted.

"He is related to Julie English," Jill said. How were they related? "A relative!" Jill replied. That wasn't the kind of answer likely to earn her a favorable mark in one of her college classes, but the lawyer wasn't about to give up. He tried again to determine just exactly who the mysterious Mr. English was.

"Father? Son? Brother?"

"No, not father. She doesn't have any brothers. I don't know the exact relationship, but I will find out the exact one . . ."

Halvorson was still reluctant to surrender and admit he was proceeding down a dead-end path with the line of questioning. He asked if Jill could pin down her benefactor's age a bit and speculate whether or not he was closer to twenty or fifty. Jill didn't know. He was simply someone who had agreed to loan her money, and she wasn't even sure about where he lived. She had a post-office box number for an address.

Twenty thousand dollars was an awful lot of money for someone to loan to a stranger, and Halvorson's puzzlement over the odd transaction was understandable. But Jill either couldn't or wouldn't provide the answers he was looking for.

The lawyer at last dropped the subject of Mr. English, and asked if there was anyone else to whom she owed money.

"Oh, I owe lots of money," she bubbled. Jill listed a few more loans ranging from $10,000 to $25,000, including $10,000 she said she obtained from her middle son, Andrew. Asked if she took out a note for $50,000 from R. L. Goodwin, Jill said she was going to get money from him but the loan was never concluded.

"Who was this Goodwin, R. L.?" Halvorson asked, sounding a bit like a military drill instructor barking names off the roster of his platoon.

"That's a friend of mine in Mississippi."

Halvorson asked if she sent Goodwin letters, and she replied that she did not. The lawyer abstained from further questions about her Mississippi friend before the exchange could deteriorate into the same kind of frustrating morass he got himself entangled in over Jules English.

Instead, he turned the questioning to more personal matters linked to her relationship with Gerry. Did Jill understand Gerry was remodeling his house in order to make more room for the baby? No, Jill said. That wasn't her understanding.

"This comes as a surprise to you?" he asked as if her response was a shock to him. It was an eyebrow-raiser.

Jill told the story about Gerry undertaking the remodeling project so she would have room to park her car inside the garage. He had been keeping his weight-lifting equipment in there, but "a garage is for parking," she said.

Halvorson asked if she was saying Gerry remodelled the garage to accommodate her, not because he wanted the room for a child they were expecting.

"I don't know why he was building a garage. I don't know his mind. But it stands to reason, so I would be able to park in the garage."

Halvorson asked her about a notation indicating a purchase made at Moonflower Birthing in Louisville, Colorado. Jill replied that when she and Gerry were in Boulder he bought a floral backpack. The lawyer wanted her to be more specific. "For a child?"

"Right," Jill said. "I think it's the only thing he

really purchased for a child. When I was with him, anyway."

"It wasn't a home delivery kit, or anything of that nature, was it?"

Jill didn't appear to be bothered by the very personal turn the questioning had taken. "I don't know. I thought, to my recollection, it was a weird-looking floral thing. I thought it was rather feminine-looking, but it wasn't for me. I usually brought presents, not Gerry."

The question-and-answer session began to bog down again when the lawyer drew closer to her claims of pregnancy. Jill blamed the stories about being pregnant with a daughter on Gerry. And she used the opportunity to fire another salvo at what she continued to claim was his secret homosexuality.

He asked if during their life together she became pregnant.

"I was not pregnant with Gerry Boggs."

The lawyer ignored the obfuscation and patiently established that she was not pregnant by anyone. He asked if she had claimed to be pregnant.

She agreed she had—because it was what Gerry wanted. Jill seemed to be trying to draw a picture of a compliant, loving woman who was manipulated by her husband into living a lie. She did it to help him create the virile, masculine, heterosexual image he wished to project for his neighbors. It made him happy.

Jill claimed at another time during the lengthy statement that although she had undergone what she termed "a partial hysterectomy" in New Orleans to have some abnormal cells removed from her uterus, she was still capable of becoming pregnant. She said she and Gerry used condoms when they had sexual relations to avoid the possibility of a tubular pregnancy. She even volunteered the brand name of the devices for her questioner.

Halvorson asked her about an earlier statement she made saying: "Anyway I am to blame. I slept with him and got pregnant before we were married."

Jill replied that was what her husband wanted her to say. "But I did sleep with him, but I was not pregnant," she added.

"So, basically this is a false statement. It's a true statement that you slept with him, but it's a false statement that you got pregnant before you got married? Is that a fair statement?"

A lot of references to "statements" were being bounced around the room, and Jill's attorney, Tremaine, objected that she had already answered the question. Halvorson didn't pursue it any further at that time and instead turned to questions about some of her business and banking dealings in Culver and Plymouth.

Jill became understandably confused at one point while Halvorson was grilling her about the judge's order in Plymouth awarding Carl $100,000 and subsequent matters relating to the Indiana educator's efforts to collect. Jill said she had attended a hearing with her husband, and Halvorson asked exactly when the hearing was.

"I have a question," Jill said. "What hearing and what husband are we talking about?"

Her confusion was understandable to the lawyer. "That's true. They're hard to follow, aren't they?" he commiserated.

"I sleep with them, I marry them, okay?" Jill shot back. "I could just sleep around."

At another point in the grueling session, Jill said she repeated her vows with DiRosa about four times. "You married DiRosa four times?" Halvorson echoed in astonishment.

"Uh-huh! Every time we went away to an island we got remarried. I'm sorry, that's just the way it was. I married W. C. six times." She followed the amazing statement up with several remarks about her respect for DiRosa as an attorney and as an individual. "Whatever he sent me, I signed, okay. There were no hard feelings. I liked the man as a person. . . . I'm sure that—because he's an attorney, whatever he's done is legal."

Halvorson asked if she read things that were printed above her signature, or if she simply signed whatever he sent her without reading it.

"Can I say something?" she responded. "Right now if he sent me something I would sign it. This man is not trying to screw me in any way." DiRosa had brought presents to her children, she said. Just because their marriage didn't work out there was no reason to be enemies. They were friends.

While discussing the promissory notes that surfaced during the process of the bitter divorce in Plymouth, Halvorson asked if Carl accused her of fabricating them.

"He accused me of fabricating everything in the whole world," she snapped.

Halvorson observed that there was some whiteout on one of the promissory notes produced as an exhibit in the Indiana divorce trial and asked if she could explain why it was there. She couldn't—but she had a suggestion: "Let's scratch it off and see what's under it?" No one scratched off the whiteout, and the deposition interview turned to other matters.

Jill and her former husband's attorney clashed over a journal which Gerry had kept during their marriage. She said it included remarks about his thoughts, opinions and what she described as his shortcomings and failures—matters that disturbed him.

The journal was discovered to be missing from the house after she left. Halvorson included the journal among other documents he asked to inspect before permitting his client to give his own depositions. Jill agreed she took the journal with her when she left, and Halvorson's plea to inspect it was a perfectly proper request to make as part of the discovery process. But Jill said she couldn't turn it over just then, because it was apparently in luggage misplaced by Continental Airlines while she was traveling between Colorado and Houston.

Halvorson asked if she had a tag on her luggage, and she said she had one which she slid her business card into. She was careful to stress that it was "a pretty tag." For a moment, she was Jill the pussycat. The Jill who was always intensely and happily feminine. It was a persona that was much more appealing and pleasant than some of the other Jills that Gerry, Carl, Clark, and other husbands had glimpsed at one time or another.

Jill had filed a claim with the airline over the luggage. And in response to a query from Halvorson, she agreed she once worked in the airline industry for six weeks. She knew a bit about the system of claims and payment for lost luggage. Jill was a woman who knew a lot about a few things and a little about a lot of things. An impressive amount of the knowledge seemed to somehow revolve either around husbands or money.

She apologized that although she couldn't produce the journal just then, she promised if and when she recovered it she would be sure to make it available to Gerry's lawyer. Halvorson wasn't about to buy that story, and he made it plain in written remarks how he felt about Jill's reputed difficulty keeping track of the journal. He wrote: "Alas, a shell game defense to discovery, first we have it, now we can't find it, so you still can't have it. But just wait because we might find it and then use it. But if it turns out that it supports your client, it probably won't ever be found." The lawyer said his client's deposition should be held off until the journal and other information were supplied to him.

The court agreed and ruled that Gerry wouldn't be forced to give his deposition until Jill had complied with the discovery process.

At long last, Jill's deposition session was ended. But she wasn't through with Gerry Boggs. Many traditional marriage ceremonies in this country incorporate the words, "till death us do part." The maxim would eventually prove to have tragic application to the mean and spiteful quarrel between Jill and her onetime husband.

It's unlikely that either Gerry, his lawyer, or Gerry's family and close friends were unaware that the bitterness and acrimony were a long way from being over. It's also doubtful any of them could have realized just how filled with anger and hate the quarrel between him and Jill had become. Unimaginable fury and savagery were about to forever blight their lives.

EIGHT

Roy and Michael

Jill was forty-eight years old and a single woman again.

Being unmarried wasn't a condition she would put up with for very long.

On Friday, February 7, 1992, about six weeks after her divorce from Carl Steely at last became final, she walked into a small wedding chapel in Las Vegas and married her ninth husband.

Roy C. Carroll was a retired US Navy chief petty officer and businessman who lived at the north edge of Houston. He was sixty-seven years old and was embarking on what was very likely the most bizarre adventure of his life. The North Carolina-born widower had exchanged vows in a marriage that was doomed to failure.

Of course he didn't know that at the time. That was the way it was with the men who walked down the aisle with Jill Lonita Billiot-Ihnen-Moore-Coit-Brodie-DiRosa-Metzger-Steely-Boggs-Carroll. On the document prepared for the quiet wedding with the retired sailor, the bride indulged her taste for fudging important information on her marriage applications and licenses.

She boosted her birthday forward to June 11, 1951,

neatly trimming seven or eight years off her real age.
In the space for her mother's maiden name, she used
her birth mother's first name, Juanita. Taney, the
maiden name of Edward Bruce Johansen's long-dead
wife, was used for the surname. A similar disregard for
the truth was used in identifying her father, who was
named as Henry Johnson. Jill's handwriting was jerky
and scratchy. It wasn't pretty to look at, but she had a
deft hand when it came to filling out marriage licenses.

She indicated she was married only once before and
was widowed. The information would become chillingly prophetic when it was compared months later
with her signature on the document. She signed her
name as Jill Boggs.

Carroll's marriage probably had even less chance of
success than those of his predecessors. That was because Jill was already playing house with a handsome
hunk of a man who was nearly twenty years younger
than the unsuspecting groom. According to some descriptions the boyfriend's hair was light brown, or
"dishwater blond." That was close enough for Jill. She
had always had a weakness for blond-haired men. It
was one of the things that attracted her to Clark more
than twenty years earlier.

Michael O. Backus was a slender, hard-bodied,
forty-eight-year-old equipment maintenance man and
troubleshooter for US West Communications, the
telephone company that serves Greeley, Steamboat
Springs, and other communities in Colorado. He was
six-foot, one-inch tall and weighed about one hundred
seventy-five pounds. Outdoor work and a fondness for
outdoor recreation helped keep him in good shape.

Like four of his girlfriend's former husbands,
Backus had strong Indiana connections in his background. He was born in Evansville, on September 9,
1945. Michael, like Gerry, was also a Vietnam veteran,
although he served his single hitch there with the US

Air Force instead of the Army. After four years of active duty from 1963 to 1967, he returned to the Evansville area and served a year with the Indiana National Guard. In Evansville, he worked with the Indiana Bell Telephone Company.

After moving to Fort Collins in 1984 and going to work for US West, he enlisted in the Colorado National Guard and began building an impressive record as a non-commissioned officer in Company C of the 140th Signal Battalion. the National Guard unit was headquartered seventy-five miles south of Fort Collins in the east Denver suburb of Aurora, but he was meticulously loyal about his attendance at evening or weekend meetings and drills and summer encampments. His duties involved the installation, operation, and maintenance of wire and cable communication systems, a vital element for making any military operation work.

One time in September 1988 when danger suddenly developed from what his supervisors referred to as "a hot shelter," he quickly shooed the men under his command away and troubleshooted the problem himself. "Staff Sgt. Backus is a good NCO and he demonstrates the principles of NCO leadership by taking care of his troops," an evaluator observed. Michael loved his work with the National Guard.

Glowing reports from a superior described him on an annual enlisted evaluation report thus: "Sgt. Backus has displayed sound judgment, initiative, and technical skills when dealing with his subordinates and peers. Sgt. Backus was a major contributing factor to the success of the switching section they now enjoy. I would recommend Sgt. Backus for any position or career field he may want to persue [sic]."

A year later an evaluator had this to say: "Sgt. Backus is s key NCO within the unit. He has distinguished himself through a consistent record of high

NCO standards including appearance, leadership, effective communication with subordinates, and being dependable to complete all assignments regardless the conditions."

His employers and fellow workers at US Communications West seemed to share much the same high regard for him. He was a dependable, hard-working, patriotic American who loyally served his country and had apparently never been in trouble with the law in his life.

He was also divorced from his wife, Kathy, and was the father of an eight-year-old girl when he met Jill. His daughter, Erin, lived in Fort Collins with her mother.

Michael was looking for a place to live in Greeley when he learned about an apartment in a house at 1309 Eleventh Avenue. Jill owned the house, and soon after he rented the downstairs apartment he fell under her spell. A short time later he moved upstairs with his lonesome landlady. She rented her boyfriend's former apartment to a young man, Rick Mott.

They were living there when Jill flew to Las Vegas to tie the knot with the retired CPO. Curiously, with her marriage to Carroll and her live-in relationship with Michael, she had completed a near-clean sweep of America's armed services, all of which were served by the main men in her life. Two were Marine corps, one was Army, one was Navy, and the other had served in the Air Force and in the National Guard of two states. Only the Coast Guard was left out.

The new Mrs. Carroll and her groom didn't waste much time honeymooning in Las Vegas before returning to Houston. While the groom attended to business and began planning a move to Colorado, his wife busily shuttled back and forth between Houston and Greeley. Even though she was away from Carroll's home in Houston much of the time, the vivacious, attractive, and smartly dressed younger woman had brought a sense of happiness and pride to his life.

Jill was as busy as a hummingbird, playing out an exhausting balancing act between two men: a husband in Texas and a live-in boyfriend in Greeley. Somehow she also made time between her roles as wife, sweetheart, full-time college student, and businesswoman to regularly make the arduous, nearly three hundred-mile round-trip drive over the Continental Divide between the "All American City" in Weld County and "Ski City USA" in Routt County to keep track of affairs at the Oak Street Bed & Breakfast and to meet with her lawyers on matters relating to Gerry and Carl.

She still had her trademark vibrant personality and driving ambition. But keeping her energy level up wasn't the piece of cake it had once been. She had lived nearly five decades, been married to nine husbands, given birth to and raised at least three children, formed or operated several businesses, and traveled much of the United States and the rest of the world.

The old silhouettes of the lithesome model's shape that helped her win photo assignments and a beauty crown were being blurred by extra pounds. Crows feet and wrinkles were taking their inevitable toll on her once-flawless, high-cheekboned face. Even her butternut-brown skin didn't have its former healthy glow and elasticity.

She had to reach for a pair of reading glasses when she was looking at small print, and she was having serious problems with her right hip. Another physician was treating her for degenerative arthritis, and she was taking cortisone shots for pain. Even her soft, silky, Southern drawl was fading, and when she got emotional or angry her voice could be as raw and scratchy as a cigarette smoker's cough. There was no avoiding it; Jill wasn't a sexy, saucy woman-child anymore. Age, an arthritic hip, and flab were ruining her beauty.

Gerry had finally released the deed of trust after being convinced beyond the shadow of a doubt he hadn't fathered a child. Jill admitted that in front of her lawyer and in front of Gerry when she finally gave her deposition. But they were still locked in a legal battle over her demands that he pay for the damage to the engine of the Mercedes and pay attorney fees and his counterclaim for defamation and demand that she repay him for remodeling the house and other expenses he incurred preparing for the birth of a daughter.

And, of course, there was the ongoing mess with Carl and his $250,000 lawsuit. The emotional pressure on her was intense, and if later accusations are to be believed, dark thoughts were running through her mind. She was still intent on making as much trouble for Gerry as she could.

Jill talked in front of her daughter-in-law about using stolen money orders to cause trouble for Gerry with the law, Julie later told law-enforcement authorities. She figured she could get him in hot water by signing his name and cashing some of them.

Gerry was deathly afraid of snakes, and Jill reportedly speculated about slipping a snake into his car or Jeep while he was working at the store or inside his house.

She also told Julie that Gerry was homosexual and talked about putting an advertisement in the personal columns of one of Colorado's daily newspapers with statewide circulation, *The Denver Post* or the *Rocky Mountain News,* to embarrass him. The ad would invite gay men to telephone or stop in Boggs Hardware when they were in Steamboat Springs looking for company and advise them to ask for Gerry in order to get a ten percent discount.

Steamboat Springs was a small town. The residents were curious and chatty and possibly less likely to show the same easy acceptance of homosexuality generally found in larger urban centers like New York, Chicago, or San Francisco.

Gerry began receiving mysterious telephone calls, including one from a man who claimed to have had sex with him. The voice wasn't familiar to him, and he taped that call and others.

Ridiculing and harassing Jill's ex-husband wasn't the worst thing Jill had in store for him, according to her oldest son, his wife, and several other people. They say Jill wanted Gerry killed. If sworn statements from family members and acquaintances are to be believed, Jill had made up her mind to employ a bloody solution to her problems. Gerry had to die, quickly and violently.

Jill telephoned Seth more than once and asked him to do a favor for his mother: murder Gerry.

Her new boyfriend had fallen under her siren spell, as so many other men had done before him. And he was apparently as determined as she was to see to it that Gerry was murdered, according to Seth's account. "We're only doing this for you kids," Michael was quoted as saying.

Statements by Jill's son weren't the only ones to place Michael squarely in the middle of a ruthless scheme to murder the Steamboat Springs merchant.

The telephone company employee did a lot of talking with one of his buddies who worked with him at US Communications West. He reportedly asked Troy Giffon at least five times to carry out a contract hit on Jill's ex and offered to pay thousands of dollars for the job. Like Michael, Giffon was a veteran of Vietnam and the shared experience helped cement their friendship.

According to Giffon's later statement to a police investigator, Michael pestered him for a couple of weeks during the early summer in efforts to enlist him in a murder conspiracy. Jill's boyfriend stopped at his friend's house four times and talked once with him by telephone about the need to get rid of the Steamboat Springs businessman because he was blocking the sale of the bed-and-breakfast. Somehow, as Michael explained it, sale of the inn had become a million-dollar deal. His girlfriend would have access to that amount after the sale was concluded, and he was lined up for a big piece of the action once the troublemaking merchant was out of the way.

Michael was telling people at the telephone company that he had been cut in as a ten percent owner of the bed and breakfast by his wealthy sweetheart. He confided a similar story to a friend from Evansville, whom he had worked with at Indiana Bell.

He offered Giffon $3,500 to do the dirty work for him. Giffon wasn't a killer and wasn't interested. But Michael wasn't ready to give up. He wheedled and promised and eventually more than doubled the bounty to $7,500. Giffon still wasn't buying. But their disagreement didn't shoot down their friendship, at least not immediately. He continued opening his door to his buddy when Michael dropped by the house, and he continued to listen.

Michael had been roaring over the Divide to Steamboat Springs on his Harley-Davidson or making the drive with Jill in one of her cars, and they were both too well known in the little town to carry out the murder themselves, he explained. Someone else had to be found who would do it for them.

As Jill had done with others, Michael painted a sordid picture of the target of their bloodthirsty scheming, according to Giffon's continuing account. Gerry was a twisted bisexual who enjoyed watching his wife have sex with other men before joining in the action,

Michael confided. Because of his respected position in the business community, he traveled outside Steamboat Springs to find male company. So when he was murdered, police suspicion would focus on one of his secret gay lovers.

Gerry's own allegedly intricately-hidden sex life would deflect the investigation and send police off on a wild goose chase, providing a perfect cover for the homicide. At least it seemed from Michael's glib explanation, that was the way the problem would be resolved.

At times, Michael called his girlfriend's former husband filthy names, especially concentrating on crude descriptions of homosexual activity. Giffon's wife, Teri listened while her husband's friend lambasted Gerry as a "son of a bitch," "faggot," and even nastier words because he was preventing Jill from selling the bed-and-breakfast. All he talked about while he was at the house was marrying Jill, selling the bed-and-breakfast and making enough money to retire, she told investigators.

She thought it was odd that he had never hung around their house before, then all of a sudden for a two-week period he was dropping by every three or four days. "Man, he must really hate Jill's ex-husband," Troy's wife remembered him saying to her one day a few minutes after Michael left. "He wants to kill the guy."

Giffon didn't want anything to do with the lunatic proposal. Michael wondered out loud if he might be able to find someone from Greeley's so-called Latin Quarter to carry out the murder for him.

It seems he never tried to follow up on that idea, or if he did, he ran into the same lack of cooperation he was faced with in his efforts to enlist Giffon. Michael left Greeley later in the summer, on assignment from the company after persistent rains and a massive flood that roared through much of the Midwest. Michael was one of thousands of skilled journeymen and technicians rushed to the area from around the country to repair damage and restore vital services.

Events in Steamboat Springs were continuing to move rapidly, however, and early in June an effort to solve the dispute out of court at a mediation hearing fell through. The Colorado Judicial Department's Office of Dispute Resolution set up a hearing at the NorWest Banks Building where the opposing attorneys had their offices. The first session was canceled because Gerry hadn't produced some necessary documents. For whatever reason, the attempt at mediation failed.

With the failure of the mediation attempt, the long-awaited trial on the suit and countersuit was at last ready to be heard in the Routt County District Court. Three days were set aside on the court calendar for the proceedings, July 28, 29 and 30.

Jill begged off. The timing was awful, and it would be a terrible burden on her if she was forced to appear in court for the scheduled proceedings, she complained through her attorneys.

She underwent total replacement of her right hip on June 23 at the Northern Colorado Medical Center in Greeley, and her attorneys explained she needed about three months to recover. Her mobility was extremely limited and she asked the trial be put back until early the next year. The motion for continuance was signed by Tremaine on June 23, the same day of the scheduled surgery.

The lawyers submitted letters from several doctors in Greeley and in Houston confirming the seriousness of Jill's medical condition and her need for a hip replacement operation. A letter from Dr. Patricia Mayer on letterhead of the North Colorado Arthritis Clinic was dated May 17 and indicated the physician had

seen "Ms. Coit-Carroll" in follow-up consultation
dealing with degenerative arthritis of her right hip. Dr.
Mayer wrote that over a period of time Jill was treated
with multiple injections of cortisone, and given anti-
inflammatories but none of the efforts eliminated the
pain for very long. X-rays revealed severe degenerative arthritis of the hip, and Dr. Mayer concluded that
the only option "for lasting relief" was hip replacement.

Another orthopedist in Houston wrote he saw Jill
on June 2 after she was referred to him for a second
opinion, and x-rays revealed degenerate joint damage
of the right hip. Jill was quoted as saying she didn't
know why she developed osteoarthritis, but she had
been in an auto accident about twenty years earlier
and suffered hip pain. The doctor concluded that total
hip replacement would be proper treatment.

Dr. Barry A. Nelms, also a Houston orthopedic sur-
geon, wrote he saw Jill Carroll in his office on June 3
and concurred that she would benefit from total replacement of her right hip. X-rays revealed osteoarthritis. The letter also disclosed Jill was on her current
husband's health-care plan.

She had suffered muscle spasms and agonizing pain.
The message was clear, Jill's condition had left her no
viable choice except to submit to an operation to cope
with the pain and to halt the rapidly continuing degen-
eration of her hip.

Gerry and his lawyer strongly opposed the continuance nevertheless. Halvorson argued she had built up
a history of acting to delay the proceedings and presented a deposition from Steely describing Jill's timely
seizure at the Denver airport. The lawyer also claimed
a delay would give Jill an opportunity to get rid of her
Colorado real estate, making any judgment against her
uncollectible.

The B&B was still on the market, and the price was

recently dropped by about twenty-five percent to $200,000 in order to make a quick sale, he added. In 1991, the property was being offered for $850,000, was then reduced to $750,000 and most recently at $650,000 before taking the latest nosedive.

Gerry's attorney also pointed out William Harold and Sylvia Boggs, who were expected to be called to testify at the trial, made it a practice to leave the area in the fall and spend the cold-weather months in Arizona. If the trial was put off three or four months the elderly couple would have to testify by deposition, rather than appear in court in person.

Reluctantly, Judge Rebecca Kourlis rescheduled the trial, setting aside three days on the court calendar beginning on Wednesday, October 27, 1993. There really wasn't much choice. Jill had undergone the operation, and it seemed obvious that she needed time to recover from such a serious surgical procedure. The ailing woman had pulled off a timely *fait accompli.*

At Gerry's request, the jurist made it a condition of the continuance, however, that Jill would again be restrained from selling or in any other way, encumbering her real estate owned in Routt County. A legal hold was back in place, once more preventing sale of the bed-and-breakfast. It would ensure her appearance at the civil trial. Nothing was said in the order about her holdings in Greeley or Alaska, but Jill's legal troubles were expanding, rather than improving. The continuance merely bought her some time, but not much.

Tremaine remarked in a motion document that his client was "optimistic that she can withstand the travel to Steamboat Springs and a trial in late October . . ."

In the meantime, the ailing woman went to Iowa with her boyfriend. She had a job to do: find herself a hired killer.

When Michael packed up his tools, extra work clothes, and other personal effects, Jill loaded her own bags with traveling clothes and necessities for the long trip. They set up temporary housekeeping in Ottumwa, a Des Moines River town of about 25,000 people. An agriculture and meat-packing center, Ottumwa is about an hour-long drive from the Missouri border, and it was water-soaked and reeling from recent storms.

While Michael was dealing with generators, fuse boxes, and a tangle of fallen telephone lines, Jill presented herself in Ottumwa as a psychologist. She was a curious kind of psychologist, who did her best to talk an acquaintance into a bigger mess than the troubled Iowa woman would have dreamed of, according to a later statement to a law-enforcement investigator.

Jill asked R. Mohee Hanley to murder a businessman in Colorado for her. It was a weird request for a psychologist to make of anyone. In the personal experience of most Midwesterners like Ms. Hanley, contract murder was a matter that was confined to what they read in books or watched on television shows and in movies. Asking someone to assassinate another person wasn't something expected to come up in casual conversation. The professional-appearing woman she met at a gay and lesbian meeting in Ottumwa was nevertheless urging her to commit a horrific crime. Jill wanted her to travel a thousand miles or so and murder a man she didn't know and had never heard of before.

Jill didn't blurt out the murder proposal all at once. She was more subtle, according to the story recounted by the Ottumwa woman. Jill claimed to be a bisexual who counselled gays and lesbians, Ms. Hanley said. Jill reportedly counselled her once a week for three or four weeks, and during one of the early sessions Ms. Hanley expressed strong feelings about the behavior of rapists.

"How would you feel if someone raped your daughter?" Jill asked her.

"I'd kill him."

Jill could hardly have created a better opening to bring up the subject of a revenge murder.

During their next counseling session, Jill explained she had a lover who was killed in a traffic accident. The dead man had a daughter who was about five years old, living with an aunt, and being sexually abused by a close male relative. It was a tragic and nasty situation to contemplate, and Jill continued to build on the story during subsequent meetings.

She described the child molester as a man who was in his mid-forties, was tall and stockily built, with dark hair and a mustache. He was the owner of a hardware store in a brick building and lived by himself in Colorado. Ms. Hanley later couldn't recall if Jill said he lived in Steamboat Springs or Greeley.

Unfortunately, the hardware-store owner was bound to get away with his disgusting abuse of the little girl because he was such a prominent member of the community. No one in authority would call him to task for his crimes, Jill reportedly explained.

Mohee Hanley had a dislike for rapists and sexual abusers of children, but murder for hire or for any other reason was something else. Jill would have to look elsewhere if she wanted someone killed, even if the grossly-detestable stories she was telling about the target of her bloodthirsty fantasies were true.

Jill asked if Ms. Hanley knew where she could buy a clean untraceable gun. Ms. Hanley didn't want anything to do with helping her strange counselor find an untraceable gun, any more than she wanted to commit a murder for her. The answer was no.

After returning to Greeley with Michael, Jill was right back where she had started when they left for Iowa. If the stories related to investigators were true, she and Michael had struck out in efforts to find someone who would agree to kill Gerry in a murder-for-hire scheme—or as a humanitarian gesture to prevent the continuing sexual abuse of a child. The trial had been rescheduled, and it was unlikely that the judge could be convinced to agree to yet another continuance.

Jill telephoned Ms. Hanley in Ottumwa, and during a series of calls, eventually offered her $1,000 to carry out the murder, the Iowa woman recounted. Jill reportedly volunteered to take an active role in the killing, and explained she knew how to get into the would-be victim's house through the back door. She also suggested he could be ambushed while he was getting out of his car. Jill would drive by while Mohee could shoot him from the passenger seat. In her final call, Jill offered to take care of Ms. Hanley's travel costs and send her airline tickets.

Ms. Hanley wouldn't budge. She wasn't going to kill anyone for Jill Coit. By late September or early October, according to the Ottumwa woman, Jill was increasingly frantic. She reportedly responded to the stubborn refusal with a statement that she was bound to find a way to have the man killed. If she couldn't find someone to do it for her, she would do it herself.

The leaves on the trees lining the UNC campus were already turning to brilliant yellows and reds when Jill walked into Bizarbor, a beauty shop on Ninth Street. She asked hair-stylist Mary Weber if she could borrow a blond wig that was on display in the shop window. Jill explained that she wanted to go to Steamboat Springs in disguise and follow her boyfriend to see if he was cheating on her.

Jill was a regular customer, and the hair stylist consented to the odd request. The next weekend, Jill returned the wig, as good as new. Nothing happened in

Steamboat Springs, she explained, because her boy-friend was sick.

According to Seth, his mother continued to keep after him to help with the killing. When he continued to refuse to kill Gerry or to help her do the job, she asked him for advice about how she could get into the house. She also asked him to pick up and get rid of the body. She could stuff it in plastic bags and leave it in a ditch near the house for him, Jill suggested, according to his statements to investigators. Then he could load the corpse into the back of Gerry's car, drive it to the airport, and dump it.

Understandably, Seth was reluctant to get involved in a murder. He had worked with her in legitimate business enterprises, and respected her for her industry. But murder was altogether a different kettle of fish.

At one point, however, he advised: "If you do anything stupid, wear gloves." It was October 8, 1993.

Jill hadn't left her daughter-in-law alone either. She once confided to Julie that she had found someone to "take care of Gerry," the young woman later reported. Jill didn't say who the mystery person was or exactly how Gerry was to be taken care of.

Jill telephoned her frequently from Greeley or Texas; Julie didn't always know where the calls originated from. Almost every time Jill called, she asked Julie to check on Gerry to find out if he was at work or at the house. When Jill was in Steamboat Springs, she had Julie drive by Gerry's house with her to see if he was at home. Jill kept herself well informed about her ex-husband's normal daily routine.

Julie recalled that Michael roared across the mountains from Greeley on his Harley one day and took her to lunch at the Steamboat Yacht Club on the river-front. He groused about all the money Jill was losing because of Gerry and how unfair it was that she was being sued. When he dropped Julie off back at the bed-and-breakfast, he told her he was going to ride by Gerry's house. He didn't say why, and she didn't ask.

During their brief meeting, Michael also mentioned how quickly he made the trip across the mountains. He kept the pedal to the metal on his bike and was behaving as if he was as obsessed as Jill was with bringing a sudden end to the angry conflict with Gerry.

Events were moving fast and time was running out. The rescheduled date of the trial with Gerry was only nineteen days away.

In Manhattan Beach, California, Jill's youngest son received a telephone call from someone he later described only as "a relative." The caller was worried about Gerry Boggs's safety, fearful that the merchant was in serious danger from Jill. William didn't take the call too seriously. He ignored it, according to his later recollection. By that time, the trial date was little more than a week away.

In Indiana, Steely and Metzger had already replied to subpoenas. Metzger was ordered to report to the law offices in downtown Plymouth of Stevens, Travis, Fortin, Lukenbill & Burbrink and produce a virtual armload of legal documents tied to his domestic and business relationship with Jill. Copies of marriage applications, marriage certificates, divorce pleadings, final divorce dissolution documents, and any legal papers related to the Oak Street Bed & Breakfast were among the material he was directed to produce.

On a deposition Carl gave, he stated that he and Jill had what he thought was a close marriage, and they spent all their free time together and didn't even quarrel. "I was utterly devastated to learn that the high ideals of marriage which we shared had been so blatantly violated," he said. "It became evident from her own deposition that Jill had been plotting from the very first year of our marriage to do me in financially."

Then he added, a bit loftily but perhaps in typical pedagogic fashion: "In the words of Thomas Jefferson, 'We are not afraid to follow truth wherever it may lead, nor to tolerate any error so long as reason is left free to combat it.'"

The two ex-husbands were learning the sad truth of another pithy aphorism: "True loves and new loves may come and go, but an ex is forever." Closer to home, the trouble shooter from Four Star Repair, Inc., on West US Highway 40, was also among probable witnesses who were subpoenaed so he would be available for questioning about the damaged Mercedes.

The pressure on Gerry hadn't eased off very much, if at all, and he was anxious to at last settle the acrimonious two-year squabble. He told his friend, Barbara Smith, on Wednesday, October 20, that although he was nervous about seeing his former wife in court he was also looking forward to the confrontation.

"I still have to know there was no baby," he told her.

Despite the findings of the private investigation carried out by Judy Prier-Lewis and her colleagues, Gerry's telephone conversation with Jill's parents, and her sworn statement at the deposition declaring she had not been pregnant and there was no baby Lara, he wanted to hear the denial of his reputed fatherhood in court from her own lips. He wanted to watch and listen as she admitted there was no baby.

On Thursday, October 21, he checked out the receipts in his cash register at about one o'clock in the afternoon, said good-bye to his fellow workers, and left for the rest of the day.

Although Friday is usually a busy time at the store because it's payday for so many people and householders are getting ready to take advantage of their weekends off to make home repairs, Gerry never showed up for work. He didn't telephone, and he hadn't said anything to anyone Thursday about taking the day off. Even through what appeared to have been the worst period of his long-going troubles with Jill, he had always managed to either keep to his work schedule or at least to let his brother and others know when he didn't expect to be on the job.

Douglas Boggs knew it wasn't at all like Gerry to simply sleep in or go off somewhere on his own and forget about his responsibilities at the store. Douglas was worried about his older brother. Gerry didn't answer repeated attempts to reach him by telephone. When Douglas went to the house to check on his brother, he walked onto a scene in his older brother's kitchen that was sickening and primitively savage. Gerry was dead on the kitchen floor.

The prophecy that was so ominously implicit in the entry on Jill's marriage application for her wedding to Roy Carroll was realized. She had come as close as it was possible, to becoming "the Widow Boggs."

Steamboat Springs Police Department Patrolman Kevin Parker arrived at the house a few minutes later in response to a telephone call indicating a possible suicide had occurred. The uniform officer barely had a chance to take a look at the crumpled body and peek around to see if there were any others, before he was asked by Detective Rick Crotz if the victim was still alive. Crotz had pulled up in his police car only moments behind the patrolman. Parker said the man on the floor was dead.

Crotz was a fourteen-year law-enforcement veteran, who spent the first part of his career with the San Diego Police Department, and he learned his job well while moving up the ranks. He was efficient, but professionally cautious. He checked out the body to confirm for himself that Parker's observation was correct and the man on the floor was dead. There was no question the diagnosis was on target. Gerry's body was cadaver-cold, there was no pulse, and his eyes were glazed over.

The corpse was blocking the back door. A ragged, scarlet gash that appeared as if it might have been caused by a gunshot, creased his high forehead. A small hole in the back of his heavy blue parka also appeared to have been made by a gunshot.

Exposed areas of the man's warmly-bundled body were also marked with ugly lacerations and bruises, including an injury to his right cheek. A huge pool of blood had formed next to the head, and other splatters extended at least ten feet away. The nearby walls were marked with more ugly rust-colored smears. A plastic bag near the body, and a small metal lump that appeared to be the slug from a small-caliber cartridge were also blood-smeared. The kitchen looked like a slaughterhouse.

Crotz took another quick look around for additional bodies or anyone who might be injured or hiding. Outside the immediate kitchen area there wasn't much to see. There were no lurking killers with a gun, no bodies, no blood, no overturned furniture, or other indications of violence or a struggle. Everything seemed to be in place, except for the answering machine on the telephone. The lid that permits the audiotape to be slipped in or out was open and there was no cartridge inside. On the surface, there was nothing especially alarming about that. It would not be very long, however, before the missing audiotape took on more significance in the investigation.

That was in the near future, however. For the present, Crotz and the uniform officer retreated outside for a war council with police department colleagues and an assistant Routt County district attorney. The street, driveway, and yards outside the attractive bi-level house on West Hillside Court were becoming very busy.

Assistant DA Kerry St. James and patrolman Jerry Stabile were among the newcomers. It was quickly agreed by St. James and Crotz that there would not be a comprehensive inspection of the interior of the house until a search warrant could be obtained from a judge. Murder is a serious crime whenever and wherever it occurs, but it wasn't something that happened in Steamboat Springs every day. Not even every year. Authorities at the scene were determined to see that no aspect of the investigation was botched.

There wasn't much of a mystery about the last previous murders that occurred in the city almost two years earlier. In September 1991, William Coleman gunned down his ex-wife Jan and her friend, Luke McKee. Coleman killed himself the next day. Crotz played an important role in investigation of the tragedy and during his career had probed several other homicides as well.

This time police were faced with a completely different kind of challenge. So far there was one dead man, and based on their cursory observation, it was obvious he was killed by someone else. Gerry didn't commit suicide. There were no other bodies in the immediate area, so it seemed to be an excellent bet that his killer was still very much alive and on the loose.

No one wanted a slick defense attorney somewhere down the line getting critical evidence tossed out of court because it had been discovered and seized without a warrant authorizing search of the house. St. James and police investigators played it safe and secured the immediate area inside and around the house to preserve the integrity of the crime scene and wait for the warrant. For the time being the interior of the house was off-limits to police, neighbors, and the press.

Reporter-photographer Brad Bolchunos from *Steamboat Today,* the sister publication to the *Pilot,* snapped pictures from the street of the house and the small group of law-enforcement officers conferring or standing just outside.

Officers dialed Routt County Coroner Dayle D. Hammock at a minute or two after four PM, and told him to get in touch with Captain J. D. Hays at the police department about a death. Hammock drove to the police headquarters, conferred with Hays for a few minutes, then hurried to the house with his deputy, Douglas Allen.

Crotz explained to him that the crime scene was secured, and after discussing the matter with St. James as well, the coroner decided to defer making an official pronouncement of death. The detective assured him the victim was dead, and Hammock chose to hold off on going inside until the search warrant was obtained.

The position taken by the police, the assistant DA and the coroner was a carefully considered good-faith decision, but it opened them to a spate of second guessing and eventually led to serious problems determining the approximate time of death.

Exactly how damaging or critical the delay would eventually become was a matter to be worked out much later before a judge and a jury. But there was no question it would make the job of police and prosecutors much more difficult in some respects. Valuable information provided by conditions such as lividity and body temperature was either already lost or soon would be. Lividity is the discoloration that occurs when the heart stops beating and gravity causes the blood to settle to the lowest areas of the body. The process of lividity stops in about two hours, or less, when the blood coagulates.

Although those factors can be a big help, even they are not sure-fire indicators of the precise time of death. Under average conditions, bodies begin to cool after the first hour or two following death. They start to feel cold to the touch after about twelve hours, and after twenty-four hours even the internal organs have usually reached the same temperature as the outside surroundings. Other elements can lead to critical variations in the speed at which a body cools, however, and must be taken into consideration in making final calculations.

Bodies cool at different rates, based on the build, how the limbs are arranged, and temperatures or weather conditions where they are found. Other conditions such as health, and how warmly someone is dressed can also be important factors. The bodies of heavier people cool at a slower rate than those of thinner people. And someone who had a fever would have a higher temperature to begin with and it would take more time for the body to reach the same cool state as a healthy person.

Skillful detectives, coroners, or pathologists must take all those possibilities and many other factors into consideration when working to arrive at a time of death. But getting a good lock on an approximate time can be critical to an investigation. Every minute of uncertainty about an exact time confronts police, prosecutors, and defense attorneys, with a wider window of time in which the murder may have been committed.

Other factors, of course, were still available to help narrow the time gap. Gerry's stomach contents could, and almost certainly would be, examined to determine approximately when and what he had last eaten. Although the rate of digestion varies with different people and can be affected by such things as anger or fear, the condition of food found in the stomach often provides valuable clues to helping pin down the time of death.

Witnesses would also be located and interviewed to determine the time he was last seen alive. Witnesses are important, but again they provide less-than-perfect tools for crime investigators. Every homicide cop knows witnesses aren't infallible. Far from it. Two witnesses describing the same individual might differ with one estimating the height and weight at six-foot and 200 pounds, and the other insisting the subject was five-foot-eight-or-ten and 145 pounds. Or one person might describe a car as a gray Ford Escort, and another will say it was a red Pontiac Sunbird.

Usually, although not always, being able to cite a close approximation of the time of death is not so helpful to defense attorneys—especially if their client is guilty.

Crotz and his colleagues didn't simply cool their heels for half a day waiting for a warrant. Not by any means. Most professionals in the field agree that the first forty-eight-hours are crucial to a homicide investigation. After that amount of time the trail begins to grow cold.

Police officers began drifting through the neighborhood, knocking on doors and talking with residents. Footwork is a tedious job, but it is a staple element of almost any homicide investigation. If anyone in the normally-quiet neighborhood saw anything unusual or suspicious on their street or around the home of the dead businessman in the last day or so, it was important for police to gather the information as quickly as possible.

Other officers got busy on the telephone, calling family members and acquaintances of Gerry's. SSPD Detective Robert DelValle talked with Thane Gilliland, who told him about a surprising discovery made during the summer of 1992 when he was trying to adjust the front seat of Gerry's red Isuzu for Jill. Two pistols were under the driver's seat. One was a .45 caliber semi-automatic handgun in a leather holster. The other was described as a small "palm gun," possibly a .25 caliber or .32 caliber blue-steel semi-automatic.

During another interview a few weeks later, Gilliland turned over a box of .22 caliber long-rifle ammunition to Colorado Bureau of Investigation, (CBI), agent Susan Kitchen. He explained Gerry told him that after the breakup with Jill he took the hollowpoint and round-nose bullets out of a car she had been driving. Gerry gave the ammunition to his friend because he couldn't use it. He didn't own a .22.

Crotz talked with Douglas Boggs. So did Detective DelValle and Stabile. The dead man's brother had discussions with all three officers during the first twenty-four hours of the probe. Boggs telephoned his lawyer's office and broke the dreadful news to Sharon Halvorson that Gerry was dead and he was with the police and about to be questioned. She passed the word to her husband, and he hurried to the SSPD headquarters. The attorney hovered protectively near his shaken friend and client as he was interviewed.

Police investigators were forced by the unhappy circumstances to ask some painful questions and carry out some unpleasant functions. The grieving brother wound up having his hands swabbed for gunshot residue, hair and blood samples were taken, and he may even have been strip searched, according to a later report in the local press.

At that stage of an investigation, a good homicide detective has to consider practically everyone who has anything to do with the victim as a potential suspect, even when he is a close family member, prominent member of the business community, and a former county government office-holder. Douglas was a one-time Routt County Commissioner. Law-enforcement officers are especially aware that there is nothing unusual about family members turning on each other, and in fact family murders are all too common. It's still more the rule than the exception, even in these days of drive-by gang shootings and drug wars, that victims are killed by someone they know.

Boggs told the officers about Gerry's marriage, the annulment and long-running quarrel with Jill, her outrageously-checkered marital background, and the approaching civil trial. He also advised them about the harassment and mysterious telephone calls. Douglas said Halvorson told his brother to save the tapes of the harassing calls from Jill and from the mystery man recorded on his answering machine. They could be important evidence in the approaching civil court proceeding.

The open lid on the empty answering machine was suddenly an aspect of the investigation that warranted a very close look.

Other, unforeseen contacts made during the sweep of the neighborhood were also turning up important gems of information, however. Stabile talked with Girl Scouts Andrea Thorne and Lisa Re and learned they had stopped at Gerry's house about four o'clock Thursday after school, hoping to sell fund-raising nuts. Although Lisa noticed vehicles parked inside the garage while she was climbing the stairs to the front door, no one answered when she rang the bell. The girl's description of the vehicles matched those of Gerry's Isuzu and his Jeep.

Debbie Fedewa was also contacted, and told DelValle about the suspicious characters she noticed lurking around the neighborhood Thursday. She described the couple who were in such inappropriate warm clothing in the balmy, early fall weather; the woman dressed as a man with the obviously false mustache and pony tail, and her tall athletically-built male companion.

Meanwhile, after conferring with the assistant DA, Steamboat Springs police called for help from the

CBI. Although the Steamboat Springs Police Department was composed of experienced and well-trained law-enforcement professionals, certain crimes sometimes occurred that strained the capabilities of a small-town organization. They didn't have the sophisticated crime laboratory or trained technicians to conduct all the ballistics, serology, and other forensic operations and tests that were so vital to a successful investigation.

The CBI also had trained crime-scene technicians who could help in the gathering of evidence and homicide detectives who had probed scores or hundreds of murders around the state. Summoning the CBI was no reflection on the professionalism of the local police department. It was a good call.

A few minutes after midnight, almost nine hours after Gerry's body was discovered, Steamboat Springs Detective Ross Kelly showed up at the house with the search warrant. Detective Kelly at last walked back into the house, accompanied by a few other handpicked colleagues from the SSPD, St. James, and a forensics team from the CBI.

Police officers fanned out to make a thorough search of the house, while forensics technicians from the CBI moved methodically through the utility room and kitchen snapping photographs, tracking, measuring and collecting samples of blood smears, and gathering trace evidence such as hair, fiber, and dirt. Photos of the back entrance were also taken immediately before the homicide team walked inside. The coroner joined the small squad of grim-faced men minutes later.

Hammock was first elected to his job as coroner in 1987. Before that he was with the police department in Austin, Texas, for four years, then served six years from 1976 to 1988 as Routt County Sheriff.

Like many of his current colleagues in other thinly-populated counties in Colorado, he had taken advantage of professional courses sponsored by the state for coroners. He had limited medical training and knew some first aid. Although he had crime-scene training during his law-enforcement career, he wasn't a forensic pathologist.

Under the circumstances, the small-town coroner did what was expected of him: the best job he could. He made a close visual inspection of the heavily-bundled body on the kitchen floor. A ragged, bloody hole was plainly visible in the victim's parka covering the upper right portion of his back, that appeared to have been caused by a gunshot. At 1:20 AM, three minutes after walking into the house, the county coroner made the official pronouncement of death.

Hammock had known Gerry Boggs for years and he recognized the dead man, but his report was properly dispassionate and professional. On a form titled "Routt County Coroner's Office Report For Case No. 93-33," he recorded the time of entry, location and position of the body, and other pertinent information. Interestingly, in a space labeled "SPOUSE," the words "Never married" were typed in.

Hammock observed that the single bloody bullet on the floor about five feet from the corpse appeared to have been discharged from a firearm "of approximately .25 caliber." The wooden handle of a shovel lying a few feet from the body, was also covered with red smears that appeared to have been left by bloody fingers.

Elsewhere in the silent, night-shrouded structure that had been Gerry's home, police were gathering a collection of articles as possible evidence. Gerry had a modest collection of weapons, and investigators took a loaded .357 Smith & Wesson pistol from his nightstand, along with thirty-one extra rounds of ammunition in a bullet wallet and dump pouch, and another handgun and two rifles from a closet.

One of the more intriguing discoveries was made in the attached garage. Several cassette tapes, a compass, trash bags, and a Denver map were collected from the top of his car. Each of the weapons and the other items were meticulously packaged or marked separately with tags identifying the location, the date, the time, and the initials of the officer in charge of the evidence at that stage. When technicians had completed their immediate work with the bloody shovel and other items found near the body or taken from Gerry's pockets, those were also carefully tagged and added to the growing mound of evidence.

After confirming his law-enforcement colleagues were satisfied with their picture-taking, studies, and inspection of Gerry's body, Hammock carefully rolled the victim over onto his back. The coroner observed what appeared to be another gunshot wound when he lifted Gerry's right arm. A third ragged bullet hole was found in the front of the parka. The slug had smashed into the victim's chest. Gunpowder spackles around the holes in his clothing and the entry wounds indicated he was shot at close range.

Gerry was savagely beaten as well as shot. The bloody shovel was obviously the weapon used as a bludgeon. The victim's forehead was marked with a curved four-inch long gash that was so raggedly deep and ugly it was initially taken by Crotz to be a possible gunshot wound. Gerry had other injuries on his nose, cheek, right temple, knee, and all over the trunk of his body. His right hand was cut and bruised with injuries that appeared to be defense wounds.

While the coroner went about his grim task of moving the body, inspecting it, and probing for information, a CBI photographer took pictures of every step of the process.

At last Hammock removed a worn black billfold from Gerry's right rear pocket. A driver's license, other identification and personal papers, and a single $10 bill was inside. A brown wallet containing $260 was removed from Gerry's left front pocket, and a leather packet of keys was taken from his pants pocket. Then Allen helped Hammock roll Gerry's cold corpse into a body bag and seal it up.

Although a few porch lights in the neighborhood were on earlier in the evening, and residents peeked for awhile through cracked curtains or stood on front porches to stare curiously toward the house, by the time Gerry's body was at last loaded into a waiting ambulance nearby residents had finally settled down for the night. The only activity was inside and immediately around the house. Even the most persistently curious snoops had given up and gone to bed, and there wasn't so much as the faint light from a television set showing in neighboring houses when the friendly hardware-store owner was driven away from his troubled home on West Hillside Court for the last time.

Gerry's body was transported to the Shearon Funeral Home on Sixth Street, but the respite was only temporary. Hammock took a short rest, cleaned up, had some coffee and a few bites of breakfast, then drove back through the crisp, early morning gloom to the funeral home.

He was met there by his deputy, who helped him load the gurney holding the dead man into a hearse. They began the long drive over the mountains, across Rabbit Ear Pass to the Jefferson County Coroner's Department in Denver. The autopsy was performed there by a team of investigators under the direction of forensic pathologist, Dr. Mike Dobersen. Jefferson County Deputy Coroners Triena Harper and John Jaungclaus, along with Tim Garner, a district attorney's office investigator, made up the rest of the team.

After x-rays were taken and photographs were snapped by both Hammock and Garner, the gurney holding Gerry's body was wheeled into the autopsy room. Dressed in crisp white smocks, and with their mouths and noses covered by white gauze masks, the forensic experts gathered around the stainless-steel slab holding the body.

More color photographs were taken. Gerry's body was weighed and measured. He was a sturdy six-foot, one-inch tall, and weighed a hefty 195 pounds. The autopsy team then made a close visual study of the body, recording the observations of Dr. Dobersen, including the location and nature of the injuries, on audiotape. The tape would be transcribed later. Samples were collected of blood, urine, other body fluids, and tissue. Hair samples were taken from Gerry's mustache, pubic area, and from different areas of his head. Variations in color often occur, especially with someone of Gerry's age, whose dark hair is frequently just beginning to turn to white. The dead man's fingers and thumbs were also inked and rolled on fingerprint cards. Scrapings were taken from under his fingernails, a critically important procedure in case he had managed to scratch an assailant and tear away tissue or blood.

Precise analyses would be made later by forensic toxicologists at the CBI laboratory on the samples, including scans for the presence of alcohol, prescription, and over-the-counter drugs. The hair samples could possibly become valuable later to match against loose hairs that may have been collected from the body or elsewhere at the crime scene and compared with those of suspects. Garner labeled and packaged the evidence, carefully signing his name or initials on each of the samples. Everyone who handled the samples from that point on would add their own initials or signatures in order to maintain the chain of evidence, a procedure that would be vital when the legal process moved into the courtroom.

As Hammock and investigators in Steamboat Springs observed earlier, Gerry was shot three times, once where his chest bones curved under his right arm and twice in the back. When Gerry's body was opened, the chief pathologist and his assistants were able to follow and determine the trajectory of the low-caliber bullets and recover two slugs.

The bullet hole on the right side of Gerry's chest a few inches away from his arm was an exit wound, made by one of the bullets fired into his back. The other bullet that sliced into his back was high and to the left of his spine and traveled along the rib cage to the soft tissue under his left arm where it was stopped. That bullet, along with one of the others, was recovered from the body. The final slug was picked up earlier from the floor during the initial search of the crime scene.

The path of the bullets indicated the killer fired from right to left, leading investigators to surmise the gunman was right-handed. The bullets also coursed slightly upward through the body. Gerry was either standing up and the shooter was shorter than he was, or he was lying down and the killer fired as he or she stood over him.

If he was lying down when all three shots were triggered, he would have had to have rolled over—or been rolled over by the killer or killers for the bullets to be fired both into his chest and in his back.

At the conclusion of the autopsy, Dr. Dobersen reported the cause of death was multiple gunshot wounds to the chest.

Hammock and Allen again loaded the body into the hearse, and drove it back to Shearson Funeral Home in Steamboat Springs. The coroner filled out the death certificate and provided copies to the police and prosecutor. This time, "Divorced," was typed in the space designated for information about the marital status of the deceased. More significantly, "Undetermined" was typed in both for the date of death and the time of death. The time and date of the pronouncement of death was filled in however, as 1:20 AM, October 23. Hammock checked a box labeled "Pending Investigation," for the manner of death.

Earlier, while police were waiting for a search warrant, news of the shocking tragedy was beginning to filter out among Gerry's friends, neighbors, and acquaintances in Steamboat Springs.

One of Jill's attorneys in the civil suit, Klauzer, was about ready to wind up business for the day and leave when a lawyer acquaintance, Ralph A. Cantafio, walked into his office. Cantafio said he had heard Gerry Boggs was dead. Klauzer telephoned his client the next day. When he wasn't able to reach her, he left an urgent message for her to call him back.

Late the next day the Boggs family attorney and his wife had an exceedingly strange experience. Vance Halvorson and his wife, Sharon, had just left the Douglas Boggs home on Routt County Road 38-A and were turning onto Strawberry Park Road when a bright-red sportscar approached them from the opposite direction.

Sharon Halvorson could hardly believe her eyes. She had seen the sports car, or its twin, before. It was either Jill's car or one just like it. But the most startling thing about the approaching vehicle was the driver. As the cars passed, Mrs. Halvorson was certain the driver was Jill. The lawyer's wife said both she and her husband saw Jill in the car and was later quoted in the hometown newspaper as saying the driver was "wearing a big, fat bushy mustache and wearing a baseball cap turned backwards." The cap was gray and the phony mustache was black.

The next day the lawyer's wife was startled by what appeared to be another Jill sighting. Mrs. Halvorson was at the Shearon Funeral Home where Douglas Boggs was making final arrangements for his brother. The lawyer's wife watched in amazement as the red Toyota Paseo cruised by the funeral home with a woman at the wheel who looked exactly like Jill. Mrs. Halvorson drew Doug's attention to the car, and as they watched, the driver peered intently at the mortuary. This time there was no phony mustache. Boggs told police he was "ninety-nine percent sure" the driver of the car was Jill.

Seth confirmed during an interview with Officer David Deschant that his mother owned a red Paseo. Jill, it was obvious, changed cars often. And she loved red.

In Manhattan Beach, William took a telephone call from his mother. Gerry Boggs was dead, she told him. Someone murdered him. It was chilling news. William was scared.

While grieving family members and morticians at the funeral home prepared for the popular merchant's last rites and burial, Steamboat police detectives and agents from the CBI were pulling together the early threads of their investigation. On Sunday, two days after Gerry's body was discovered, Detectives Crotz, DelValle, Kelly, Officer Deschant, Hammock, St. James, and DA's investigator Tim Garner met with CBI agents Robert C. Sexton and Kitchen at the police department to share information and discuss their battle plan.

They had been busy looking up people who knew Jill and Gerry for interviews. They were especially anxious to talk to Jill—when the time was right.

For the time being, police were necessarily keeping a tight lip with the local and state press. They refused to comment to reporters about a motive for the murder or possible suspects and said nothing about the strong focus the investigation was taking on the activities of the former Mrs. Boggs and her handsome boyfriend.

Douglas Boggs and Halvorson had already informed them that the civil trial was scheduled for Wednesday. It was less than a week away. As it turned out, that was one day after Gerry's family, friends, neighbors, and fellow employees from the store gathered at the United Methodist Church at Eighth and Oak streets, only three blocks from the courthouse and two blocks due west of Jill's bed-and-breakfast, to remember him and to mourn at his final rites.

When they assembled for the two PM funeral service, the pews were filled. Some time later most of the mourners joined in the grim procession of vehicles that followed the hearse carrying Gerry's body to the local cemetery for burial.

Boggs Hardware was closed. A message on letterhead stationery, advised in large black type:

> "In memory of Gerry Boggs.
> We are closed today for funeral
> services."

At the request of his family, memorials were made to the Yampa Valley Foundation Hospice Fund in Steamboat Springs.

When Jill returned Klauzer's call he informed her that Gerry was dead, and she told him she would be in Steamboat Springs Sunday and stop in at his office Monday morning. She spent a big portion of Monday with her lawyer conferring about the mysterious slaying of her former husband and the effect of the murder on the civil trial that was to begin Wednesday. It would obviously have to be postponed once more, but that was a problem to be worked out between the attorneys and the judge.

Jill indicated she was going to drive to Denver, but promised to stay in touch. She kept her word, and talked with Klauzer by telephone at least once a day on Tuesday, Wednesday, Thursday, and Friday. Judge Kourlis postponed the trial as expected. There really wasn't any other viable alternative.

A week to ten days after Jill talked with her lawyer at his office she telephoned and asked if authorities investigating Gerry's murder had placed any travel restrictions on her that would prevent her from taking a previously planned trip. Klauzer said he didn't know of any.

In that event, Jill responded, she would be away traveling for awhile. But she promised to keep in touch through the mails with Klauzer, and through the law office with her son, Seth, in order to take care of business matters.

When investigators from the Steamboat Springs Police Department and the CBI were finally ready to look up Jill Coit-Boggs-Carroll for a long, serious talk about her ex-husband's murder it was too late.

NINE

John Law

Solving the shocking slaying of the local merchant was top-priority business in the Steamboat Springs Police Department, among the CBI agents assigned to assist them, and Assistant DA St. James.

The law enforcement officers moved fast and cast a wide net in their search for the killer or killers who had bushwhacked Gerry Boggs in his home. Investigators began snooping through courthouse records in Steamboat Springs and questioning people in Colorado towns and cities from the Routt County seat to Denver, Westminster, Fort Collins, and Greeley.

They contacted Judy Prier-Lewis, who shared information with them collected during the investigation she conducted for her friend. Very quickly, the law enforcement sleuths expanded their probe far outside the boundaries of the Centennial State to Texas, Indiana, Louisiana, and Iowa.

Much of the early activity was focused on Greeley, where the odd couple who had rapidly become the principle suspects in the dreadful crime was living. After checking in with local Greeley police and enlisting their cooperation to avoid stepping on jurisdictional toes, DelValle interviewed the tenants who rented the downstairs portion of Jill's house. The young men described their landlady and her live-in boyfriend as best they could for the officer.

Michael was described by Rick Mott as being in his middle-to-late thirties, between five-foot, eleven-inches and six-foot, one-inch, with a slim build, dishwater-blond hair and no beard or mustache. Steve Giamberdine told the detective Michael was about forty years old, six-foot-tall, and had his blond hair cut short. There was no beard or mustache.

Mott said his landlady was in her early forties, with large breasts, big hips, and dark brown hair almost to her shoulders. Giamberdine described her as about five-foot, seven-inches or five-foot, eight-inches tall, with brown shoulder-length hair, a "flat rear" and "kind-of-wide-in-the-hips." Interestingly, both men's description of their landlady's "flat rear" fit in perfectly with Debbie Fedewa's observation about the oddly-flat bottom of the strange cross-dresser lurking outside Gerry's house.

After the interview on the Tuesday following the slaying, Michael telephoned Mott and said Jill wanted to talk with him. Mott conversed with his landlady for a few minutes, and she said she was coming to the house to pick up some clothes. She walked up to the house about five minutes later, and they greeted each other while he stood on the front porch. Mott didn't see her red Paseo parked anywhere nearby. Jill didn't want to go inside the house after all. She preferred to take a walk with her young tenant and have a little talk.

While they strolled slowly down the quiet street a few moments later, Jill peppered Mott with questions. She wanted to know what the police officer said to him, and exactly what information the investigators were after. As Mott recounted the odd encounter to yet another detective, Don Eyer of the Greeley Police Department, Jill cautioned that the lawmen were trying to harass him and advised him not to talk with them. He should get himself a lawyer, she said.

Why should he hire a lawyer, Mott asked? He hadn't done anything wrong. But Jill insisted he needed legal representation. Her former husband was a homosexual who only married her to put up a front, she explained. But she was involved in a divorce and lawsuit with him, and several of his friends killed him in order to avoid personal embarrassment at the approaching trial.

It was a weird story that was difficult to swallow. The entire matter was very strange, in fact, like a children's game of cops and robbers or an exceedingly-poorly written mystery yarn. Mott didn't take his landlady's suggestion that he find himself an attorney or avoid police. In fact, he disclosed one other especially-important fact to the same Greeley detective. He saw Jill about nine o'clock Friday morning, October 22, when she knocked on his door. That was only a bit more than six hours before Gerry's body was discovered.

There was no question that Jill and her boyfriend were feeling intense pressure from the fast-moving police investigation. It was becoming more intense every day, and the stress was getting to them. The fallout from the savage slaying was also getting to other people, according to a story passed on by *Houston Chronicle* reporter Susan Bardwell to Worth Weller in North Manchester.

Houston police reportedly opened Clark's old case file after an anonymous woman caller began telephoning them to inquire about the two-decades-old murder. Police pulled the file and traced the call. Then they telephoned the Oak Street Bed & Breakfast and Jill Coit answered the phone. In a follow-up call, the Houston police spoke with Julie Coit. When she was confronted and accused of being the mystery caller, she told the police her mother-in-law's ex-husband in Steamboat Springs had just been murdered.

In Steamboat Springs, police descended on the Oak Street Bed & Breakfast with a search warrant. Among the items collected in the sweep were a cashier's check with the name "William Clark Coit" on it and another paper with the name "Jill C. Metzger." Another warrant was served on U S West Communications, which turned over Jill's telephone records. Eventually more than a dozen search warrants would be issued and served during the rapidly-broadening probe.

On the Tuesday after Gerry's death, Michael was summoned to the US West Communications offices a few miles outside Greeley in unincorporated Weld County. A CBI agent wanted to talk with him, he was advised by Neil Wilson, manager of US West's Network & Technology Services in Greeley and Michael's immediate supervisor. Robert Sexton was waiting at the office to discuss a murder in Steamboat Springs. Michael told the CBI investigator he wasn't talking; any questions about the affair should be directed to Jill's attorney.

Sexton told him he had been seen, and it was already "a done deal!" The agent also pointedly observed that it was obvious Michael was wearing new boots. The telephone-company worker wouldn't budge however. He wasn't talking to the CBI about a murder.

Michael had walked into a tense confrontation, but he stuck by his guns. Before Michael left the office his boss informed him the company was keeping the US West truck he usually drove. A different truck would be provided for him later. Being temporarily without company wheels wasn't the problem for Michael. It was obvious why his truck was taken away. The CBI had a search warrant and was planning to comb it for evidence.

About eight-thirty the next morning, Michael telephoned his friend, Troy Giffon, and asked for a lift to work. He explained that police had his company vehicle tied up. On the way to work he pulled his wallet from his pocket, opened it up, ripped out a handful of papers and tossed them outside the window of the truck. He was becoming an emotional basket case, and Giffon was alarmed.

Michael had continued to show up for work, but he was jumpy, erratic, and his distraction was obvious. He told his friend that Jill's ex-husband had been found dead of multiple gunshot wounds the previous Friday. Giffon reminded Michael about his efforts that summer to talk him into killing, or helping to murder the victim. "I was hoping you'd forget that," Michael said. "This is the only thing that could hang me."

Did anyone else know about the hit, Giffon asked? Michael said there was someone in Ottumwa, Iowa, and police were pretty sure to talk with the individual because the name was written down in the vehicle investigators were searching. At times while he was talking about the murder and the interest of police in him and his girlfriend, Michael choked up. Tears formed in his eyes.

Firmly gripping Giffon's shoulder, he soberly advised: "Vietnam buddies don't rat off their buddies." Although it went unsaid, Gerry Boggs was also a Vietnam veteran, twice over, and he had suffered a much more terrible betrayal.

After the appeal to Giffon's loyalty as a fellow veteran, Michael launched into a spirited explanation of the alibi he and Jill had for the period immediately surrounding the time of Gerry's death. They went camping at Kelly Flats between Greeley and Steamboat Springs the Wednesday night before Gerry was found dead at the house. Michael said the campground was empty, and he filled out an envelope, wrote their name on it, and dropped it into a collection box along with a $4 fee.

He didn't learn of the murder until after he and Jill had temporarily gone off in separate directions, and she telephoned him from Steamboat Springs to leave a message on his answering machine, Michael said. When he checked his messages Sunday, he heard Jill's voice telling him, "Something's happened at Steamboat. Don't talk to anybody about anything."

According to Giffon's account to investigators, his friend was concerned about how accurately it was possible for law-enforcement authorities to pin down the exact time of death. Giffon said he thought they could figure it out to within about an hour and that got his pal upset.

"They can't tie me to the murder. I wasn't there," he declared. Several times he repeated that he didn't own a light-tan jacket. Giffon listened, and for the most part, kept his own counsel while his friend rambled on. He knew that despite what Michael was saying, he had indeed owned such a jacket with a corduroy collar and details. He might not still have the jacket at that very moment, but he had owned one, and not very long ago.

Michael reportedly said the murderer would be bound to have blood on his shoes and could be "burned" if they weren't disposed of. The killer, whoever that might be, would definitely destroy the shoes.

"There's no way anyone could have evidence against me," he was quoted. "I wouldn't hide the stuff, and I wouldn't save the stuff."

Giffon glanced at Michael's feet. The shaken man was wearing a pair of workboots that were sparkling new. Michael explained he needed new boots and bought them during the weekend.

The two men discussed which foreign countries had criminal extradition treaties with the United States and which ones would refuse to extradite. Giffon thought Argentina and Brazil would refuse to send someone back.

Michael was behaving as if he was going through a checklist in his mind about the evidence in the murder investigation. At one point, in mid-afternoon, he seemed to lose control and his emotions overwhelmed him. He was raving and waving around a knife he used on the job. Michael was "livid and going nuts," according to Giffon, and begged him to slap and punch him, to beat him up. Giffon figured Michael's conscience was bothering him, and he wanted to be punished.

He didn't beat Michael up. He listened. When he got home, he told his wife about his unsettling day with Michael and about the camping alibi. They agreed the story was ludicrous. Later, when Susan Kitchen met with the couple, he told the CBI agent about the disturbing conversation. The Giffons also told her, in considerable detail, about Michael's earlier efforts to enlist Troy as a hit man.

CBI Agent Scott Mundine talked with US West worker Bern Barry Boker while he was on the job. Boker, whose friends usually called him "Bud," had known Michael since 1991 and never noticed him with a tan jacket. Michael referred to Jill's father as his father-in-law and talked about owning ten percent of the bed-and-breakfast, a share that was worth a whopping $100,000, Boker recalled.

Michael never once talked in front of him about murdering Jill's former husband in Steamboat Springs, Boker said. When he talked about wanting to kill someone, it was his ex-wife, Kathy who was named as the potential target. Sometimes when Michael talked about wanting to find someone to kill Kathy his anger was obvious. At other times he discussed it calmly.

In other discussions Michael said Jill would only

stay at B&B's when the couple was driving around Colorado, Boker revealed. She wasn't the camper type. Michael's reported remarks fit in with Jill's history; she liked cleanliness and comfort and wasn't known as a woman who looked forward to roughing it in the mountains or a woodland campsite.

As lead investigator, Rick Crotz was assuming much of the responsibility for coordinating the fast-moving probe. While interviews were conducted and other aspects of the investigation were carried out by CBI agents and other law-enforcement officers from cooperating police departments, reports were typed and filed with the Steamboat Springs detective. Somehow Crotz made time to conduct his own interviews while he and Captain Hays fought to keep up with the flurry of paperwork and information that was flooding in.

One of the people Crotz talked to was Sue Heiser, a Greeley manicurist who works out of her home. She told the SSPD detective a woman telephoned her about eleven AM on Friday, October 22, identified herself as Jill Coit, and asked for an appointment. The client showed up about three PM. Ms. Heiser described the woman as nervous and chatty. While her nails were being filed and polished, she confided that she was on her way to Steamboat Springs where she owned a B&B, and had to go to court Monday morning because her ex-husband was suing her for slander. The woman, who identified herself as Jill, added that she had gotten her marriage annulled after learning her husband was a homosexual.

Just before leaving, she asked Ms. Heiser if she knew a good lawyer. The manicurist recommended a local attorney and offered to permit her client to telephone him from there. The woman declined and said she needed to make the call from a public phone. She left the manicurist's home about four PM.

That was about twenty minutes after Douglas Boggs

reported finding his brother dead. Two people, Mott and the manicurist, had reported seeing Jill in Greeley on the day her former husband's body was discovered, one in the morning and one in the afternoon.

If investigators expected to show that Jill was either the killer or was present when Gerry was murdered in Steamboat Springs, developing a close determination of the time of death was absolutely imperative. Her alibi for Friday was growing stronger as the investigation progessed. Judging from the way the situation was shaping up, she was more than a hundred miles away from Steamboat Springs on the day the murder was discovered. If Gerry died on Thursday however, she would have a big time-window to account for.

While investigators were developing new leads and sorting out such details, Crotz and Hays were continuing to deal with the shower of information and the steadily-rising mound of paperwork. Some of the most important aspects of the paperwork they were concerned with was tied to search warrants.

As searches were being conducted of the house the couple shared in Greeley and of his work vehicle, Michael asked his supervisor for a day off on Thursday so he could talk with his attorney in Steamboat Springs. Wilson was agreeable and told his troubled employee he could also have Friday off if he wished. Michael agreed that was a good idea and added that he might decide to take a vacation the following week, beginning November 1. His supervisor told Michael to be sure and let him know if he decided definitely on taking the work break.

In Denver, CBI laboratory ballistics experts determined that the bullet recovered at the crime scene and one of the slugs taken from Gerry's body were .22 caliber round-noses, with copper color coating. Tests were still being conducted on the other bullet.

Also downstate, Detective Tim Palmer of the Fort

Collins Police Department interviewed Michael's daughter and his ex-wife, Kathy Backus at the elementary school in Wellington. Eight-year-old Erin Backus was a student there. The school girl told Palmer she was with her father from six o'clock Friday night, October 22, until six o'clock Sunday night. Jill was with them from about the time it began to get dark on Saturday night, and they drove to William Andrew Coit's house in Denver, she added. Jill and Andrew left in a small, new red car.

A few days later when Detective Crotz interviewed Andrew in the office of the Denver apartment complex where the young man lived and worked as manager, he heard a different story. Andrew said he hadn't even seen his mother since sometime before Gerry Boggs was killed, although he talked to her by telephone a few times after the slaying. So far as he knew, his mother's red sportscar wasn't parked anywhere near the apartments, and he didn't see her on that weekend.

The conflicting stories told by Michael's daughter and Jill's son, were typical of the frustrating discrepancies investigators often run into when conducting interviews with different people. The inconsistencies posed a problem to be worked out in subsequent talks, sworn statements—or in a courtroom.

Investigators were faced with other problems. Michael didn't return to work after his long weekend. The first couple of weeks of November came and went and there was still no sign of him—or of Jill. In Steamboat Springs, rumors spread that the couple was out of the country. The stories were right on target.

She was in Mexico. Jill's youngest son, William Clark Coit III and his wife Robin were new parents. On her flight south of the border, Jill had a layover in California, and she telephoned William at his home in Manhattan Beach. William drove to the airport with his four-month-old son, so his peripatetic mother could see her first grandchild.

On November 9, Jill was at the US Embassy in Mexico City where she signed a document giving power of attorney to Seth so he could sell the B&B and the house in Greeley.

Two days later Michael telephoned his boss at US West and left a message asking for a two-year leave of absence. In two years he would be eligible for retirement and a pension. He was a bit tardy making the call. After he failed to return to work on time and didn't get in touch as he had promised, Wilson advised a labor-union representative that the missing employee was going to be fired. But Michael had always been a dependable worker who compiled an excellent attendance record until his recent troubles. Wilson began looking into the matter of the leave of absence for him.

Robert DelValle executed a warrant for the search of one of the three Toyota 4-Runners Jill had driven at various times. One was black, one pewter-gray, and the other red. Her constantly changing fleet of vehicles during that period also included the red Paseo and a red Ford pickup truck. DelValle searched the first of the rugged, boxy, utility vehicles for a false mustache, hairs and fibers, and a pair of blue jeans. Nothing that appeared to be blood stains was observed by the detective and evidence technicians when they looked through the vehicle. And there was no false mustache or blue jeans.

On November 20, Crotz had a long talk with Ms. Hanley, and the Iowa woman recounted her story of Jill's repeated efforts to talk her into carrying out a murder in Colorado. Incriminating evidence was piling up.

There was even more reason for police to be pleased over the way the investigation was shaping up.

They received a tip that Jill and her boyfriend were returning to Greeley. The tipster was Jill's youngest son. When his mother telephoned him from Mexico to say she was coming home, William quietly passed on the message to police. He was afraid she would get away.

Jill's sons were shaken by the news of the brutal slaying in Steamboat Springs and the realization their mother was a principle suspect. William III telephoned his uncle, Charles Coit, to talk and to ask questions. Jill had raised her sons to believe that Clark died of a heart attack. The Episcopal minister, who was in semi-retirement in Orange Park, Florida, at the south edge of Jacksonville, knew better than that. But he wasn't anxious to be the bearer of bad news.

"I was beating around the bush," he says of the talk with his nephew. But as he later recounted, William was persistent. He wanted to know what happened to his father, and he continued to press his uncle for the truth. According to Charles the young man asked:

"My mother did it, didn't she?"

The clergyman reluctantly confessed what he knew about the story. William's father was shot to death in his home in a murder that was never solved. The Reverend Coit was so emotionally rattled by the developments, he went into therapy for awhile. He said his nephew did the same.

The tip was just what police were hoping for, and they began closing in on the couple. On November 22, Fourteenth Judicial District Judge Richard P. Doucette issued arrest warrants for Jill and Michael. They were ordered picked up on suspicion of first-degree murder for the gunshot slaying of Gerald W. Boggs.

The bulky twenty-three-page documents related the manner of Gerry's death, the way his body was found, the witness's sighting of strangers lurking in the neighborhood, and detailed some of the background of the bitter lawsuit fought out between him and his former wife. Significantly, the warrants indicated the date of death was Thursday, October 21. But they also noted the murder weapon, a .22 caliber handgun, was not recovered.

Sixteen names by which Jill was believed to have been known by at one time or another were listed on her arrest warrant. She was identified as: Jill Coit, aka Jill Johansen-Coit, Jill Lonita Billiot, Jill Steeley, Jill Steely, Jill Coit-Steely, Jill Boggs, Jill Johanson, Jill Carroll, Jill Kisla, Jill Billiot, Jill Ihnen, Jill Brodie, Jill Metzger, Jill Moore and as Jill DeRosa (sic). Although Jill had used Michael's surname at least a time or two, it did not appear on the list. There were three dates of birth, all June 11, in 1944, 1946, and 1950.

Her companion's arrest warrant was less exotic. He was named simply as Michael O. Backus, and a single birthday was listed, September 9, 1945. He was described as a white male, about six-foot, one-inch, 175 pounds, with brown eyes and blond hair.

At dusk Monday night, November 22, a cadre of law-enforcement officers from the Steamboat Springs and Greeley police departments and the CBI positioned themselves at various locations in the neighborhood surrounding the two-story house at 1309 Eleventh Avenue. Jill's pewter-gray, 1993 4-Runner was parked in the driveway.

Ten hours later, around four AM, a couple drove slowly down the street in a car recognized by the license plates as a rental vehicle. A tall, bearded man and a woman were inside. As they got almost in front of the house, the waiting stakeout team pounced. Two police cars pulled up behind, the spotlights trained on the rental vehicle.

In moments, Michael and Jill were outside with their hands on the roof of the rental car and their legs spread while they were patted down by police. Moments later they were handcuffed, advised they were under arrest, and helped into separate police vehicles. Jill was carrying her passport. The couple also were carrying $3,000 with them. The arrests occurred just more than a month after the murder was discovered.

While they were driven to the Weld County Jail on Tenth Avenue and locked up on suspicion of first-degree murder and conspiracy to commit first-degree murder, the Toyota and the rental car were towed to the Greeley Police Department Auto Pound at 1300 A Street.

This time, authorities had Jill and her newly-bearded boyfriend solidly in custody. She wouldn't be running to New Orleans and committing herself to a psychiatric hospital.

The police officers moved fast to take every bit of advantage of the situation they could, and by seven AM they were sitting down to an interview with her at the jail. It had already been a long, exhausting night for her and for the detectives. The gray late autumn sky that was just beginning to show slivers of light over the eastern horizon would have a bright mid-morning glow before she returned to her cell.

Jill had invited the interrogation team, Sexton and DelValle, inside the cell, but they insisted on using the interview room. They weren't there for a five-minute chat about the accommodations.

It was Jill's decision whether or not to talk with the officers, and she agreed to the tape-recorded procedure. But simply reading her the obligatory Miranda Warning which advises criminal suspects of their constitutional rights against self-incrimination was an ordeal. Jill repeatedly interrupted DelValle's recitation with questions and comments.

Through the first ten minutes or so of the interview, she peppered the lawmen with questions and remarks including: "What is the fastest way to get me to trial so that I can get out?" "Okay, I don't want to talk to you. I was gonna ask you one question though" "I don't sign anything. That's what Randy says" "Okay, and I get to ask questions, too?"

Jill apparently wanted to ask questions more than she wanted to avoid answering them. After a period of fitful starts and stops, DelValle finally completed the reading and wound up with Jill's consent to the interview. She had always been a woman who liked to talk.

The lawmen began the deadly-serious procedure on a light note, joshing with the suspect and establishing as friendly an atmosphere as they could, considering the grim job ahead. Jill was still smarting from the coldly-efficient process of the arrest and booking and pleaded with Sexton and DelValle not to treat her "like the other cops."

She complained about her bad hip and the fact that she almost ended up at the hospital the previous night because of her reputed rough treatment during the arrest.

Jill was also concerned about publicity that was so sure to be sparked by her arrest back in Steamboat Springs. "I want to get this over with as quickly as possible because the Steamboat paper is gonna come out and they're gonna say I've been arrested," she announced. "And it's gonna be on the front page. And when I am released it's gonna be on the little bitty back page so nobody will notice it."

Klauzer advised her on the Saturday after the murder not to talk to police until she knew what time Gerry died, she said. For awhile the woman and the police officers verbally fenced over the subject. But the detectives couldn't quote an exact time when it was believed Gerry died. They didn't know. If the accusations made in the warrant for her arrest were correct, she knew more about it than they did.

She talked about her annulment, and she repeated

her accusations that Gerry was bisexual or gay. All of a sudden, because Gerry was dead, he was suddenly no longer bisexual, Jill scoffed. "One of the main reasons why Gerry hated me was because of me getting— when we finally broke up, okay, people were going around saying he was gay. That's the only reason Gerry married me. Gerry didn't marry me because he loved me. It was all surface."

In Jill's version of the story, it was other people who were spreading tales that Gerry was gay. Other people who heard the stories, however, were pointing their fingers at her as the originator. Sexton pointed out she hadn't answered the question: Did she get the annulment because Gerry was gay?

"For double fold," she said. Although Jill never provided a complete explanation, she claimed to have obtained the annulment because Gerry was gay, and she was still married.

Moments later the suspect had the interrogators on the defensive. She accused them of being out to get her. She was an easy target because she had been married so many times. Sexton tried to get the message across that multiple marriages weren't the point "Hey, we're talking murder, not bigamy," he said.

Suddenly, the interview veered back to the question of an alibi. "Let me tell you what. I have enough witnesses that are normal people that saw me there. There's no way in hell I could have killed him Thursday or Friday," Jill declared.

DelValle asked if she was saying the witnesses would confirm her story. Just give her attorney the time of death, she said. He took depositions from her witnesses.

DelValle asked if it was correct that it took four hours to get from Greeley to Steamboat Springs. Jill replied that was what she had figured, but her lawyer told her someone could make the trip by air in an hour and return in two hours. "So there's one four-hour period that I'm not covered."

The SSPD detective asked exactly when that four-hour period was, but Jill didn't fall into the trap. "No, see, that's what I'm not telling you because that's when Gerry had died."

Sexton asked if Michael could account for his whereabouts during the critical time period. Jill said he was with her part of the time and other people part of the time. DelValle asked if it was true she and Michael went camping. She agreed they camped out at Kelly Flats on Thursday, October 21.

Later in the interview, Jill flatly denied killing Gerry or asking anyone to murder him for her. "I was out of the country. I came back to clear up this shit," she snapped.

Her irritability flared again when the subject turned back to her domestic relationships. "You know what was in the paper, okay, that I'm a bigamist? That I was living with two men! I wasn't living with two men," she declared. "Give me a break, okay?"

"You're married to Roy Carroll and you're living with Mike Backus," Sexton pointed out.

"I have a question. I'm living . . ." Jill began, before starting over. "How do you know I lived with Roy Carroll? How do you know I even slept with him?"

"You're married to Roy Carroll," the CBI agent repeated.

"Just answer your question. Answer my question," she demanded. Once more the suspect and the police officers were tilting over who was controlling the interview. Who was there to ask questions and who was there to answer them?

"Can I say something?" Jill asked.

"When I knocked—" the CBI agent began.

Jill was steaming and she interrupted him before he

could finish the sentence. "You're probably fucking wrong."

Sexton ignored the profanity and pointed out that when he looked her up earlier for a talk he knocked on her cabin door and Carroll was inside with her. Jill agreed. He was in Colorado for her civil trial, which at that time was scheduled only three days away.

A bit later, Jill veered back to Gerry's sexuality, asking if police had checked out any of his former lovers. DelValle answered the question with a query of his own. Who were the dead man's former lovers? Did she have names?

Jill told him to look in Gerry's address book. What names should they look for? DelValle asked. He pointed out there might be hundreds of names in an address book. Look for entries with initials and telephone numbers, she suggested.

The suspect claimed a family member of Gerry's told her he was sexually abused by a teacher when he was in high school. "How many psychologists would put two and two together?" she asked. "If a person can only have sex from the rear, with the lights out, the person that I didn't want [undecipherable word] here." Jill said she had long hair when she first came to Steamboat Springs, and Gerry made her cut it off so she would look like a boy. "Totally like a little boy."

It must have been difficult to believe that the big-breasted woman who spent a lifetime exploiting her femininity could ever be mistaken for a boy. Even with the lights out.

Before Gerry had her cut her hair it was so long she wrapped it around her head, she said. "I'm French. I've always had long hair." No one bothered to bring it up, or perhaps it simply wasn't considered important enough, but she had claimed at least one time in Steamboat Springs that she was being picked on because she was an American Indian. On the other side of the family, her mother's maiden name was Engleman. If the surname was French, it had an oddly Germanic sound to it.

During a return to the question of alibis, Jill disclosed another ailment to her interrogators. She said she left her bed "super early" in the mornings. "By six o'clock in the morning I am wide awake. Wide awake, okay?"

"Okay." Sexton was already convinced, or at least he seemed to be.

"Wide awake because I have to have food. I have hypoglycemia. If I don't eat from the time of midnight to six o'clock, if I don't have food in my mouth by six o'clock I get shaky and can't function," she blurted.

Jill complained that while she was standing with her hands on top of her car one of the policemen suddenly kicked her legs out to spread them further apart.

"Immediately I went down," she said. There was just time for mental images to form of a helpless woman recovering from a major hip operation knocked to the ground, when she asked, "Well, you know how you're the nice guy and he's the bad?" When she said "nice guy," she looked at DelValle. She glanced at his companion when she said "he's the bad."

Sexton sputtered, in mock surprise, "I'm the bad guy? I thought I was the nice guy."

"Yeah," Jill soberly confirmed. "You're the one who is supposed to. Nice guy, bad guy."

DelValle protested that they didn't play that game. Jill began to resume her story about the policeman kicking her legs out when Sexton interrupted. "I'm too tired to hear this," he groaned. He heard it anyway.

"Don't do that. I've had hip surgery," Jill recalled saying to the roughneck lawman. That was when another officer stepped in and stopped the leg-kicking.

Jill then proceeded to tie the story about the arrest

and the trouble with her hip to her claim of innocence in the brutal attack on Gerry. "Because that's the reason I couldn't have killed him. Because the paper—Jan Boggs told the manicure lady that he was beaten, okay? Either by the fist or with a shovel or something, okay? And something about abrasions and stuff. If you so much as push me hard you would knock my hip out. The total hip surgery took a solid year, because the first six months if I even step in a hole, my hip popped out." Jill said it would have been impossible for her to have fought a 200-pound man.

It was an interesting scenario, but in drawing the picture for her interrogators, Jill had unwittingly offered a wide opening to follow up. She seemed to know an awful lot about the brutalities of the slaying. "Who told you that the guy was beat up?" Sexton asked.

Jill stammered for a moment, but eventually managed to put together a reply that pointed the finger at her onetime sister-in-law. Jan Boggs told a manicurist in Steamboat Springs. That was Jill's story. "That's the gossip around town, is that Gerry was beat up," she added.

"Okay," Sexton said.

"And that he was either beat up with a fist or a shovel. And he was cut up with a knife or something. Okay? And he was shot. Okay, I'm guilty, you know. I said I am capable." Jill wasn't stammering anymore. She had turned to sarcasm.

Sexton moved the interrogation to the question of handguns, asking what kind of gun she carried in her purse. Jill replied that she had a .45, but she didn't even carry a purse. "Do you have a chrome Derringer with pearl handles?" the CBI agent asked. She said she didn't know; her gun was a .45.

She also said she didn't know if she had a .22, when she was asked. Her interrogators knew Gerry was shot with a .22, and they pressed her for more information. Sexton pointed out she had a box of .22 shells in her car.

"In my car? Twenty-two?" she responded in surprise.

"Uh-huh," Sexton said, nodding his head.

Jill said she didn't have a .22. "My gun is at—the gun that I use, and would use in case of anything is a great big .45," she said. "Because that way if I shoot you, you're not moving."

"That's probably true," DelValle agreed.

Jill said she had a gun dealer's license and knew how to shoot a .45. DelValle wanted to know how she received her firearms training.

It was the result of being raped, she replied. The rape was also tied into the hip surgery, she related. "Yeah, I was raped and beaten approximately ten or eleven years ago," she continued. "The guy did not get an erection . . . and so he proceeded to kick the shit out of me. I had a concussion . . . I had damage, uh, broke the ribs, did damage to my hip."

The dreadful attack was bad enough, but apparently she was still suffering repercussions according to her tale. She confided she had a bad hip ever since and sometimes had seizures. She cautioned the two lawmen not to touch her in case she had a seizure while they were with her.

"Just leave you go?" DelValle asked.

"Yeah," she said, "because it only lasts for . . . It's going to be grand mal. It's three minutes. If you touch me, if I fight, if I fight with this hip I'm in a body cast for six months. So please, I mean, I know you would want to help me," she pleaded. "But I won't die. Just don't let anybody touch me."

The officers were presented with a sobering thought. No one wanted the suspect flopping around helplessly on the floor with a grand mal seizure. For

someone who was so frenetically active, however, it
seemed Jill had suffered from a bewildering cornuco-
pia of ailments; she had everything from a degenerative hip and grand mal to hypoglycemia and dyslexia.
It was a virtual medical miracle that she was able to
lead such an active life.

While tracing her ailments, Jill became so caught up
in the subject she forgot what they had been discussing
a few moments before. "What were we talking
about?" she asked.

"The training, after the rape," DelValle prompted.

Jill said she took firearms training after the rape, "a
policeman's course." Later she took additional in-
struction with Captain Hays in Steamboat Springs, she
explained. (Months later, Carl Steely would testify in
court that she attended a paramilitary school in Georgia. She boasted that the training made her "more
conniving," he said.)

Sexton tried to slip in a quick change-of-pace question. "Can I ask you: Who is Thadius Brodie?"

If Jill was caught off-guard, she didn't show it. "You
don't want to know," she said.

"Why don't I want to know?"

"Because I'm not telling you."

With the subject of Thadius so firmly disposed of,
the officers returned to the subject of firearms. If she
was going to shoot someone, she would use her .45
caliber, she remarked at one point. "I would, too,"
DelValle agreed.

"Okay, what caliber of gun was it? You can't tell me
what caliber of gun was used," she asked. "Okay, no, if
I was going to shoot somebody it [would] be with my
.45."

The two experienced officers weren't interrogating
the suspect in order to provide her with information
about what they knew about the investigation. She was
there to answer questions, not to ask them. DelValle

responded with a cautiously neutral "uh-huh." If Jill was the shooter, or present when the shooting occurred, it was obvious that she knew the caliber of the gun that was used anyway.

Sexton asked what kind of .38 caliber pistol she owned. Jill replied that she thought she had a .38 in her safety-deposit box, and when the CBI agent asked where that was she snapped, "You know where it is. It's all over the *Pilot* from Steamboat." Jill clearly didn't appreciate the storm of publicity that had erupted since the murder.

She wasn't sure about the location of the .38, however, and suggested that Seth might have it. If he didn't have the pistol, then it would be in the safety-deposit box, she said. "Was he [Gerry] shot with a .38?"

"Where is the .45?", DelValle asked in response. Neither he nor the CBI agent were there to spar with Jill over word games. She said the .45 was in her house, then hesitated and said she wasn't sure. A moment later she switched direction again, and accused her interrogators of already knowing where the pistol was. Police saw the gun when they served the search warrant on her house. DelValle and Sexton claimed they didn't go in the house. But Jill had been reminded of something that got her dander up.

"Okay, the people laid my dildo next to my .45 to be funny," she accused. Jill was properly offended.

Sexton reacted with apparent shock to the outrageous accusation. "Somebody do that?" he asked as if in disbelief.

Jill didn't think the low-class antic was at all funny "Yeah," she said.

Both officers denied again they were even at the house when it was searched. DelValle said they were across Oak Street from the B&B in front of the Bell

Telephone Company building. Sexton agreed. They weren't at the house.

The suspect's pique at the crude prank seemed to subside, and she veered away from the subject. Her girlfriend was also standing across the street watching the activity at the house during the search, she said. Jill had asked her to see what was going on, after being advised by her lawyer that the search warrant was going to be executed. Jill complained about officers rummaging through her desk and taking a pair of Seth's blue jeans. It was illegal to take the jeans, she claimed.

Jill conceded that she didn't blame the two officers for what went on at the bed-and-breakfast. DelValle agreed. They were down at US West, he said. The remark opened a brand new can of worms.

"Oh," Jill responded. "Then it must of been you guys that told one of the people that . . . if they couldn't pin it on me, they were gonna pin it on Michael."

Michael was telling her a bunch of nonsense, DelValle replied. Sexton said it wasn't their job to pin anything on anybody.

Jill asked if Klauzer had provided them with her alibi. "He doesn't tell us anything, you have to," Sexton said.

"Okay, then I have to tell you till after y'all charge me, because as soon as you charge me and I provide my alibi, then y'all can never harass me again?" she asked. "Is that right?" The officers said it was up to her, that she didn't have to tell them anything.

"The only thing is that the alibi, if you got a good alibi . . ." DelValle began.

"I've got nine alibis," Jill shot back, chuckling at her own awkward joke.

Her mood changed abruptly a few moments later when Sexton asked if she ever solicited anyone to murder her husband. Jill had enough. "Let's stop the question, okay?," she snapped. "No, I did not." The question was ridiculous and tacky, she declared. The question wasn't tacky at all, Sexton defended. "That is tacky," she insisted.

The interrogation was almost concluded when one of the most startling moments occurred. Jill seemed to have a woeful misconception of just how much trouble she was in and how slowly it took the wheels of justice to grind out a conclusion to a matter as serious as she was faced with. Observing that she was already in jail, Jill said she figured she had seventy-two hours to be formally advised of the charges against her and another three weeks to wait until the trial. "So I'm looking at one month," she concluded.

Both lawmen were taken aback by the naive assumption. It was an astounding remark.

"Ho, Jill, it's not gonna come to trial in three weeks," DelValle corrected.

It was a disappointing revelation, but Jill rolled with the punch. "Well, I guess I'll be a bit longer than a month in jail," she said. Sexton told her "a speedy trial" takes about six months. It went unsaid that although criminal suspects have a right by law to a speedy trial, it is usually their own attorneys who drag out the process. Long delays are generally much more advantageous to the defense than to the prosecution, as memories fade, witnesses die or drift away, or evidence is misplaced.

Six months didn't go down as well with Jill.

"Okay, then I'm looking at six months in jail," she conceded. "Am I allowed to have my glasses and reading material? Or do I just have to sit in this fucking jail?" The two lawmen surmised she would be permitted to keep her glasses with her.

"Well, good, as long as I can have my glasses and

carry my computer, then I'm in good shape," Jill said. "I can spend six months in jail."

Before the matter of her guilt or innocence was decided in court, she would mark hundreds of days off her calendar. She had far more than six months in local jails to anticipate while awaiting trial. There was the grim possibility of years behind bars—or execution by lethal injection—if she was convicted of the murder.

Jill had apparently been back in Colorado with her boyfriend at least a day or so before they were apprehended and one or both of them had already been in the house. Mott gave police a photograph of Jill he found on the floor near an overturned garbage bag after Backus was inside cleaning up. Several bags were filled with refuse. Michael also sold his motorcycle back to a Harley-Davidson dealer in Fort Collins and cashed the check the Saturday before the arrest.

Police tracked the fast-moving couple's movements to a rented room at Lowry Air Force Base at the east edge of Denver between the Mile High City and suburban Aurora. Jill and Michael stayed in Room C232 in Building 1400 of the Mile High Lodge, which was set aside for rental to visiting families and civilian dependents of military men and women.

Base Commander Major General Jay D. Blume Jr., signed a search warrant for the room. Jill's 1992 red Paseo, parked behind the three-story brick building, was also searched.

Considering Jill's later claims that she and Michael returned to Colorado to face the music and straighten out the mess over Gerry's murder when they were suddenly thrown in jail, the couple's temporary living and driving arrangements were exceedingly strange. They had at least two of their own cars available to them, as well as a house in Greeley. Yet they rented a car to drive, and also rented at room a Lowry AFB. It was curious behavior for someone who wasn't trying to hide something.

Special Agent Richard Griffith, of the Air Force Office of Special Investigation at the base, was in charge of the searches, which were carried out at night. Air Force authorities pointed out that civilian private investigators had been snooping around the lodge trying to get into the room.

The searches at Lowry yielded a plastic bag containing two wigs, one brown and one a darker brown; two pairs of surgical gloves; maps of Mexico and Europe; a hotel receipt from Cancun, Mexico; two Aero Mexico tickets for trips to Spain; EuroRail passes which would permit each of them to travel through Europe fast and cheap; a Continental Airline employee ID issued to Jill Boggs; a MasterCard issued to Jill C. Backus; an Alaska voter-registration card issued to Jill Boggs-Coit; a US Embassy document from Mexico giving power of attorney from Jill Coit Steely to Seth J. Coit; the military dependent ID card issued to Jill Coit-Brodie; a photocopy of a military ID card issued to Chief Petty Officer Roy C. Carroll; an empty envelope addressed to Jill Coit-Backus; and a pair of international driving permits.

Jill's international license was issued on November 1, 1993 at Heathrow, Florida. It was signed "Jill Coit (Boggs)." Jill was behaving strictly in character, utilizing a confusing combination of names on important documents.

She may have known her way around the jet-set world, but if reports about her behavior are true, Jill didn't know a crucially-important rule of behavior for people who are locked up in prisons or jails. Never talk about your troubles with the law or reveal your personal business to your cellmates.

Two women inmates who were locked up with her passed on information to police about conversations

with Jill while they were locked up together in Weld
County jail. One said Jill claimed she established an
alibi for the time of Gerry's slaying by writing checks
at different businesses in Greeley. The other said Jill
posed a rhetorical question about how she could be in
Steamboat Springs at two o'clock if she was somewhere else. At that time, police had not told Jill the
date or time frame when they believed Gerry was murdered.

The suspects appeared at a brief court hearing in
Greeley where they were formally advised of the
charges against them. Each was charged with first-degree murder and with conspiracy to commit murder.
The homicide charges carried maximum penalties of
execution in Colorado's death chamber or life in
prison with no parole. The conspiracy counts carried a
maximum prison sentence of forty-eight years. They
were also liable to fines totalling nearly $1.5 million
each on the charges.

Colorado is one of thirty-seven states with the death
penalty, and specifically permits execution by lethal injection for first-degree murder, felony murder, and
kidnapping when the death of the victim occurs.

On Saturday, Jill and her co-defendant were driven
back across the mountains to Steamboat Springs in
separate Routt County Sheriff's Department cars, the
possibility of the death penalty looming ominously
over them.

Before being led to their cells in the Routt County
Detention Center, they were run through the booking
process, posing for mug shots and standing quietly
while their fingers and thumbs were inked and rolled
onto fingerprint cards. Jill's SSPD booking number
was 934966A. Michael's was 934966B. The couple also
exchanged their civilian clothes for baggy orange jail-
issue jumpsuits.

As accused killers, they were locked in maximum

security areas of the jail, and held on temporary bail of $5 million each.

Jill's shoulder-length, reddish brown hair was curly, but news reporters who later wrote about her appearance seemed to be more impressed with her eyebrows. She was described in nationally-distributed press reports as "stocky" and "heavy-eyebrowed." Michael's hair, beard, and mustache were cut short and neat. Sometimes he wore glasses, and at other times he didn't.

The same law firm Jill had depended on to handle most of her legal matters during the past two years continued to represent her immediately after her arrest. But Klauzer and Tremaine had built their practice with strong focus on civil law. Criminal matters, especially when such critical charges as first-degree murder were involved, were another thing altogether.

The talk in taprooms, coffee shops, and courthouse corridors began to speculate that Jill would call in a big-time criminal lawyer. Staff at *The Steamboat Pilot* and the *Steamboat Today* were pestered for collections of news clips on the story by journalists from other cities and by lawyers whom Dodder described as "name-brand attorneys."

Michael didn't have any property or cash to speak of. Even his Harley was gone. And in an application for a court-appointed attorney, he stated he was on leave without pay from his job at US West. Judge James Garrecht appointed Deputy State Public Defender William S. Schurman to represent him.

Schurman was in his corner when Michael and Jill appeared in court on the Monday morning after their arrival back in Steamboat Springs for an advisement hearing. At the proceeding, Judge Garrecht soberly explained to the defendants the charges against them and the possible penalties. About twenty people witnessed the brief hearing, including five sheriff's deputies.

Bob McCullough was also among the spectators for the appearance of the couple accused in the slaying of his longtime friend and business colleague at Boggs Hardware. He was astonished when Jill turned to look at him and said, "Hi."

A request by Schurman and Klauzer asking that their clients be released on their own recognizance was denied. The motions were based on claims the defendants were not formally charged within seventy-two hours of their arrest as the law required. Garrecht disagreed, pointing out the court appearance in Weld County the previous Friday. It was one of those go-through-the-motion motions, and it seemed doubtful anyone really expected it to succeed.

The pair wore their bright orange jail jumpsuits and were handcuffed during the hearing. The roomy rear-end of the suit on the woman who had once impressed acquaintances in Indiana with her fashionable clothes slumped into a weary mass of wrinkles. The defendants didn't look at each other during the hearing, or if they did it wasn't noticed by most observers.

Before the proceeding concluded, Judge Garrecht set Thursday morning, December 16, 1993 for the preliminary hearing to determine if there was sufficient probable cause to continue the prosecution. Unable to even come close to raising the staggering $5 million bail, both defendants were returned to the detention center. They traveled the same way they were transported from the center to the court, handcuffed in the back of separate sheriff's cars.

In the meantime, Detective Eyer, and other officers and technicians had already searched the impounded 4-Runner. According to the warrant, they were looking for .22 caliber firearms and ammunition, bloodstains, body fluid and tissue, footwear, false mustaches

or false-mustache hairs and adhesive, baseball caps,
including a cap with a ponytail, a light canvas
rancher's jacket, camping gear, maps, soil and vegeta-
tion, and other items.

They came up with a treasure trove of potential evidence, including an Omega stun gun. Stun guns come
in different varieties and have different shapes, but the
job they are designed to do is the same. They stop and
temporarily incapacitate people or animals they are
used on. Contact of only three or four-seconds from
one of the more powerful stun guns can shock nerves
and muscles with up to 4,700 volts of electricity and
deliver a blow like a horse's kick.

They were initially developed to provide police and
corrections officers with a non-lethal means for subdu-
ing unruly or dangerous criminal suspects or convicts.
Inevitably, stun guns spread from law-enforcement
and corrections agencies to the civilian market where
they can be legally purchased by anyone. Police also
seized a stun gun from Seth. Discovery of the weapons
were significant to investigators because marks on
Gerry's body appeared to have been inflicted with a
stun gun. No fingerprints from the stun gun found in
the car or the package it was in, could be traced to Jill
or to Michael.

The search team recovered a wealth of less dramatic
items from the vehicle that were of interest nonetheless. Texaco and Chevron credit cards issued to Roy G.
Carroll, a photo of Jill, and a vehicle registration made
out to Jill Coit were taken from the glove compart-
ment. The Colorado license tag was also issued in Jill
Coit's name. A floor mat was tagged, and hair, fiber,
and other debris were carefully vacuumed from the
front and back, then placed in nine marked envelopes.

No firearms or ammunition were found, and there
were no obvious bloodstains, although laboratory ana-

lysts would make the final determination after concluding their examinations.

While police continued to press their investigation and Jill and Michael cooled their heels at the jail, important changes were being made in their legal representation. The earlier speculation was right on target.

Jill's local lawyers bowed out of her criminal case, and were replaced by one of the best-known defense lawyers in Colorado. Joseph Saint-Veltri took over the defense chores after Klauzer and Tremaine left. Saint-Veltri was a grizzled twenty-five-year veteran of the legal wars who had a reputation for defending clients hauled into federal court on various drug charges.

At the time Saint-Veltri's entry into the sensational murder case was publicly disclosed, Joanna Dodder wrote a piece in the *Steamboat Pilot* based on an interview with a pair of noted Colorado trial lawyers and law partners, Walter Gerash and Scott Robinson. Referring to Gerash as the man Saint-Veltri called his "mentor," the reporter quoted him as saying the Denver law firm was considering taking on Backus as a client.

The big-time city lawyers had compiled a glittering record of murder acquittals, including that of former policeman James King, accused of killing four guards during a holdup of the Mile High City's United Bank in 1991. Robinson was quoted as saying the firm was contacted by Backus's family, and the lawyers expected to take the case if they could work out the details.

"I like Michael Backus. He seems like a decent guy. I'm hard-pressed to see him as a murderer," Robinson added.

Jill's longtime Steamboat Springs lawyer also pulled out of the civil case after Tremaine explained to Judge Kourlis he wasn't being paid. The judge gave Jill until the middle of the following month to get herself a new lawyer or else she would have to defend herself in the continuing dispute with the Boggs family. Douglas Boggs was executor of his brother's estate and was working with Halvorson to defend against Jill's lawsuit and to continue to press Gerry's claims.

Money was rumored to be the bait reputedly used to lure Jill and her boyfriend back to Colorado and interrupt a planned trip from Mexico to Europe. She was forced to return to try and free some of her money or possibly pick up valuables that were stashed away and could be converted to cash.

Significantly, during the same hearing where Jill's former lawyers were permitted to step out of the civil case, Judge Kourlis refused to release the restraining order preventing sale of the bed-and-breakfast. Speaking for his clients, Halvorson argued vociferously against lifting the ban. If the Boggs family won the countersuit, he declared, the B&B might be needed to pay off the award. The lawyer added that although some of the allegations in the countersuit were now void because of Gerry's slaying, it was possible a wrongful-death suit might be lodged.

The development meant Saint-Veltri was taking a chance Jill wouldn't be able to pay him for his work. She needed the money from the sale for her defense. Judge Garrecht warned the high-powered criminal defense lawyer that if things went the wrong way for his client in her efforts to sell the B&B, Saint-Veltri might wind up as her court-appointed attorney. That would mean, of course, that his normal fee would probably be drastically reduced.

Saint-Veltri didn't talk in open court about his exact fee schedule, but it seemed safe to assume it was somewhere between the $140-per-hour that was the going rate for Steamboat Springs lawyers practicing civil law and the whopping $475-per-hour commanded by big-time Washington lawyer Robert Bennett for defending President Clinton in the Paula Jones sex-harassment case. But when a complicated and long-drawn-out defense like Jill's promised to be was at hand, even fees based on the lower end of that spectrum could be staggering.

After all the years Jill spent accumulating wealth, it seemed the orderly transfer of her riches to lawyers was inevitably underway. And her already desperate situation was becoming even more complicated.

Her new criminal defense attorney's entry into the fray added another odd element into the equation as well. For people who concern themselves with such matters, there promised to be an interesting matchup in the courtroom, if for no other reason, because of the similarities in the surnames. St. James would be on one side of the courtroom, and Saint-Veltri would be on the other. St. James was a recent arrival in Colorado from Palm Beach county, Florida, where he was also an assistant district attorney. In one of his more high-profile cases there, he assisted in the successful prosecution of members of a gang of contract killers who advertised in *Soldier of Fortune Magazine,* and of a boatyard owner who hired them to murder his wife. But there was more at stake than idle interest in surnames. St. James's boss, District Attorney Paul McLimans, joined his subordinate and began assuming an increasingly important role in shaping the prosecution's case.

Michael also changed lawyers, dropping his public defender. But he didn't sign on with Gerash and Robinson. He replaced Schurman instead, with Leonard E. Davies, another Denver-based lawyer with a respected record in Colorado for criminal defense. In the 1960s and 1970s, Davies drew considerable attention to himself in Colorado for his work in several high-profile civil-rights cases, and he was author of a book dealing with cross-examination. Details of the financial arrangements were not publicly disclosed, but stories circulated that members of Michael's family were providing money for his defense.

Settling down with a pair of experienced criminal-defense lawyers would appear to have been a plus for the defendants in their efforts to make their pleas of not guilty to the horrible charges against them stand up. On the negative side, perhaps the most discouraging development occurred about as close to home as possible. After talking in early January with Agent Kitchen, Jill's son, Seth, and daughter-in-law, Julie, agreed to a deal with authorities to testify as prosecution witnesses at the trials. In return for their cooperation, they would be given immunity from prosecution. The immunity pact was not further identified publicly by St. James or by police at that time.

The first public notice of the drastic turn taken in the case occurred less than three weeks into the new year when the preliminary hearing for Jill and Michael was postponed. They had already been led into the Routt County Courtroom for the proceeding when St. James disclosed that two new witnesses had surfaced with evidence that was tremendously damaging to the defendants.

St. James didn't identify the witnesses during the hearing, and it was a few days before the names came to light through public documents. The prosecutor also declined to identify the nature of the information, but he did reveal the witnesses were given immunity from prosecution.

The development was so recent, the prosecutor wasn't yet able to provide the defense with transcripts of the statements by the new witnesses. That was a necessary legal requirement as part of the discovery process, which according to American rules of law requires sharing of information developed by the prosecution with the defense. The process is governed by strict rules, and prosecutors can't hand the information over at the last moment in order to take the defense by surprise. Discovery is one of those elements of the system that provides a distinct advantage for the defense, but is so necessary to ensure a fair trial. It is in keeping with the long-established legal reality of the American system of criminal justice which requires that the burden be on the prosecution to prove guilt, not on the defense to prove innocence.

The defense had already been complaining that the prosecution was slow in complying with the discovery process. "Mr. St. James won't even tell me when Gerald Boggs died," Davies complained. "How am I supposed to determine an alibi without the time of death? I'm flabbergasted not to be told this. A preliminary hearing should be to determine probable cause, not a trial by ambush."

Davies pointed out that information available at that time left a glaring twenty-six-hour window between one PM Thursday when Gerry was last seen alive leaving the store and about three PM Friday when his body was discovered. Saint-Veltri asserted that the prosecutor could do better than that. Forensic science was sufficiently sophisticated to pin down the time of death within an hour, he claimed.

The assistant DA disagreed. "It is the state's theory that only three people know when Gerald Boggs died," he responded. "Jill Coit, Michael Backus and Gerald Boggs." Nevertheless, the legal fallout over the failure or inability to be more exact was already beginning to be felt.

The defense lawyers also appealed to the judge to permit their clients to appear at hearings without their shackles.

"My client is brought in here shackled like he's a convicted criminal. I think it's highly prejudicial," Davies carped. "Mr. Backus must be presumed innocent, and we must preserve that."

The judge denied the motion. He pointed out that Routt County Sheriff's Department officers considered the shackles to be a necessary security measure. Later, when a trial or trials began and a jury was present, the defendants would appear in civilian clothes without handcuffs, ankle, or belly restraints. Judges are not as likely as juries to be swayed or impressed by defendants who appear in court in cuffs and chains.

The exchange was one more replay of a contest that occurs in courtrooms throughout the United States practically every day, when defendants are involved who are charged with major felonies. Jurists usually rule as Judge Garrecht did. The wishes of the defendants to appear unshackled at preliminary hearings must give way to security requirements as decided by the local sheriff or other experienced and knowledgeable law-enforcement and judicial authorities.

Judge Garrecht postponed the hearing until the middle of February to give defense attorneys an opportunity to examine the new information. Jill and her co-defendant were driven back to the detention center where she was marking time reading and studying languages and psychology.

When the preliminary hearing finally occurred on schedule a few weeks later, Kitchen's testimony about her conversation with Seth and Julie was devastating.

Between three-thirty and four PM, a couple of hours or so after Gerry was last seen alive, she said, Seth received a telephone call from a woman whose voice he recognized as his mother's. The caller relayed a message that was chillingly blunt, according to the testimony, and advised, "Hey, baby, it's over, and it's messy."

It was a critical statement, that if accepted as true, could become a vital element in helping the prosecution pin down the time of Gerry's death. The time window between one PM when he was seen leaving the hardware store, and three-thirty or four PM, was considerably less than the twenty-six hours investigators were previously faced with. There would be a time period of only a few hours on Thursday, October 21, for proving the whereabouts of the defendants that would be crucial to both sides facing off in the courtroom shootout.

The CBI agent recounted the other conversations between Jill and Michael and the younger couple that were tied to the alleged murder plot against Gerry sparked by the civil dispute. Seth told her Michael claimed to have an untraceable .22 caliber pistol, the witness said. She also quoted Julie as talking about watching her mother-in-law trying on scarves and a wig she planned to use as disguises.

During cross-examination, Saint-Veltri quickly followed up on disclosure that Seth and Julie claimed to have known in advance that Gerry's murder was being plotted, then kept quiet about their knowledge for months after the slaying.

"If what they told you is true, they both knew an impending murder was going to take place in Steamboat Springs," he observed of the couple. "Did they tell you what benefit they stood to gain?"

Kitchen said Seth and Julie would never be prosecuted for any role they may have played in the murder, and were also given immunity for an alleged insurance scam. No details were provided about the affair involving the insurance. Julie was also planning to write a book about the case, the witness added.

Agent Kitchen also testified about the statements by Giffon, tying Michael to the alleged murder scheme through a $7,500-offer for a contract hit and other remarks.

Members of the Boggs family crowded into the

courtroom with scores of Gerry's friends and other spectators. It was an ordeal, and some of the testimony was especially agonizing. When a police photo of Gerry's body was introduced and described by a witness as "messy," although the picture was shielded from the audience, William Harold and Sylvia Boggs leaned against each other in horror and pain. Douglas Boggs cried.

Jill watched the proceedings from the defense table, and frequently smiled.

When it was Rick Crotz's turn to testify, he brought up the statements by Ms. Hanley in Iowa about Jill's reputed efforts to talk her into killing a man in Colorado. But the lead detective on the case ran into stiff cross-examination from the defense. He had to concede no physical evidence had yet been turned up that positively linked either of the defendants to the crime scene.

The defense lawyers established that police did not have a murder weapon, blood-stained clothing, or identifiable fingerprints or footprints, despite the execution of at least thirteen search warrants. And once again, they criticized initial handling of the investigation that led to the difficulties establishing a more exact time of death.

Two other law enforcement officers and Sharon Halvorson also testified at the hearing. Mrs. Halvorson recounted her two sightings of the red Paseo in the days immediately following Gerry's murder, including observation of the weirdly-costumed woman both she and her lawyer husband recognized as Jill at the wheel.

St. James and his team of law officers were constructing a solidly-impressive case. With Seth's devastating revelation, so far the prosecutor had three people lined up who were ready to testify they were solicited by either Jill or Michael to carry out the murder. And circumstantial evidence was piling up from the searches, laboratory tests, and other sources.

The assistant DA told the judge that statements from the witnesses about being solicited to carry out the slaying was proof the crime was premeditated. It was not a crime of passion, a spur-of-the-moment act. "Each of these defendants had a long-standing desire to kill Gerald Boggs or to have him killed," St. James declared. "They had motive, opportunity, and method, and the evidence confirms the great premeditation of this act, the premeditation of two evil minds."

Saint-Veltri passed on his opportunity to make a closing statement. Davies, however, claimed there was a woeful lack of evidence against his client. He insisted there was nothing in Michael's background to indicate he would commit such a "heinous act," and he called the case against the bearded defendant "singularly circumstantial." Davies asked the court to dismiss the charges.

Judge Garrecht didn't comply with the defense attorney's proposal for dismissal. At the conclusion of the tedious six hour proceeding, he declared that the prosecution had established its case and bound the matter over for trial. There would be no quick or easy out for Jill and Michael, not that anyone really expected there to be. They were one big step closer to a first-degree murder trial.

TEN

Lady Justice

The arrest of Jill and her boyfriend as suspects in the grisly murder of the prominent hardware store owner was big news in Steamboat Springs. Jill had been an exceedingly busy woman during the past three decades of her life, and the dreadful accusations were also big news around the country.

At various times she lived in a half-dozen states or more, married nine different men, romanced others, obtained divorces in the United States and in Haiti, was adopted once, raised three sons, and made loyal friends and bitter enemies.

Her myriad romantic and domestic entanglements and business dealings left a trail that was untidy at best. At worst, it was a nightmare for any investigator to follow, whether law-enforcement officer, private detective, journalist, or author. The path she took was twisted, and diffused into an impenetrable fog like a haze of smudged fingerprints. Some of the questions about Jill and her life will probably never be fully answered.

People who knew her and the men and women she interacted with, reacted with a mixture of emotions ranging from anger and disgust to pity and relief.

Private eye Stan Lewis bestowed on her a classic

nickname that is commonly used for women who are suspected of murdering their husbands.

"She's a psychotic, vicious, ruthless black widow," he told a reporter. "She takes a sadistic, fiendish delight in preying on well-meaning men to facilitate her ultimate goal of furthering her financial welfare."

Lewis had delivered a solid verbal spanking, but he hadn't yet exhausted his descriptive repertoire. "She was very manipulative and knew how to press the right buttons. She's no doubt a psychopath and a very sick person," he added to *Steamboat Pilot* reporter Joanna Dodder.

Dodder was quoted, in turn, in an interview with *The News-Journal* in North Manchester. "Everyone here is saying she did it . . . It's really bizarre. Everyone kept coming to us with all kinds of stories, and now we are finding out a lot of them are true."

"I think she got to the point after twenty years of scams, she got this false sense of security of what she could get away with," Judy Prier-Lewis, the Denver P.I. remarked to another journalist.

"She was able to turn men's brains to mush," *Chronicle* reporter Bardwell told Weller of the accused murderess.

In Ottumwa, reporter Alan Pierce of the *Chronicle*, hurried to Mohee Hanley's house after learning of the local connection to the bizarre story. The house was locked up and it sounded like a big dog was raging inside. He left and didn't go back.

"I'm thankful to be alive," said Carl V. Steely in Culver. "If you were to meet her and talk to her, you'd think she's just the greatest person you ever met. Why would all these people marry her if she weren't that way?" he added in another statement.

"She's a master of dirty tricks," he told the author in additional remarks. "I mean it was so funny, the things she'd think to do, you wouldn't take her seriously."

"The Houston murder was my brother and I've always thought that she did it," said Charles Coit. "She's ruined a lot of lives, whole families."

"He grabbed his chest like he was going to have a heart attack," Houston Police Department Detective Sgt. Binford said of Roy Carroll's response when he was told about the trouble his wife was in. "He's in total shock." After his first stunned reaction, the retired Navy chief reportedly clammed up and responded to police efforts to interview him by telling them to talk to his attorney.

In New Orleans, Judge DiRosa was "unavailable for comment," according to a report in *The Times-Picayune*. He ducked inside a house when he was tracked by television cameras.

"She was a beautiful damn woman, and cold clear through," added B. B. McCurdy in Houston.

Twenty years of fast living had apparently changed that, according to the observations of a woman at the North Manchester Library after seeing a picture of a frizzy-haired Jill being led away in handcuffs by police. "She was so dramatic and beautiful when she was in business here. Then people saw her on television after her arrest and the reaction was: 'Oh my. She didn't age well!'"

Even Eldon Metzger spoke out, and when he at last broke his silence, it was to defend the woman he was once married to. He complained to *The News-Journal* the information compiled by private investigators in Colorado was slanted against her. "Most people didn't really know Jill. There was a side to her that isn't being reported that was very kind," he said. ". . . She gave, and gave and gave."

"I just can't believe she had in her whatever it takes

to be a murderer," said her friend, Nancy Reed, the
North Manchester town clerk.

Michael's longtime friend from US West also joined
in. Troy Giffon telephoned Denver's Channel 4 news
and reported he had received a threatening telephone
call after talking with police. He wouldn't let the
threat keep him from testifying at the trial, he insisted,
however. When reporter Rick Sallinger asked what he
was doing to protect himself, Giffon replied, "Guns,
caution, watching. The Greeley police will take care of
it." He accused Jill of being responsible for a "river of
tears."

Greeley police confirmed they were investigating a
call that contained what Sgt. Carl Alm described as
"moderately threatening language." He refused to be
more precise, and added that police couldn't confirm
it was specifically related to the murder case. The police department refused to release a report on the incident, and another sergeant said there weren't even any
officers assigned to investigate it.

The news coming out of Steamboat Springs and
Houston was an astounding story, even without occasional inaccuracies in some reports that gave the
slightly erroneous impression Jill was married at various times to ten or eleven different men. Some early
reports indicated Michael was her tenth husband.

To most men and women who may have been married once or twice, she was a record setter.

Throughout her life, Jill managed to be many different women to many different people. As the year-end
holidays of 1993 approached, she was still playing multiple roles.

To the prosecutor and police, she was a ruthless
woman who was accused of the grisly murder of her
husband in Steamboat Springs—and was a strong suspect in the disturbingly similar murder of another
spouse in Houston twenty years earlier.

Police in Houston responded to queries from news agencies and other interested parties about the status of the investigation into Clark's murder, however with oddly divergent statements.

During a telephone call to the Houston Police Department, Joanna Dodder says she was told it was too late to reopen the investigation. The file on the case was lost. The small-town reporter was astounded by the statement.

"You mean you lost the file?" she asked again, in disbelief.

"Well," the anonymous Houston PD spokesman explained, "we have lots of homicides here."

DelValle told *The News Journal* in North Manchester he talked with Houston police and reported they might re-open the old murder case there.

Months after Jill's arrest when the Houston Police Department was petitioned through the Texas Open Records Act for information about the case for this book, the request was forwarded to the City Legal Department. The legal department passed it up the ladder to Texas State Attorney General Dan Morales in Austin for an opinion. The city's legal experts stated in their letter to Morales they believed the request should be exempted from the act because "the case has remained open" and was "now under active investigation by the Homicide Division of HPD due to new information . . ."

Disclosure of the information could interfere with the investigation into Clark's slaying and potential prosecution of the suspect in the case. The Steamboat Springs Police Department had also asked the investigative file be kept confidential while the SSPD established the case against their suspect.

The opinion was pending as the murder charges against Jill and Michael were about to go to trial in Colorado.

Twenty years after leaving Houston, following his brother's funeral, Charles still hadn't heard anything from police about the matter. "I don't know why they won't open the case," he says.

The behavior of Houston police department bigwigs is curious for people with nothing to hide. There were various reasons that would seem to justify reopening the investigation and actively seeking information. The telephone calls to the Houston police department that were traced back to Jill's bed and breakfast in Steamboat Springs were one. The similarities in the manner of Clark's murder and Gerry's slaying were another.

In Colorado, the Steamboat Springs Police Department, the Greeley Police Department, the CBI, and other cooperating law-enforcement agencies conducted a sparklingly professional investigation they could be proud of. Of course, the investigation didn't end with the arrests.

While St. James and defense attorneys began the demanding task of preparing for one of the most dramatic, sordid and highly-publicized criminal trials in the history of Colorado's Fourteenth Judicial District, investigators still had much work to do. New witnesses were contacted, and people already interviewed were talked to again. Every lead had to be followed up.

A few weeks after the arrests, Judge Doucette imposed a gag order on police, prosecutors, defense attorneys, and others involved in an official capacity with the case. The court order didn't slow the rush of publicity, however, and stories about the lurid affair were prominently featured as far away as London, England, where the popular tabloid, the *Sunday Mirror* printed a photograph of Jill in custody, and a major story headlined, "Murder Cops Unravel Real Black Widow's Deadly Web." The article predicted a quickie Hollywood film would be made on the subject.

Jill helped fuel the firestorm of publicity by giving a

few carefully-selected interviews. She talked to a reporter for the TV tabloid show, *A Current Affair,* and she did a far-ranging interview with Denver's *Rocky Mountain News.*

When she met at the jail with a reporter for the tabloid TV show, Jill had trouble keeping straight the dates she married and divorced her husbands, and was occasionally forced to consult a crib sheet she brought with her for the interview. One matter she was firmly consistent about, however, was her insistence she never murdered anyone.

Ignoring twenty-year-old divorce records, she denied there was any trouble in her marriage with Clark before his murder. She was waiting in New Orleans with the boys where the family was planning to relocate when she learned the dreadful news he was dead, she said.

Her youngest son, as well as the Reverend Coit and B. B. McCurdy also appeared in the two-part television presentation. Coit spent about three hours hanging around for the interview and appeared for a couple of minutes on the show. McCurdy was on for a longer period. But with the exception of his mother, William was the most dramatically-riveting appearance on the show.

Jill's youngest son vowed to have no more to do with his mother if it was proven she was involved in his father's murder. "This is my mother. People are calling her the black widow, the most poisonous spider there is," he said. "Maybe it's true."

When Jill chatted with a reporter for the *Rocky Mountain News,* she apologized for the way she looked. She was dressed in the usual baggy orange trousers and a gray sweatshirt with the words "ROUTT COUNTY JAIL" stenciled on the back in ugly black capital letters. Her current appearance wasn't the real Jill, she explained. The real Jill Coit had class.

During the talk, she traced some of her background and insisted she didn't kill Gerry. She explained she married him because of his intelligence, despite hearing stories he was bisexual. He stood out in Steamboat Springs because most of the available men there were "ski bums," she explained.

She agreed she was not pregnant while she was married to him, but begged off going into much detail about the matter because the civil suit was still pending. She hinted, however, that plans for an adoption of a child may have been involved. Her new attorney in Denver had wisely counseled that some subjects were, by necessity, off-limits.

Jill took a verbal potshot at Steely, whom she referred to as "the ugly part," and scoffed at his intimation she may have tried to kill him or to have him killed.

Stories circulated in Steamboat Springs and elsewhere that Jill was charging for interviews, and was paid thousands of dollars for the television appearance. Although Klauzer and his partner were no longer working for Jill in her criminal or civil case, the Steamboat Springs lawyer was representing her in efforts to peddle her story to television and movie producers and book publishers.

Douglas Boggs called reports of her efforts to sell broadcast, movie, and book rights to her story "bizarre." In written remarks, the murder victim's relatives declared: "The Boggs family is extremely disappointed that Jill Coit and her lawyers are seeking to profit from the sensationalism of either this case, the death of Gerry Boggs, or the events of her life. We are confused about why her attorneys withdrew from her case, yet they continue to represent her in the film, book rights, and the story of her life."

When Worth Weller telephoned the SSPD from Indiana, Rick Crotz explained he couldn't talk because a

defense request for a gag order had been approved.
The detective suggested the reporter talk to someone
at *The Steamboat Pilot,* according to Weller. The en-
terprising Indiana reporter and newspaper publisher
did that. He also drove to Steamboat Springs and interviewed Jill at the detention center.

They barely had time to settle down on opposite
sides of a heavy clear-glass barrier in the sparkling
clean, brightly-lighted room and begin to talk through
telephones, before she boasted about how she was losing weight on the jail food. It wasn't very good or very
plentiful, she said, as she stood up and patted her hips
to show how she had slimmed down.

Getting down to more serious talk, she traced her
version of her troubles with Gerry Boggs and firmly
denied she had anything to do with his murder. At the
trial, her attorney would either pinpoint the real killers
or at least provide details about the type of people
they were and reveal their motive, she claimed. Jill
complained she was being picked on because she was
an outsider in a close-knit community run by people
close to the Boggs family.

When Weller asked about the reports she tricked
Gerry into believing she was pregnant by him, Jill explained it away by saying they were planning to adopt
a child. "We were very happy about that," she told the
reporter. "I don't do fake pregnancies. I have real
children. You know who they are."

At the conclusion of the hour-long sit-down, Jill said
she expected to be back in North Manchester in
March, after the trial, to visit with her mother and
friends who have stood by her.

The baptism of fire for the defense attorneys and
the prosecutor occurred weeks before the *News-Journal* interview when they at last squared off at the
downtown courthouse in a preliminary hearing before
Routt County Judge James Garrecht.

The most devastating testimony came second-hand
from Seth, when CBI Agent Kitchen recounted her
interview with him. The CBI agent quoted him as telling her about the efforts to enlist him in Gerry's murder and in the disposal of the body. Seth was called to
the witness stand for brief questioning by the defense
and conceded he was granted immunity from prosecution in return for his testimony in the case.

Although Seth appeared in court, as far as reporters
were concerned it seemed he and his wife had gone
underground. They cleared out of the Oak Street Bed
& Breakfast, and workers there refused to reveal
where the couple was or to answer any other questions. For awhile, at least, they were reportedly in At-
lanta where Julie's parents lived. Roy Carroll also
pulled up stakes in Houston for awhile and went to
Gulfport, Mississippi.

Investigators continued interviewing witnesses and
collecting new evidence well into the new year. Steamboat Springs police served a warrant and opened a
bank safety-deposit box rented by Jill and found several handguns inside. None of them were the .22 caliber pistol they were looking for, however, and none of
them were seized.

Other warrants were served to: the American Telephone & Telegraph Company in Denver for records of
calls made on an AT&T calling card made out to Jill
Backus; the NorWest Bank in Greeley for Michael's
personal banking records; and the J. C. Penny Credit
Service Center in Littleton for an account in the name
of Jill Coit.

A .22 pistol surfaced from an unexpected location
hundreds of miles away about that time, however. The
couple who bought the bed-and-breakfast in Culver
found the firearm in a box of possessions left behind
when Jill and Carl split up. They turned it over to Culver Town Marshal Steve Michael, who telephoned

Steamboat Springs police and told them about the discovery. The weapon, which was believed to belong to Jill, was old.

Initially, a detective in Colorado talked about flying to Indiana to pick up the unregistered weapon, but later advised the town marshal to contact authorities in Houston where another husband of Jill's was also shot to death in an unsolved slaying. The pistol was at the bed-and-breakfast in Culver at least two years or more, and couldn't possibly have been used in the Steamboat Springs homicide. Marshal Michael wound up packaging the handgun and mailing it to the Houston Police Department, which had ballistics tests conducted on it.

Small caliber firearms such as .22s have a history of being difficult for ballistics experts to work with, but recent advances have made the job easier. Nevertheless, the tests on the pistol found in Culver reportedly failed to show a matchup with the bullets recovered after Clark's murder.

Back in Colorado, Crotz and Kitchen paid another call on the Giffons, this time carrying an audiotape along with them. It was the telephone message left by the mystery male caller who claimed to be Gerry's homosexual lover. After Agent Kitchen and the husband left the room, Crotz played the tape for Mrs. Giffon and asked if she recognized the caller's voice. She didn't. Before the tape was played for her husband, however, she told the detective about his frightening brushes with Michael riding to work and on the job with him after Gerry's murder.

After Mrs. Giffon left the room, her husband was brought inside and the tape was played for him. He was a bit hesitant when he was asked if he recognized the voice, but told the detective it sounded like Mike Backus.

On another front, Judge Kourlis finally released the

restraining order preventing sale of the Oak Street
Bed & Breakfast, freeing up Jill's assets to pay for her
defense. The hostelry wound up being sold for a fraction of the amount she and Seth originally sought.

At the request of Gerry's family, the civil trial itself
was put on hold until the murder case was decided.
Through their attorney, the Boggses argued that publicity over the civil lawsuit might prejudice the murder
trial. Police and prosecutors also had custody of the
files in the civil suit. Jill was representing herself in the
case, since her previous attorneys were given court ap-
proval to pull out.

In the criminal case, the defendants publicly disclosed their alibis through documents filed in the middle of May. They claimed they were together at the
national forest campground in Poudre River Canyon
during a critical four-hour period on the Thursday afternoon of the day Gerry was most likely believed to
have been slain. They said they checked into Kelly
Flats about one PM, but left about four hours later and
drove to Fort Collins, then to Thornton where they
stopped at the Cactus Moon nightclub. They stayed at
the club for about a half-hour from ten to ten-thirty
PM, before driving to the house they shared in Greeley.

According to their account they were together at the
house from about eleven-thirty PM until six-thirty the
next morning when Michael left for work. He attended
a training class until about ten AM then worked the rest
of the day.

Jill talked with Ricky Mott downstairs about eight
AM and left approximately forty-five minutes later to
meet with a State Farm Insurance agent. She was back
home again by nine-fifteen, then left at ten-thirty for
the law offices of Greeley lawyer William Cresher. By
eleven AM, she was beginning an hour-long class at
UNC, and was back home again by twelve-fifteen. She

left home about three PM to get the manicure from Mrs. Heiser.

The couple had an impressive array of witnesses to back up their account of their activities on Friday, October 22. But during the crucial hours the previous afternoon and evening there was a glaring lack of witnesses. Their attorneys were reportedly looking for someone who might have seen the pair at the Cactus Moon or elsewhere Thursday night or earlier in the afternoon.

Mott also threw a damper on the alibi when he told DelValle he thought it was odd that Jill left a note for him Thursday, advising him that she and Michael were camping. Michael had a nasty cold, and Jill was still on the mend from her hip surgery, and neither of them indicated before that they were camping enthusiasts, Mott related. The tenant thought Jill was making a special effort to be noticed at the house when she dropped in on him Friday morning.

Dozens of motions were filed and considered in the criminal case against Jill and Michael. A request by the defense to separate the trials was rejected. So was a move to suppress evidence and another defense request to dismiss the charges because investigators hadn't more closely pinpointed the time of death. Judge Doucette stated there was no evidence of bad faith involved in the delay because investigators were waiting for a search warrant. "The danger of going into the house without a warrant is that all of the evidence obtained may have been suppressed," he pointed out.

But a motion for a change of venue because of the pervasive publicity, the victim's prominence in the community, and the reputed inability to select an impartial jury was granted by the court. Saint-Veltri cited an opinion poll conducted by the defense indicating forty-three percent of potential jurors in the district believed Jill was guilty.

The decision was only a partial victory for the defense, which had asked for the trial to be moved completely out of the Fourteenth Judicial District which embraces Routt, Moffat, and Grand counties. Jurisdiction remained in the district, but Judge Doucette moved the proceedings seventy miles southeast of Steamboat Springs to the Grand County Courthouse in Hot Sulphur Springs on the other side of the 9,426-foot high Rabbit Ears Pass. (The pass gets its name from a geological formation that gives it the appearance of a *Playboy* magazine logo.) Pretrial hearings continued to be held in Steamboat Springs, but it was a convenient move for the jurist, nevertheless. Both he and District Attorney McLimans lived in Grand county.

Jill's hope of getting the show on the road and disposing of the trial within six months was not to be realized. The trial was originally set to begin on July 13, then set back to August 29, but even the later effort to comply with her desire for a speedy trial was hopelessly ambitious. When Judge Doucette moved the trial out of Steamboat Springs, he also rescheduled it to begin at 8:30 AM on February 6, 1995. He set aside four weeks on his court calendar for the proceeding. Once more, summonses were mailed out to expected witnesses in the case. Carl Steely was looking forward to the trip back to Colorado. He planned to take his skis along.

In October 1994, almost a year from the day Gerry's body was found at his house, a large two-column display advertisement appeared in the *Pilot* with the headline: "INFORMATION WANTED." A private investigator working for lawyers for one of the defendants was looking for information to help identify the killer or killers, the ad stated. An 800 number was provided for callers.

The defendants continued to wait out the long process at the Routt County Detention Center still held under $5 million bail each. Jill was keeping occupied with her books, helping other prisoners study for GED examinations, and reading her news clippings. Outside the jail, the man whose life they were accused of ruthlessly snuffing out, was still being mourned by his family and friends.

Inside Boggs Hardware, a framed photograph of Gerry was hung as a tribute. An inscription by his friend, Judy Prier-Lewis, read: "A practical man with a heart of gold leaves much behind. He leaves memories and a place in the hearts of each of us who were touched by his gentle hand."

ELEVEN

Guilty

Jill and Michael were found guilty of twin charges of first-degree murder and of conspiracy to commit first-degree murder after a six-week trial extending from early February to the middle of March 1995.

All three of Jill's sons testified as prosecution witnesses during the grueling proceedings in the Grand County Courthouse in Hot Sulphur Springs. Each of them said their mother had talked of killing Gerry.

But the nine men and seven women making up the jury, and four alternates, never heard about Jill's sordid string of marriages, some of them bigamous. Defense objections to the efforts of prosecutors to detail her many marriages and divorces to the jury with a chart were upheld by Judge Doucette.

The judge also refused to allow the prosecution to enter into evidence the tape of the 911 telephone call made by Douglas Boggs after finding his brother's body at the house. Douglas accused her of the crime during the call, and Judge Doucette ruled out the tape because he didn't want to prejudice the jury.

The influx of reporters from newspapers around the country and tabloid television shows previously expected to descend on the quiet little mountain town for the trial never materialized.

There were plenty of empty seats for spectators in the small courtroom gallery. The County Seat Restaurant, the only public eatery in the little mountain town, was a bit more crowded than usual but the staff managed to get everyone served quickly enough for them to get to court on time for the morning and afternoon sessions. Hot Sulphur Springs is busier during the annual hunting seasons.

The attention of much of the nation's conventional and tabloid media had been diverted from the reputed "black widow" and her co-defendant to Los Angeles and the O. J. Simpson trial. After attracting widespread interest at the time of the arrests, the trial of Jill and Michael raised scarcely a ripple among the press outside Colorado.

District Attorney Paul McLimans used his opening statements to paint Jill as a scheming woman who manipulated Gerry and others in order to realize her own aims. Gerry was killed after showing "a resolute commitment to steer his own course," the prosecutor declared.

Defense attorneys claimed, however, their clients were nowhere near the location of the shooting and added that investigation of the crime scene was so woefully bungled that the real killer may never be found.

Saint-Veltri declared that a "massive, intense, panoramic investigation" produced hundreds of items, and none of them could be tied to the defendants. The murder weapon was never found.

Although his brothers also testified, Jill's oldest son, who had moved with his wife to Idaho, was the star witness. Seth said his mother became increasingly angry over her civil-court dispute with Gerry during the last summer of his life and began talking about having the businessman murdered.

A week before Gerry was shot to death, both Mi-

chael and Jill made separate trips to Steamboat
Springs, Seth continued. He said his mother stayed at
the bed-and-breakfast and before leaving she instructed him not to clean the room because she was
planning to return.

Seth also recounted taking the telephone call from a
woman whose voice he recognized as his mother's,
telling him, "Hey, baby, it's over, and it's messy." He
ordered her not to talk to him and slammed the receiver down. The call occurred between three-thirty
and four PM, October 21, according to the witness.

Continuing his testimony, Seth said he told his wife
about the call and they went out to a restaurant to eat
that night. "We wanted people to see us," he explained.

He also checked Room 7, which his mother had ordered him not to clean. "I just had a feeling she had
been there," he said. There was an unpleasant odor in
the room, and the sink was spotted with drops of
blood.

Seth testified that he sopped up the blood with towels, and washed and bleached them. Asked why he
cleaned the room, he replied, "I don't know. I related
it to the Boggs murder."

That Sunday, his mother telephoned and demanded
to know what questions he was asked by police, the
witness added. "She kept asking if they knew when the
time of death was. She said she did not have a seven-
hour alibi and a three-hour alibi. "I was scared!"

A surprise witness later provided testimony for the
defense that seriously questioned the timetable Seth
laid out in his statements about the "hey baby" call.
Jan Bertrand said she waited on Gerry at the Pilot
Computer and Office Supply Store in Steamboat
Springs during the time period Seth gave for receiving
the call.

Prosecutors, however, produced sequential sales

tickets showing that Gerry made his purchase at the store closer to one PM.

During cross-examination of Seth, Davies attempted to tie the the witness to the murder instead of his own client.

"I submit to you that when it became evident that Mr. Backus would not participate in the killing of Gerald Boggs, it was in your best interest to kill him," the lawyer declared.

"You're wrong," Seth calmly replied.

"Isn't that true?" the lawyer persisted, pointing his finger at the witness.

"No," the husky young man responded.

During William's testimony, Jill's youngest son said his mother discussed Gerry's death with him during her brief stopover in Southern California and told him not to talk to police about it. They were driving to his home from the airport when he advised her he had already talked to police, and she became enraged and started hitting him, he testified.

William said his mother ordered him not to continue on to his house in Manhattan Beach because she was afraid police already had it under surveillance, so he drove her and Michael to a motel. He said his mother was still upset later in the day when they met at a mall, and she carried her four-month-old grandson under her arm like she was lugging a sack.

Steely also flew in to testify at the trial and take advantage of the opportunity to get in a little skiing. He told the jury Jill had bragged of taking mercenary training that made her "more conniving."

Some of the most intriguing testimony, however, revolved around the contention of prosecutors that Gerry was attacked with a stun gun before he was murdered. Investigators testified that injuries found on Gerry's body were consistent with those that could be caused by a stun gun. And a stun gun was found in Jill's car twelve days after his death.

Defense attorneys countered that police didn't test the gun to determine if it was fired. They argued that no fingerprints from the weapon itself or from the package it came in were traced to either Jill or Michael.

The lawyers also pointed out that Seth owned a stun gun and offered into evidence a weapon seized from him by police.

Dr. Robert Stratbucker, an Omaha, Nebraska, cardiologist, testified as a prosecution witness to back up the state's contention Gerry was assaulted with a stun gun before he was killed. Dr. Stratbucker, considered one of the nation's leading experts on stun-gun injuries, stated that testing the weapon taken from Jill's car may not have revealed anything of use.

Stun guns are tested at the factory where they are manufactured, he pointed out. They do not have individual signatures (such as the rifling inside the barrels of firearms), so testing the weapon wouldn't have revealed if it was used in the attack.

During summations, McLimans said the defendants killed Gerry after he had threatened to open a "closet door" that would reveal the secrets of Jill's past. "And that closet was brim-full of skeletons," the district attorney declared.

After all the testimony was over and the summations delivered, the jury deliberated only five hours before returning verdicts against both defendants of guilty to all counts.

"She picked the wrong town, she picked the wrong man, and she picked the wrong family," Douglas Boggs told reporters of his former sister-in-law after the verdicts were revealed.

Jan Boggs described Michael, whom family members said they believed was a willing participant in the murder but who was duped by his co-defendant, as Jill's final victim.

The Boggs family, including Gerry's heartbroken parents, his brother and sister-in-law, faithfully attended each day of the trial. Family members of Jill's and Michael's also made the trip to the little Colorado town and attended the proceedings.

In Culver, Carl Steely said he was relieved the ordeal was over and that he believes justice was served. "I feel sorry for her. I pity her for what she's going to have to go through, but she certainly had to be stopped," he said.

Gerry's persistence in pressing the civil suit against Jill wasn't motivated by money, Steely observed. The businessman was determined to stop her from continuing to prey on other men, the Indiana educator added.

Reflecting on his own star-crossed relationship with Jill, Steely remarked, "I think I was more bewitched— love is too strong a word. I was very vulnerable at that time. She told me all the things I wanted to hear."

In Houston, Sgt. Binford told reporters that police had gathered volumes of information about Jill, and he or some of his colleagues expect to eventually meet with her in prison to discuss Clark Coit's unsolved slaying. The meeting wasn't expected to be set up for several months, sometime later after the appeals process ran out on her conviction.

Although at this writing sentencing hearings were still a few weeks away, there was apparently no question that Jill and Michael would be ordered to spend the rest of their lives behind bars. Life in prison without the possibility of parole is the mandatory sentence for conviction of first-degree murder in cases where the prosecution did not seek the death penalty.

Jill was expected to be sent to the Colorado Prison for Women at Canyon City. It is not a prison with a reputation as a country club. The cunning woman with the talent for business and the sordid history of obsessively misusing the men in her life can be expected to live out the rest of her days amid the harsh surroundings of one of the nation's toughest prisons for female felons.

There will be no ski trips, scuba-diving expeditions or sports cars for Jill at the grim fortress-like prison at Canyon City.

APPENDIX

A Celebration of Men

Jill Lonita Billiot changed her name many times during the first half-century of her life. She married nine different husbands, some of them more than once. This is a list of her husbands with the date of marriage and the date the marriage was dissolved by divorce, annulment or death. The name of her co-defendant, whom she lived with, also appears on the list.

LARRY IHNEN, apprentice bricklayer.
Married 7-24-61 in Wabash, Indiana.
Divorced 6-12-62 in Wabash.

STEVEN MOORE, college student.
Married 5-5-64 in Mississippi.
Divorced 3-23-67 in Louisiana.

WILLIAM CLARK COIT, JR., Tenneco engineer.
Married 1-29-66 in Orange County, Texas.
Shot to death 3-28-72 in Houston.

DONALD CHARLES BRODIE, US Marine Corps major.
Married 11-3-73 in Orange, California.
Divorced 7-8-75 in California.

LOUIS A. DIROSA, lawyer (later a New Orleans civil district court judge).
Married 10-11-76 in Wilkinson County, Mississippi.
Divorced 11-4-78 in Haiti; divorced again 7-26-85 in New Orleans.

ELDON DUANE METZGER, auctioneer and realtor.
Married 3-27-78 in Lima, Ohio.
Divorced ?

CARL V. STEELY, prep-school teacher and administrator.
Married 1-6-83 in Culver, Indiana.
Divorced 12-29-83 in Haiti; divorced again 12-23-91 in Plymouth, Indiana.

GERALD W. BOGGS, merchant.
Married 4-4-91 in Steamboat Springs, Colorado.
Annulment 12-3-91 in Sterling, Colorado.

ROY C. CARROLL, retired US Navy chief petty officer and businessman.
Married 2-7-92 in Las Vegas, Nevada.

MICHAEL O. BACKUS, telephone company maintenance and repairman.
Met in late 1991 or early 1992 and lived with Jill in Greely, Colorado. Reports they were married are apparently untrue, although Jill is known to have used his last name.